Capsicum spp.

(Sweet and Chile Peppers)

Herb of the Year™ 2016

International Herb Association

Compiled and edited by Karen O'Brien

IHA HERB OF THE YEAR™

EACH YEAR THE International Herb Association chooses an **Herb of the Year**™ to highlight. The Horticultural Committee evaluates possible choices based on their being outstanding in at least two of the three major categories: culinary, medicinal, or ornamental. Herbal organizations around the world work together with us to educate the public throughout the year.

Herb of the Year™ books are published annually by the
International Herb Association
P.O. Box 5667
Jacksonville, Florida 32247-5667
www.iherb.org

Copyright 2016. International Herb Association. All rights reserved. No portion of these books, text, prose, recipes, illustrations, or photography, may be reproduced in any manner without written permission from the International Herb Association.

This book is intended as an informational guide. The remedies, approaches, and techniques described herein are meant to supplement, and not to be a substitute for professional medical care or treatment; please consult your health care provider.

The International Herb Association is a professional trade organization providing education, service, and development for members engaged in all aspects of the herbal industry.

978-1-4951-7416-2

"Uniting Herb Professionals for Growth
Through Promotion and Education"

THE INTERNATIONAL HERB ASSOCIATION has some of the most dedicated volunteers who keep the organization afloat, giving their time and talents to ensure that IHA continues to share herbal knowledge and connect those in the profession of herbs. We are deeply indebted to the IHA board of directors, the IHA Foundation members and our webmaster. Thanks for all you do, and for caring enough to move us forward.

IHA BOARD MEMBERS
Diann Nance, President
Larri Parker, Vice President
Karen O'Brien, Secretary
Marge Powell, Treasurer
Matthias Reisen, Past President
Susan Betz
Gert Coleman, Newsletter Editor
Maribel Rodriguez
Skye Suter

IHA FOUNDATION BOARD OF TRUSTEES
Davy Dabney, Chair
Ann Sprayregen, Secretary
Marge Powell, Treasurer
Chuck Voigt
Diann Nance
Donna Frawley
Stephen Lee

WEBMASTER
Jason Ashley

Chile Pixie, Skye Suter

ACKNOWLEDGEMENTS

THE INTERNATIONAL HERB Association, in its mission to promote herbs and unite herb professionals, selects an herb to highlight and advertise each year. Since 1995, IHA has encouraged not only its members, but the world, to focus on and investigate this particular herb. This book aims to disseminate pertinent, timely information on one of the most interesting family of herbs, *Capsicum*.

It goes without saying that putting together a book such as this is no easy task, and there are a number of people to thank. Special kudos to Jean Berry and Gert Coleman, who helped enormously with proofing and editing, catching those spelling and punctuation errors that pop up mysteriously.

Each and every contributor deserves special thanks, for taking the time out of their own busy lives to share their love of *Capsicum* with us. Some of these are past contributors, who are truly passionate about herbs and will research and write about each herb, adding their own personal experience and knowledge to the piece. Then there are the writers who are new to our publication, and they add a fresh perspective to the book as we expand and reach out to new audiences. Our photographers and artists are to be commended for their contributions – their work enhances our effort and illustrates that we really have a multi-talented group of individuals to make this book extraordinary. I appreciate all the support and willingness to make this book a reality.

Thanks also to Heidi Lowe and Marty Jenkins of Litho Printers for all their assistance in compiling and printing. Jason Ashley of That Hosting Place deserves kudos for getting the preview on the website, and for working to ensure that ordering the HOY™ books is simple and effective.

In any herbal community, there are always those whose support and encouragement are the catalyst that moves us forward. I would not be as involved in writing and editing, or as interested in herbal books, if I had never met Lucille Dressler. She is the archivist and librarian for The New England Unit of The Herb Society of America, and she has a wealth of knowledge of herbal history, lore, facts, and so much more. We both share a love of books, and I thank her for allowing me to select many volumes from her extensive and varied collection as she downsizes. Thanks, Lucille!

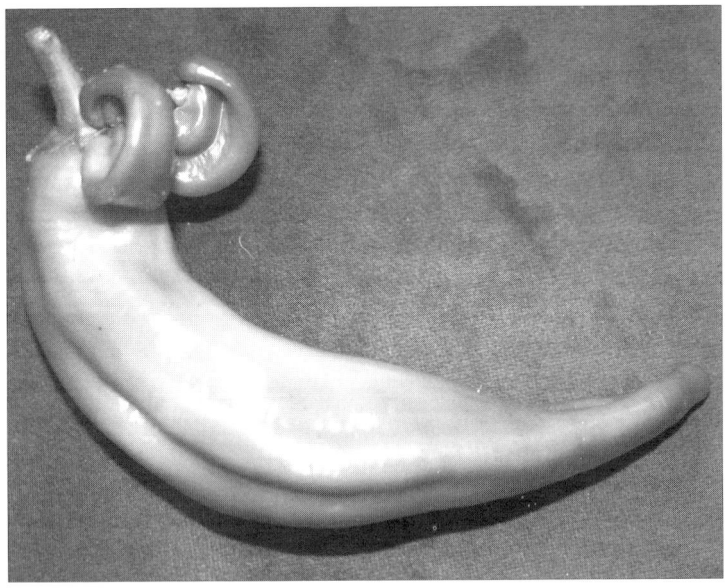

Funky Pepper, Karen O'Brien

Table of Contents

Capsicum Nomenclature: Is it Chile, Chili, or Chilli? 1
  Susan Belsinger

Capturing Capsicum 5
  Mary Ellen Warchol

Captivated by the Capsicums 11
  Rosemary Roman Nolan, LMT

Cheers to Chiles 23
  Tamara Huron

Ginger Cayenne Ointment 29
  Marge Powell

In the Kitchen with Capsicum 37
  Carol Little R.H.

Chile Pepper Shrub 47
  Susan Belsinger and Tina Marie Wilcox

Pappas' Peppers Pizza Oil 51
  Diann Nance

The Amazing Medicinal Properties of Cayenne 55
  Daniel Gagnon

Holy Mole! 69
  Arthur O. Tucker and Susan Belsinger

Fueling the Flames of Capsicum Confusion 83
  Pat Crocker

What's Really Hot? 95
  Jim Long

Fire in the Garden 99
  Charles E. Voigt

Capsicum Cuisine 109
    Skye Suter

Capsicum—Experiencing Peppers 119
    Donna Frawley

Smoked Peppers—A How-To Primer 127
    Kathleen Connole

A Chile by Any Other Name Would Taste as Hot? 131
    Art Tucker

Herbed Chili Sauce 171
    Marge Powell

Red Pepper Paste—One of Life's Culinary Secrets 173
    Stephen Lee

Calling All Capsicums 179
    Karen O'Brien

But Really, Why on Earth Do We Love Chiles Anyway? 191
    Conrad Richter

Some Like it Hot, Some Don't—Paprika, the Sweet Spice 201
    Gert Coleman

Hot Sauce or Salsa? 213
    Jim Long

Paprika Promises 221
    Pat Kenny

Cayenne—A Fiery Friend in our Herbal Apothecary 235
    Carol Little R.H.

Green Farmacy Medicinal Spices - Pepper 243
    Dr. James A. Duke

Herb of the YearTM Selection 275

Join the IHA 276

Recipes 277

Color Insert credits 279

Small chiles waiting to be dried or infused—though they are little—they pack a powerful heat. Susan Belsinger

Dried chiles and ground red chiles in molcajete. Susan Belsinger

Capsicum Nomenclature:
Is it Chile, Chili, or Chilli?

Susan Belsinger

FOR THOSE OF us, who are celebrating *Capsicum, Herb of the Year 2016*,™ and are teaching and writing about these veritable pods, it would behoove us to use a consistent spelling of the common name for this plant.

I'm attaching the quote (which is part of a discussion on the confusion of *Capsicum* nomenclature) below because I also concur that we should refer to peppers as *Capsicums*—however, we do want the general public to know what we are talking about.

> *It would be so much less confusing if they were called what they are—capsicums— but getting Americans to call peppers Capsicums would be like getting us to use the metric system; "chilli" instead of "chili" or "chile" is more realistic.*
>
> —Jean Andrews
> *Red Hot Peppers*

The three spellings that we see most often for the common name of hot peppers are *chile, chili,* and *chilli*, all of which are recognized by different dictionaries as being correct.

In Spanish the word is "chile"; there is no "chili" in Mexican Spanish. In present day Mexico and throughout the southwestern U.S., chile is the accepted and preferred spelling (chiles is the plural).

The anglicized spellings of **chili** or **chilies** are sometimes used to refer to capsicum pods, however when spelled with an "i" chili commonly refers to the popular Southwestern American dish—also known as *chili con carne* (literally chili with meat)—as well as to the mixture of cumin and other spices (chili powder) used to flavor it. Chili powder is different from ground chile in that the former is the seasoned blend of ground chiles combined with other herbs and spices, while ground chile, is simply that—dried chiles ground to a powder. There is also chili sauce, which is a condiment rather like ketchup which is seasoned with chile peppers.

In South America, hot peppers are occasionally called chile or chiles, although more often they are referred to as *ají, locoto,* or *rocoto.*

The usage of **chile** or **chiles** refers specifically to the fruits of the *Capsicum* plant; these are the common Spanish spellings in Mexico, as well as some parts of the Americas and Canada. The chile pepper industry uses the terms chile and chiles as evident in the promotion of Hatch Green Chiles, which are advertised and marketed throughout the U.S. In the southwestern U.S. and especially in New Mexico, green chile and red chile are terms used for long-simmered sauces, which are served over everything from *huevos rancheros* to enchiladas.

Chilli derives from the Romanized interpretation of the word for hot peppers from the original Náhuatl language. According to the Oxford English Dictionary, it is the preferred British spelling although it also lists *chile* and *chili* as correct. Chilli is still occasionally used in the British Isles and India. However, this spelling is discouraged by capsicum enthusiasts since it would be pronounced differently in the Spanish language.

In 1985, when I co-authored *New Southwestern Cooking* with Carolyn Dille, after much research and consideration, we stated on the first page: "We refer to the plants and their fruits in general as *chile, chiles, pepper* or *peppers. Chili* is a stew or powder compounded of spices as well as ground chiles."

If one searches on the Internet "books on *chile* peppers," there is a huge list of books by experts (from growers, botanists, agronomists, and cooks) such as Dave DeWitt, Paul Bosland, Mark Miller, Gary Paul Nabhan, and many more who all use the term chile pepper. Further searches for "books on *chili* peppers" leads one to the rock band Red Hot Chili Peppers.

In conclusion, for the sake of clarity and consistency, let us agree as professionals in the industry to use the current, commonly used Spanish spelling of the words *chile* or *chiles* when we are speaking of hot peppers.

Red Serranos, Susan Belsinger

Susan Belsinger teaches, lectures, and writes about gardening and cooking, and is a food writer, editor, and photographer who has authored and edited over 25 books and hundreds of articles. Recently referred to as a "flavor artist", Susan delights in kitchen alchemy—the blending of harmonious foods, herbs, and spices—to create real, delicious food, as well as libations, that nourish our bodies and spirits and titillate our senses. She has been blogging regularly for Taunton Press' www.vegetablegardener.com for the past five years. Look for her newest informative and colorful *The Chile Pepper Calendar* featuring, Capsicum, Herb of the Year™ 2016. *The Culinary Herbal: Growing & Preserving 97 Flavorful Herbs* co-authored by Susan Belsinger and Dr. Arthur Tucker will be released in January 2016 by Timber Press. www.susanbelsinger.com

Hot Peppers in Sherry, Karen O'Brien

Capturing Capsicum

Mary Ellen Warchol

During my formative years, peppers only came in green, they were a bit sweet, and were almost always paired with onions and celery. Yesterday, I visited a local farmstand and was greeted by a display of thirty-six varieties of peppers. They ranged in taste from mild, sweet bells to ultra-hot ghost peppers and came in every color of the rainbow. What culinary opportunities! Our own garden holds all of the typical varieties that I use frequently, but I couldn't resist bringing home a few more to try. Golden cayenne, sweet banana, super poblanos—so many choices, so many flavors—where to begin?

There is a pepper for everyone. We all know someone who delights in eating the hottest pepper without flinching. Then, there's that friend who absolutely can't tolerate anything more potent than a sweet red bell. In between, all the rest of us test our limits and enjoy the complex, rich flavors that members of the *Capsicum* family allow us to experience.

Over the last few days, I've noticed how prominent a role peppers play in my family's menu. It's canning season, and yesterday I made jalapeño jelly spread and peach-jalapeño jam. Today's accomplishments included peach salsa, *fra diavolo* sauce, and spicy tomato-lemon marmalade. It seems that capsicum is one ingredient I cannot do without. Here are a few of my favorite recipes. I invite you to try them and hope they help convince you to come over to capsicum.

Stuffed Peppers á la Tony and Michael

This recipe came from friends who ran a fine-dining restaurant. When they entertained at home, the food they served was earthy and delicious and often reminiscent of Mom's cooking. These stuffed peppers are simple, flavorful, and satisfying.

SERVES 8

4 bell peppers, any color, cut in half, seeds and ribs removed
2 anchovy fillets, preserved in oil
1/4 cup whole milk
1 clove garlic, finely chopped
1/4 cup extra-virgin olive oil
2 cups dried, unseasoned bread crumbs
1 tablespoon chopped fresh parsley
1 tablespoon chopped fresh basil
1 teaspoon dried oregano
1/2 teaspoon kosher or sea salt
1/4 teaspoon freshly ground black pepper
1/2 cup toasted pine nuts
One lemon, cut into 8 wedges

Preheat the oven to 375°F.

Flatten the pepper halves with your palm and place them, skin side down, on a baking sheet. Soak the anchovies in the milk for 15 minutes. Drain them and place them in a bowl with the garlic and olive oil. Mash the ingredients until they are well-incorporated. Add the bread crumbs, parsley, basil, oregano, salt, and pepper and combine. Stuffing should be fairly wet in consistency. If needed, add more oil. Taste and add more salt and pepper if desired.

Divide the stuffing among the pepper halves and lightly press on the top of each pepper to fit the stuffing into the pepper shell. Bake for 15 minutes. Test to see that the pepper is cooked through. If needed, cook for another 5 minutes. Remove from the oven.

Peppers may be served hot, cold, or at room temperature. Garnish with toasted pine nuts and a wedge of lemon.

John's Spicy Eggplant

Each summer, my husband, John, grows the most beautiful eggplants. It's not his favorite vegetable, though, so I had to find a way to prepare them so that he could enjoy this wonderful gift from his garden. Capsicum to the rescue!

SERVES 4

2 eggplants, peeled (if desired) and cut into 1-inch cubes (about 4 cups)
3 tablespoons sugar
2 teaspoons crushed red pepper flakes
3 tablespoons cider vinegar
2 teaspoons soy sauce
1/2 teaspoon kosher or sea salt
1 tablespoon toasted sesame oil

Place the eggplant onto a rack over boiling water and steam until tender, 5 to 7 minutes. Remove the eggplant from the heat and allow it to drain.

Put the sugar, crushed red pepper, cider vinegar, soy sauce, and salt into a small saucepan. Bring to a boil and stir until the sugar has dissolved. Remove the pan from the heat. Pour the sauce over the drained eggplant and toss. Drizzle the sesame oil over the eggplant and toss again.

Put the eggplant into the refrigerator until it is cool. This dish is best served cold or at room temperature.

Liptauer Cheese

A recent trip to Eastern Europe brought back childhood memories of this paprika-filled cheese spread.

MAKES A GENEROUS CUP

8 ounces cream cheese, at room temperature
2 tablespoons unsalted butter, at room temperature
1 tablespoon Hungarian sweet paprika
1 teaspoon dill seed, coarsely chopped
1 teaspoon capers, drained, rinsed, and coarsely chopped
1/2 teaspoon kosher or sea salt

Place the cream cheese, butter, and paprika into a bowl and beat with a whisk until ingredients are well-incorporated. Fold in the dill seed, capers, and salt.

Put the cheese mixture into a serving bowl, cover with plastic wrap, and refrigerate for at least two hours to allow flavors to blend.

Remove the cheese from the refrigerator 20 minutes before serving. Liptauer is especially good when paired with toasted dark bread or rye crackers.

Honey-Glazed, Super Chile Chicken

This is a recipe I developed when we were asked to give a cooking demonstration at a local honey festival. Our garden was bursting with a variety of pepper called 'Super Chile'. It is an Asian-type pepper, well-suited for stir-fry use. The recipe was a hit, and it's one I use frequently in pepper season.

SERVES 4

4 tablespoons honey
1/2 cup warm water
1 tablespoon soy sauce
2 teaspoons cornstarch
1 to 2 teaspoons vegetable oil
2 to 4 chile peppers—fresh or dried (use the 'Super Chile' variety if available)
2 cloves garlic, chopped
1 tablespoon fresh chopped ginger root
1 pound boneless chicken breast cut into 1/2-inch slices (use boneless chicken thighs if preferred)
1/4 cup fresh basil leaves, torn (use Thai basil if available)

Make a sauce by mixing together the honey, warm water, soy sauce, and cornstarch. Set aside to use later in the recipe.

Heat a sauté pan over medium heat; coat the bottom with oil. If using fresh chiles, make a small incision into the side of each one. Add chiles to hot pan. Stir fry for a few minutes until aromatic. Add chopped garlic and ginger; sauté for 1 minute. Add chicken slices and stir over medium high heat until cooked through.

Stir the prepared sauce mixture and add it to the cooked chicken. Stir until sauce has thickened, about 3 to 4 minutes. Fold basil into mixture and remove chiles if desired. Serve over steamed rice.

Mary Ellen Warchol runs Stockbridge Farm in Deerfield, Massachusetts with her husband, John, and her sister, Denise Lemay. Their herbal enterprise is dedicated to exploring the flavors and wonders of herbs through educational programs, culinary instruction, and cooking demonstrations throughout the Northeast. stockbridgeherbs.com, lavendergrower.tumblr.com.

Capsicum flower, Pat Kenny

Captivated by the Capsicums

Rosemary Roman Nolan, LMT

I AM GLAD to say that the only *complete* culinary failure I have ever suffered occurred as a young cook, still innocent of the awesome powers of the spice rack, and in particular, hot peppers.

One dreary, cold Sunday, at around the age of fourteen, I decided to make dinner. Perhaps it was a recipe in the *Boston Sunday Globe* that inspired me; in any event, there was a cabbage sitting on the counter, and ground beef in the icebox. The intricacy of assembling a stuffed cabbage appealed to me; there is nothing like food with a surprise inside to motivate a young cook. Plus, I thought, I'm Eastern European. This is my heritage, my folklore, my destiny! I can do this blindfolded!

The directions for the meat stuffing, albeit simple, called for "a few dashes" of Tabasco. I had never used the condiment for anything. In fact, I don't even know why we had it in the house; my family didn't cook or eat food that included hot peppers. Takeout Chinese was about as exotic as we got in those days. Seeing how tiny the "dashes" were as I shook them into the meat mixture, I thought, "That can't be right." But best to be safe—I tasted the Tabasco. I liked it. I liked it a lot. The capsaicin sting suddenly transported me to a crowded quay in Calcutta, the humid air reeking of exotic spices, with assorted adventurers like Marco Polo in the background.

This recipe is wrong, I decided. It's been toned down for timid souls reading the Sunday paper who *fear flavor*, who don't know how to LIVE when they make a stuffed cabbage. I shook in many more dashes, hesitated, then briskly shook in most of the bottle, along with a vigorous quantity of paprika and a goodly sample of everything else in the spice rack. No one uses this Tabasco stuff in our house anyway, I reasoned, so why not jazz up this humble cabbage and start my culinary career with a triumph. None of these bland, rubbery, insipid, cowardly stuffed cabbages for MY family!

It baked up beautifully. Really, I had interlined the leaves with my nuclear-powered stuffing using a surgeon's level of care, tucking and draping the final leaves like a mother dressing her only daughter for the wedding. It unmolded perfectly from its bowl, and loomed, steaming, and benevolent, on an appropriately decorative platter. It sliced like a dream, the stuffing perfectly melded with the crisp-tender cabbage, not overcooked, still green and inviting. A gleaming, nutritious triumph of food architecture!

I cut big first servings with palpable pride. I waited for my mother and sister to try it before I took a bite—being polite, you know, as the gracious chef. Go on, *you* first—really! Tell me how it came out. I wanted to see their faces, the better to savor my triumph. I think my sister got down one bite. My mother, being what mothers are, actually choked down at least two bites and then murmured something vague about how zesty it was. Forks were laid down. Silence fell. I took my first bite and there was really no flavor at all; only unmitigated fire carried by hopelessly contaminated ground beef. To say I was crestfallen would be putting it mildly. I let my slice of volcano cool a little, thinking woefully of that mostly empty bottle in the refrigerator door, and tried again. No use. I couldn't eat it. I even tried some the next day, cold, thinking perhaps the wildfire would have burnt itself out overnight and we could salvage the wretched thing somehow. No luck. To my everlasting shame (wasting food was, and is, a serious sin) I think we had to heave the radioactive cabbage into the woods. It could still be glowing menacingly there as we speak.

As an adult, however, I've always adored spicy foods; I love to cook them and I love to eat them. I sometimes wonder if I had a slice of that same cabbage today … perhaps I'd think it was just fine?

But my mother and sister still dislike spicy dishes. In darker moments, I wonder how much I contributed to that with my Capsaicin Cabbage of Doom.

Capsaicin (methyl vanillyl nonenamide), the oily chemical that puts the fire in hot peppers, is not easily water soluble; only protein, fat, or alcohol will dissolve its attack on the taste buds of an unwary diner. (I should have served at least two pints of sour cream with that dratted cabbage.) Sweet pepper hybrids are "sweet" because they have a recessive gene that prohibits capsaicin formation in the seeds and membranes of the fruit. Some modern hybrids such as the 'Mexibell' have been developed to combine the size and growth habit of a sweet pepper with a touch of the capsaicin gene for mild heat in what looks like an ordinary bell pepper.

Along with turkeys, pumpkins, cacao, tobacco, and potatoes, peppers are one of the gifts of the New World to the Old, and also to Africa. It's difficult to imagine a Thai or Indian curry without hot peppers today, but until the Spanish and Portuguese explorers brought them back to Europe and to colonies in Africa and Asia, peppers did not grow in those locales. Once introduced, they became a vital part of these regional cuisines. By the 1600s, peppers were firmly entrenched around the world.

We now associate families of capsicums with geographic locations: sweet peppers with Italian, Hungarian, and American Creole cooking; jalapeños, poblanos, and serranos with Southwestern and Mexican cooking; Scotch bonnets and habaneros with Caribbean fare; and cayenne and bird chiles with Indian and Pacific Rim cuisine.

The Mesoamerican peoples were well acquainted with peppers and cultivated them extensively over 4,000 years ago, combining chiles with chocolate in a beverage fit only for the ruling elite. The original wild chiles from which our modern varieties descend are small, berry-like, fiercely hot varieties variously named the Chiltepin, wild bird pepper, or flea pepper. "Wild bird pepper" as a name makes perfect sense as these early fruits were and are good food for birds, which do not have the sensitivity to capsaicin that mammals and insects do. This is why loading your birdseed with chili powder can successfully repel squirrels. As with corn, the variety of capsicum hybrids is quite staggering today, with research on new hybrids appearing regularly from programs at New Mexico State University (for more information, see www.chilipepperinstitute.org), Cornell University, and others.

Wilbur Lincoln Scoville (1865–1942) was an American pharmacist, researcher, and author who developed the scale we now use to grade the "hotness" of capsicums. Scoville devised a clinical method for diluting capsaicin at measured intervals and using human subjects to taste-test the diluted chemical to grade its potency. SHU (Scoville Heat Units) are the unit of measure, starting with zero for the innocent bell pepper and rising over 2,000,000 for modern super-hot hybrids such as the 'Trinidad Moruga Scorpion' and 'Carolina Reaper' (SHU 2,000,000 and up is also the concentration in commercial pepper sprays used for self-defense). The number of units is defined as the number of units of fluid needed to offset one unit of capsaicin from the pepper under examination, to the point where its heat cannot be detected in the solution by taste.

Jalapeños, probably the most common hot pepper familiar to the average eater, can register between 2,500 and 8,000 SHU. Why such variance? I can attest from having grown peppers for many years that it is part of the wondrous variety of nature. How "hot" a hot pepper is going to be depends on a variety of factors: Genetics. Soil quality. Climate. Water supply. Weather of a particular growing season. Possible cross-pollination (or lack thereof). Ripeness. I have had peppers vary widely in hotness even when harvested from the same plant—one jalapeño will taste exactly like a sweet pepper and another will be quite spicy. Or one will be spicy throughout and another will have sweet flesh but spicy seeds and ribs, where capsaicin is primarily generated.

Capsicums, having come to us from the semi-tropic and tropic climates of the New World, love warm soil (at minimum 60°F). They prefer well-drained soil rich in organic compounds, full sun, heat, and an even water supply. A soil Ph of 6.2 to 6.6 is ideal, along with enough space for proper air circulation between plants to maximize yield. Irregular watering, plant crowding, or extreme hot weather may cause capsicums to drop their blossoms and fail to set fruit. For Northerners, there are cold-hardy hybrids; in a semi-sheltered location I have continued to harvest both sweet and hot peppers well into the New England autumn until frost. They may be tropical in nature, but capsicums are tough plants.

Being unattractive to most mammalian and many insect predators, hot peppers can still fall prey to some bacterial, fungal, and viral infections. The best defense for your capsicums, and for that matter any plant in your garden, is to ensure that your soil is vibrant in terms of its mineral content, proportion of organic matter, and presence of friendly soil organisms. A healthy plant grown in healthy soil is naturally resistant to both disease and insect damage, whereas plants grown in depleted or overly disturbed soil will usually require more artificial intervention.

Medicinally, all peppers, because of their membership in the Solanaceae or nightshade family, have been identified as possible triggers for those who suffer from migraines (along with tomatoes, potatoes, and eggplant, all nightshade cousins). On the positive side, however, hot peppers are particularly high in Vitamin C—even more so then citrus fruits—and their capsaicin content is demonstrably effective at increasing circulation to aid the body's own healing processes. There is ongoing research demonstrating that capsaicin may be a powerful natural aid in healing gastric ulcers by encouraging the regeneration of gastric mucosa and discouraging the bacteria that trigger ulcer formation. Capsaicin is also turning up in many over-the-counter liniments and muscle rubs as a circulatory stimulant, counterirritant, and topical pain reliever.

Chile powder is one of the first-line ingredients of your home first-aid kit, especially since it lives in the kitchen. If you cut yourself while prepping dinner, which usually means you have a nasty, freely bleeding cut in a very inconvenient place on your hand, apply a hefty gob of chile powder to the cut before bandaging; it is instantly styptic and also antiseptic. The "burn" you feel upon eating capsaicin is not actually a chemical burn; it is simply massive local overstimulation of the nervous system. It is possible, if a particularly high-SHU pepper were consumed or applied to the mucous membranes, to suffer acute respiratory distress and/or require emergency medical care—which is why that self-defense pepper spray is so effective.

In the Ayurvedic system of health care (which had its beginnings in India approximately 1500 B.C.E.), capsicums are utilized both as food and as medicine. For some human constitutions or doshas, hot peppers in particular are thought to be too stimulating, while for other body types both hot and sweet peppers are utilized in the diet to treat inflammation or congestive conditions.

In the kitchen, capsicums are stars—so many varieties to choose from, so many ways to prepare them: stuffed, baked, sautéed, dried, smoked, ground up, raw, pickled, infused, turned into condiments—so many ways to celebrate the captivating capsicums! Just be careful next time you try a stuffed cabbage…

Hot Pepper Mustard

This mustard is perfect for gift giving! The recipe may easily be halved. The spiciness of the final product may be adjusted by leaving out the jalapeños, or adding more as desired. It is wonderful on roasted meats, grilled kielbasa, or sausages; as a dip for pretzels; or as a sandwich spread. Try mixing a dollop with regular mayonnaise when making potato salad or pasta salad!

MAKES 16 HALF-PINT JARS

40 hot banana peppers, seeded and stemmed
1 large onion, chopped
6 cloves garlic, chopped
4 cups prepared mustard of choice
3 cups sugar (a mix of brown and white sugar is optimal)
1 cup honey
4 cups raw apple cider vinegar
1 tablespoon salt
1 teaspoon ground turmeric
3 medium jalapeños, seeded and stemmed (optional)
1 1/2 cups flour
1 cup water, vegetable stock, or chicken stock
1 teaspoon fresh ground black pepper

Blend the peppers, onion, and garlic in a blender or food processor and process until fairly smooth. In a large saucepan, combine the pepper mixture, mustard, sugar, honey, vinegar, salt, turmeric, and hot peppers (if using). Bring to a boil.

In a large bowl, stir together the flour and water/stock until smooth. Add a few spoonfuls of the hot mustard mixture to the flour and whisk together thoroughly in the bowl to prevent the mixture lumping when it goes into the pot. When it is smooth, add the flour mixture and the rest of the mustard mixture to the saucepan. Continue to boil, stirring constantly, for 5 minutes.

Pour into sterile jars and seal with new lids and rings. Process in a steam or hot water bath for 10 minutes.

Ethiopian Berbere Paste

This fiery paste is far fresher-tasting than any prepared mix you can buy. Use as a table condiment; as a rub for roasted and grilled meats; in chili; a little mixed with mayonnaise as a spicy aioli dip for steamed vegetable crudités; a little shaken up with lemon juice and olive oil to dress roasted or grilled vegetables.

MAKES ABOUT 2 CUPS

5 tablespoons dried red pepper flakes
2 teaspoons each: ground cumin, fresh ground black pepper, and kosher salt
1 teaspoon each: ground cardamom, fenugreek, nutmeg, clove, cinnamon, allspice, and coriander
1 1/4 cups ground cayenne
3 tablespoons smoked paprika
6 cloves garlic, minced
2 cups water or chicken stock
4 tablespoons peanut oil

Toast all the ground and flaked spices, dry, in a heavy nonstick skillet over medium heat for about 4 minutes, stirring occasionally, until you can smell their aromas. Be careful not to scorch them.

Blend the toasted spices with the garlic, water or stock, and oil in a blender until completely paste-like, about 3 minutes. Add more oil or water as needed if it is too thick. Return the paste to the skillet and cook for another 10 minutes over low-medium heat, stirring occasionally. Cool and store in a jar, refrigerated, for up to three months.

Mole Poblano de Guajolote

Pre-Conquest Mexican nobility drank chocolate not with sugar and milk products as we know it today—that was a European invention—but with chiles, a combination our modern palates may find strange. The echo of that royal beverage is the rich and exotic mole sauce below. Traditionally the early Mexicans would have served this sauce with turkey, but it's fine with any sautéed or roasted poultry or pork.

*NOTE: Dried chiles to use if you can find them: pasilla, mulato, or ancho—5 to 10 total. If you can't find dried chiles, 4 to 5 fresh jalapeños plus 1 to 2 fresh poblanos will work also. I usually use fresh because I think they taste better and are less expensive, but either fresh or dried are fine.

For those who do not like chiles or hot food, the sauce could certainly be made without hot peppers entirely; but keep in mind that mild chiles such as poblanos (called anchos when dried and poblanos when fresh) can add authentic body and flavor to the sauce without a great deal of hotness.

MAKES ABOUT 4 CUPS

5 to 10 dried chiles (rehydrated) OR 4 to 5 fresh chiles* (See note)
1 cup boiling water or chicken stock to soak dried chiles, if using
3/4 cup green pumpkin seeds (pepitas)
3/4 cup blanched almonds
1 cup onions, chopped
1 cup canned, diced plum tomatoes, drained
1/2 cup raisins
2 tablespoons sesame seeds
5 cloves garlic, chopped
1/2 teaspoon each: cinnamon, ground clove, coriander, and fennel seeds
Salt and fresh ground pepper
1 teaspoon smoked paprika
2 tablespoons apple cider vinegar

To finish the sauce:

- 2 tablespoons olive oil or butter to grease the skillet while cooking the mole
- 2 ounces chopped semisweet chocolate
- 2 cups chicken stock or just enough to thin the sauce to your liking
- 4 cups of cooked meat of choice, shredded, minced, or diced

Cut open the dried chiles if using and discard their seeds. (If fresh, do the same, removing the inner ribs of the pepper as well if you want less spice). Soak the dried chiles in the hot water for about 30 minutes to soften and then drain.

In a food processor or blender, blend the chiles (fresh or dried and soaked) and the rest of the sauce ingredients, except the olive oil or butter, chicken stock, and chocolate.

Put the sauce in a deep skillet with the remaining 2 tablespoons of oil or butter and simmer, stirring, for 5 to 10 minutes. Add the chocolate and some chicken stock and continue to simmer uncovered over low heat until the chocolate has melted. The sauce shouldn't be too thin. Taste for hotness and salt and adjust seasoning.

Now add your leftover sautéed or roasted meat of choice to the pan and simmer for about 15 minutes, turning to keep coated with the sauce. Serve sprinkled with more sesame or pumpkin seeds if desired.

The mole sauce, prior to adding the protein, can be refrigerated in a tightly covered container for 2 to 3 days.

Mexican Chocolate Cookies

These are a dark and delicate palate-tingling cookie that will have you reaching for just one more. Decadent with an excellent cup of coffee!

MAKES APPROXIMATELY 3 DOZEN

2 1/4 cups all-purpose flour
1/2 cup unsweetened cocoa powder
2 teaspoons cream of tartar
1 teaspoon baking soda
1/2 teaspoon salt
1 cup (2 sticks) unsalted butter, room temperature
1 3/4 cups sugar
2 large eggs, beaten
2 teaspoons cinnamon
1/2 teaspoon chili powder, either cayenne powder or chile powder
1 teaspoon ground cardamom

Preheat oven to 400°F. In a medium bowl, sift together the flour, cocoa powder, cream of tartar, baking soda, and salt. In another bowl, cream together the butter and 1 1/2 cups of the sugar until light and fluffy, either by hand or with a mixer. Add eggs and mix well. Gradually add flour mixture and beat well until all is combined.

In a small bowl, combine the remaining 1/4 cup of sugar, the cinnamon, and the chili powder. Using heaping tablespoonfuls of dough, form balls by rolling between your palms and then rolling each in the sugar-spice mixture. Place a few inches apart on parchment-lined baking sheets and bake until cookies are set and begin to crack, about 10 minutes. Let cookies cool and store in airtight containers as needed.

REFERENCES

Bremness, Lesley. *Herbs.* New York, NY: DK Publishing, Inc., 1994.

Castleman, Michael. *The Healing Herbs.* Emmaus, PA: Rodale Press, 1991.

Duke, James A., Ph.D. *The Green Pharmacy.* Emmaus, PA: Rodale Press, 1997.

Gordon-Smith, Clare. *Basic Flavorings: Chiles.* Philadelphia, PA: Running Press, 1996.

Hazen, Janet. *Turn It Up!* San Francisco, CA: Chronicle Books, 1995.

Jones, N. L., S. Shabib, and P.M. Sherman (1997), Capsaicin as an inhibitor of the growth of the gastric pathogen *Helicobacter pylori.* FEMS Microbiology Letters, 146: 223–227.

Keville, Kathi. *Herbs: An Illustrated Encyclopedia.* New York, NY: Michael Friedman Publishing, Inc., 1994.

McIntyre, Anne. *The Medicinal Garden.* New York, NY: Henry Holt and Company, Inc., 1997.

Personal notes, Proceedings of the 4th International Herb Symposium, Norton, MA, 1998.

Stewart, Amy. *Wicked Plants: The Weed That Killed Lincoln's Mother & Other Botanical Atrocities.* New York, NY: Algonquin Books of Chapel Hill, 2009.

Tiwari, Maya. *Ayurveda: A Life of Balance.* Rochester, VT: Healing Arts Press, 1995.

Rosemary Roman Nolan, LMT, grew up in a family of herbalists and green thumbs and maintains a messy but vibrant organic garden in Central Massachusetts. When not finding new excuses to avoid weeding, and planning for the next big endeavor—beekeeping and chickens—she is a Massachusetts licensed massage therapist and Reiki Master. She has also been an adult education teacher for over ten years, offering food folklore classes, Tribal Fusion belly dance, and many hands-on workshops including soapmaking, cheesemaking, and papermaking. To learn more about her or to obtain contact information, visit her website at www.amtamembers.com/rosemarynolan.

Pickled Peppers, Susan Belsinger

Cheers to Chiles

Tamara Huron

I WAS INTRODUCED to the many wonderful members of the Capsicum family by living in Colorado for many years. My experience comes from working alongside Colorado country club and restaurant chefs who highlighted the beautiful chiles in their delicious recipes.

I love the heat of chiles and create recipes that showcase the levels of capsaicin. Fresh chiles, whether roasted or grilled, add a complex flavor to my recipes. Dried chiles complement my recipes with their robust flavor notes. Fresh, dried, or smoked, there is always room for a chile in my kitchen.

My garden reflects my love for *Capsicum annuum* as I am growing poblanos, pasillas, Anaheims, and jalapeños. It's a great feeling when you visit the garden looking for that perfect chile for your recipe. I encourage you to use chiles in different types of recipes as their complexity will enhance any meal.

Cream of Poblano Soup with Jack Cheese Crust

Poblano chiles offer a pleasing flavor and are readily available. This soup is thick and rich with a nice balance of heat and delightful in summer as well as cooler months. It is a great first course or accompaniment to a salad.

MAKES 4 SERVINGS

3 tablespoons olive oil
3 medium poblano peppers, seeded and chopped
2 onions, chopped
1 carrot, chopped
4 cups vegetable stock
1 large potato, diced
1/2 cup plain yogurt
1/2 teaspoon salt
1 tablespoon cilantro, chopped
8 large tortilla chips
4 slices Monterey jack cheese

Heat the oil in a large saucepan. Add poblano peppers, onions, and carrots and sauté slowly for 5 minutes. Stir in the stock and add the diced potatoes. Bring to a boil, then reduce heat and simmer for 30 minutes.

Remove from heat and puree in a blender until smooth. Return to the pan. Stir in the yogurt, salt, and cilantro.

Preheat broiler. Ladle soup into ovenproof bowls and top with 2 tortilla chips. Lay a slice of jack cheese over chips and place under the broiler briefly until cheese melts. Carefully, remove bowls from oven and serve.

Breakfast Migas with Anaheims

Migas is a traditional dish in Mexican cuisine that uses leftover bread or tortillas. It is served as a first course for lunch or dinner in restaurants in Mexico. With Southwest cuisine being popular, migas is now a preferred breakfast dish. Add your favorite ingredients for a remarkable morning meal.

MAKES 4 SERVINGS

8 eggs
1/4 cup milk
1/2 teaspoon each salt and black pepper
3 tablespoons olive oil
3 corn tortillas, cut into strips
1/2 medium onion, diced
1 large Anaheim pepper, seeded and chopped
1 large tomato, chopped
1 teaspoon ground cumin
1 cup crumbled feta cheese
Cilantro and sliced avocado, optional garnish

Combine eggs, milk, salt, and pepper in a medium bowl. Whisk just enough to combine. Set aside.

In a large skillet, heat the oil over medium heat. Add the tortilla strips and sauté until lightly crisp, about 4 minutes. Add onion, Anaheim pepper, tomato, and cumin. Stir and cook for 3 minutes.

Pour egg mixture over ingredients in the pan, stirring lightly with a spatula as it cooks. Add feta cheese, stir once more and remove pan from heat. Garnish with cilantro and avocado. Serve immediately.

Southwest Broken Spaghetti

I created this recipe after trying fideos, a Mexican dry soup; it is a delicious healthy side using no oil or butter. The reduced-fat feta cheese complements the pasta. Serve with shrimp or chicken.

MAKES 4 SERVINGS

1/2 pound whole-wheat spaghetti
4 cups vegetable broth
4 Hatch green chiles, roasted or grilled and peeled
3 tablespoons fresh cilantro, chopped
1/2 teaspoon black ground pepper
Salt, to taste
1/2 cup reduced fat feta cheese crumbles

Break spaghetti into 2-inch pieces. Remove stem and seeds from chiles and chop them.

In a large oven-safe sauté pan, add vegetable broth and bring to a boil; add spaghetti and chiles. Reduce heat to a simmer and stir occasionally. Cook for 10 minutes.

Remove sauté pan from heat. Preheat broiler. Add cilantro and ground pepper to the spaghetti. Add salt to taste. Stir well. Top with feta cheese crumbles. Place under the broiler until cheese browns slightly.

Remove pan from oven and serve.

Blackberry Chipotle Fool

With my love for chiles, why not have chiles for dessert! The chipotle chile adds a subtle spicy note that enhances the sweetness of the berries. Fools are easy to make and a light dessert. Always a favorite with my family and friends.

MAKES 4 SERVINGS

1 1/2 cups fresh blackberries
1 chipotle chile (from a can of chipotles in adobo sauce), stemmed
3 tablespoons light brown sugar
Juice of 1 lime
1 cup heavy cream
1 1/2 tablespoons confectioners' sugar
1/2 teaspoon pure vanilla extract

Set a mesh sieve over a medium bowl. Use the back of a wooden spoon to push 1 cup of the blackberries and the chipotle through the sieve, smearing the berries and chile back and forth across the mesh until only seeds and pulp remain. Scrape any purée from the bottom of the sieve. Stir the brown sugar and lime juice into the purée.

In a chilled medium metal bowl, combine the cream, confectioners' sugar, and vanilla and beat with an electric hand mixer on high speed until soft peaks form, about two minutes.

Pour the blackberry mixture over the cream. Use a butter knife to gently stir the mixture so that thin streaks of dark purple run through the cream.

Spoon the mixture into four glasses or small dessert bowls and top with the remaining blackberries. Serve immediately.

Tamara Huron, BA, MA is a graduate of Nazareth College and the University of Kansas. Originally from Binghamton, New York, and living for many years in Colorado, she now calls Alabama her home. Tamara furthered her culinary knowledge working at country clubs and restaurants. She creates recipes that highlight herbs and has written for numerous magazines and publications. Tamara's fondness of herbs and cooking led her to develop Organic Herbal Cooking, Inc. Her company offers an organic herb of the month, which arrives with beautiful photo recipe cards. She writes Organic Herbal Cooking's blog and shares the benefits of cooking with herbs in simple healthy cooking. Tamara enjoys doing cooking shows and teaching her audiences about fresh herbs. She has cooking videos on www.YouTube and is followed on Facebook and Pinterest. She is a member of the Huntsville Herb Society and is chairman of the Tea Bed at the Huntsville Botanical Garden. Tamara grows many herbs from seed or cuttings. Herbs are always present in her kitchen adding a healthy freshness to the recipes she creates. Visit www.organicherbalcooking.com

Hatch Chiles. Susan Belsinger

Ginger Cayenne Ointment

Marge Powell

HOT PEPPERS BRING to mind images of Mexican dishes, Thai food, and maybe even chutney. But let's venture a little further afield from food and think about hot peppers and what they can do for our skin and joints and circulation. Penelope Ody recommends the infused oil of hot pepper for use in chills, and if the skin is not broken, the oil can be heated and applied AROUND a varicose ulcer to encourage blood flow away from the ulcer. She also advises it as a massage oil for arthritis.[1] Vicki Pitman cautions against prolonged use in pregnancy but advises that hot pepper can counter shock and normalize blood pressure, though she notes the ability of hot pepper to quickly penetrate tissue her only recommendation is a preparation to be taken internally of "1/4 –1 teaspoon (powdered dried peppers) … mixed with juice or water".[2] Robin Rose Bennett says she sprinkles cayenne powder mixed with dusting powder into socks or shoes in winter to keep feet warm. She does warn that it will stain your socks.[3] These authors generally refer to cayenne pepper as hot pepper or red peppers. But there are far more hot peppers than the common cayenne and they are not all red. Some are yellow, some are orange or purple. The effective element of these peppers is capsaicin. Jim Duke notes that an ointment with capsaicin has successfully treated postherpetic neuralgia in shingles as well as arthritis and has been effective in treating psoriasis.[4] Clearly the external use of hot peppers has a significant and beneficial history.

The following is a formula for creating an ointment used externally that takes advantage of the capsaicin in hot peppers. Technically, an ointment,

---

1 Ody, Penelope. 1993. *The Complete Medicinal Herbal.* New York, NY: Dorling Kindersley, Inc.,
2 Pitman, Vicki. 1994. *Herbal Medicine: the Use of Herbs for Health and Healing.* New York, NY: Barnes & Noble, Inc..
3 Bennett, Robin Rose. 2014. *The Gift of Healing Herbs.* Berkeley, CA: North Atlantic Books.
4 Duke Ph.D., James A. 1997. *The Green Pharmacy.* New York, NY: Rodale, Inc.,.

or a salve, has no water as an ingredient. However, this formula calls for the addition of two different tinctures. Tinctures are made by infusing alcohol with herbs; the alcohol I use is 100 proof vodka which is 50% water. This is not a lot of water but it does move us out of the definition of an ointment. Because the water and alcohol used is less than would be used in a lotion and because this formula is intended to be used as an ointment would be used, I call it an ointment, though it is really a hybrid.

As we grow older, and we are all aging—some of us just further along the path than others—our joints and our circulatory system necessarily age with us. And while the access to conventional medical intervention for these issues is available to many of us, there are many reasons for using herbal remedies in our self-care. It's important to note that we all need to recognize when self-treatment ceases to be an option and seek conventional medical assistance.

I have used this treatment for arthritic reasons. My feet seem most afflicted by this condition, so when they bother me, I apply the ointment all over my feet, put on my socks, and then I am set for the day. I have found this to be helpful, and my customers tell me they find this balm useful for joint pain and muscle aches.

Making this ointment takes time, because unless you have them on hand, you must first make the ginger tincture and pepper oil. These both need to infuse for six weeks before they are used in the formula. The willow bark tincture can be easily purchased at a health food store.

While the name of this preparation is Ginger Cayenne, any hot pepper can be used. It is preferable to use hot peppers you have grown yourself but if this is not available to you, dried cayenne peppers should be easy to find. I would not use powdered cayenne pepper as it is likely to be old. The formula also uses emu oil. Emu oil was used historically by the Australian aborigines for the treatment of burns, wounds, and bruises and as a pain reliever for bone, muscle, and joint disorders. The emu oil enhances the benefits of the ointment and can be found through online sources. The olive oil is not only a good moisturizer but has also been found to have a beneficial effect on arthritis. The use of organic olive oil is preferred but it should not be extra virgin olive oil because of the scent. The essential oils in the formula—wintergreen, nutmeg, clove bud, and cinnamon leaf all have a purpose. Wintergreen and nutmeg are good for muscular pain; cinnamon leaf and clove bud are both anti-infectious and antifungal and have a role in preserving the ointment. However, any one or all of these essential oils could elicit a reaction in some people. Therefore, it is wise to mix a drop of each essential oil individually into 10 drops of olive oil. Then apply these mixtures to the inside of your elbow one at a time. If there is any reaction within 24 hours DO NOT USE THAT ESSENTIAL OIL. The ointment can be made with any combination of the essential oils or none of the essential oils depending on your reaction. If you omit the wintergreen and nutmeg oils, the preparation will have less than its full potency; if you omit the cinnamon leaf and clove bud oils, store your product in the refrigerator.

GINGER CAYENNE OINTMENT

Because of the infusion times, carefully read the formula so you can plan accordingly and be sure that all of the necessary ingredients are on hand when you need them. If you are using your own peppers you will need to dry them first because infusing fresh peppers in the oil will cause mold to grow and render the infusion unusable.

The Pepper Oil

Makes about 9 ounces

Disposable gloves
1.55 ounces dried hot peppers
12 ounces olive oil
A blender
A quart glass jar with lid

Put on the gloves before handling the peppers. Assemble approximately 1.55 ounces of dried hot peppers. These can be all one variety such as cayenne or a combination of varieties. In my last batch I used .4 ounces rooster spur peppers, .35 ounces cayenne peppers, .15 ounces hot Thai peppers, .25 ounces 'Aji Lima' peppers*, .15 ounces 'Aji Eschbeche' peppers*, .25 ounces 'Aji Cristal' peppers*.

Place the dried peppers in a blender jar with 12 ounces of olive oil. Be sure the pepper stems have been removed but not the seeds and ALWAYS use gloves when handling the peppers. Blend the oil and the dried hot peppers until the peppers are in very small pieces. Place the pepper oil in a quart jar and set in a dark place for 6 weeks. Check occasionally to be sure no mold has invaded the mixture. This will only happen if the peppers were not completely dry and if it does happen you must start over.

After six weeks, strain the oil into a clean jar. The oil should measure about 9 ounces. Press firmly on the remaining peppers in the strainer to be sure all of the oil has been squeezed out.

*South American heirloom hot peppers

The Ginger Tincture

MAKES ABOUT 4 OUNCES

3 1/2 ounces fresh ginger, sliced
4 ounces 100 proof vodka
A regular size blender or a mini blender (a mini blender is easier to handle for this)
A small glass jar with lid

In a mini blender, place 3 1/2 ounces of the sliced fresh ginger. There is no need to peel the ginger but do cut off any old ends on the ginger where it may have been previously cut. Cover this with 4 ounces of 100 proof vodka. Whir the blender until the ginger is in very small pieces. Put the ginger vodka mixture in to a glass jar and cover and let sit in a dark place for 6 weeks.

After six weeks strain the oil into a clean jar. The oil should measure about 4 ounces. Press the ginger bits firmly to be sure all of the tincture has been squeezed out. Discard the bits of ginger.

The Ointment

Makes approximately 20 ounces

What you will need:

Disposable gloves
Glass jars and lids to hold the 20 ounces of finished ointment—I find a 2 to 4 ounce size works well
Isopropyl rubbing alcohol – 70%
Cotton pads or a spray bottle
The strained pepper oil
The strained ginger tincture
A glass jar to hold the strained ginger tincture
2 ounces emu oil
3.2 ounces unbleached beeswax
.8 ounces willow bark tincture
.2 ounces wintergreen essential oil
.2 ounces nutmeg essential oil
.1 ounce clove bud essential oil
.1 ounce cinnamon leaf essential oil
An instant-read thermometer
2 strainers
A stick blender
A saucepan large enough to hold 24 ounces
A spatula for scraping out the saucepan
Labels for the jars of finished ointment

Put on the disposable gloves. This protects your hands as well as prevents contamination of your product.

Place about an ounce of the alcohol in the spray bottle and heavily spray the alcohol on the inside of the jars and the inside of the jar lids then set aside for the alcohol to evaporate while you proceed with the ointment. If you do not have a spray bottle use cotton pads to wipe the inside of the bottles and lids with the alcohol.

Use one of the strainers to again strain the ginger tincture into the glass jar. There should be no ginger particles in the strained tincture. Use the other strainer to again strain the pepper oil into the saucepan. There should be no pepper bits in the strained oil.

Measure the emu oil into the saucepan.

Add the beeswax into the saucepan.

Heat the oil gently until the beeswax has melted. This should be at 165ºF. Remove the saucepan from the heat. Watch the oil closely, do not leave it unattended. Hot oil will ignite. If the oil gets hotter than 165ºF, let it cool back down but the oil should be between 165ºF and 170ºF in order to proceed to the next step.

Add the willow bark tincture and the essential oils to the jar with the ginger tincture.

Using the stick blender, blend the contents of the jar with the ginger tincture and essential oils into the oil mixture in the saucepan until it is fully emulsified. You will know you have reached this point when you cannot distinguish between the tincture mix and the oil mixture; it will be homogenous. Continue blending if you think you have not reached this point. Now the ointment is finished.

Use the spatula to scrape the ointment into the jars that have been treated with alcohol.

Label the jars with the contents and date.

Lovingly use as needed.

This ointment will keep indefinitely but it is always a good idea to store any extra jars in the refrigerator until they are needed.

Marge Powell has been an herbalist for over 25 years and an avid plant person her entire life. Her herbal interests span both the culinary, medicinal, and body care. She completed a medicinal herbal apprenticeship with Susun Weed and was introduced to herbal body care in workshops conducted by Rosemary Gladstar. In 2000 she incorporated Magnolia Hill Soap Co., Inc. (www.magnoliahillsoap.com) where she sells soap, lotions, and ointments with plant-based ingredients. She is currently a board member of the International Herb Association (IHA) and the International Herb Association Foundation and is past president of IHA's former Southeastern Region. She has also contributed to previous Herb of the Year™ publications.

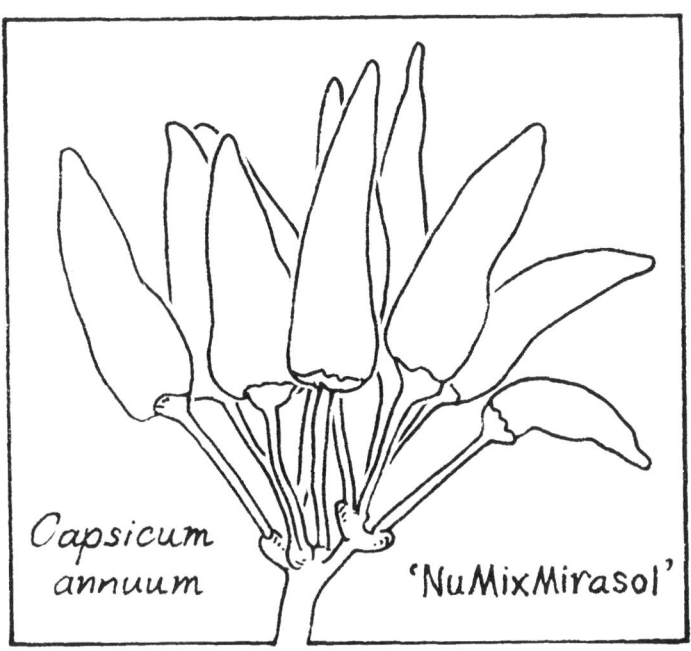

Capsicum annuum 'Nu Mix Mirasol', Pat Kenny

In the Kitchen with Capsicum

Carol Little R.H.

"Some like it hot"... goes the saying. I wasn't born into a family of folks who eat hot food. In fact, aside from the occasional packaged hot chile flakes, I don't think my early days included any spicy food! I remember one week, twenty years ago, spent in Santa Fe, New Mexico. I think that there was ONE dish that I could eat, the entire time! Everything else was just too hot!

Along the way in my herbal education, it occurred to me that it would benefit me to learn to manage some additional heat. I've come to believe this benefits one during the cold and flu season (which may be longer for me than for you as I live in southern Ontario). Probably that trip to Santa Fe, years ago, was a motivation too. So I have steadily increased my tolerance to heat, bit by bit over the last decade or so. I tell my family, friends, and clients; just eat or drink something every day which makes your nose run and your eyes water. It's just my own opinion, but I have noticed that when I detoxify my eyes and nose each day, not only am I obviously eating good nourishing, warming foods, but I am allowing my mucous membranes to possibly release any invaders. The healing attributes of cayenne and others from the *Capsicum* family are many. Why not incorporate some of these famous (and not so famous) members of this plant family into your week?

I've developed a series of condiments, sauces, and soup recipes, which with a little planning, I can have on hand all year and especially in the cooler months, when they are most welcome and needed.

Here's a delicious infused olive oil to have on hand to add a picante edge to soups, stews, sauces, and marinades! It takes two hours to make but it's easy and the result is a delicious infused oil with lots of flavour!

Chile-Infused Olive Oil with Herbal Healers

Friends love this recipe! I've made it for a couple of years and it is an unusual but thoughtful hostess gift or special treat for a heat-seeking foodie!

MAKES ABOUT 3 CUPS

6 cloves garlic, local and organic when possible
1 piece of raw ginger (1 to 2 inches long)
3 cups cold-pressed olive oil
1 cup dried chiles—whatever you grow or an assortment of chiles with the level of heat you like**
1/2 cup your favourite hot peppers, black peppercorns, cinnamon sticks, cardamom pods or possibly star anise, optional

Crush the garlic and grate the ginger.

In a heavy-bottomed saucepan over low heat, heat oil, plus half of the garlic and ginger and chosen spices on medium heat for 2 hours. Do not boil, do not allow the garlic to brown. Check occasionally.

After 2 hours, raise temperature until bubbles form in oil. Add the remainder of the garlic and ginger root at this point and simmer for two to three minutes.

Place crushed chiles (and any additional flavourings, if using) in a large metal bowl resting on two to three tea towels.

Strain hot oil over crushed chiles. This can be tricky. Be careful! You may notice a "frothing" and a wonderful aroma. Keep your face away from the bowl.

Let stand for 20 minutes, transfer to a glass canning jar. Cap the jar.

Store in the fridge for up to three weeks.

**I tend to use a combination of guajillo, cascabel, ancho and poblano. I've also made this with cascabel alone. Very tasty; hot, but not over the top.

Hot Pepper Infused Vinegar

Here's a quick and easy way to add delicious flavour and healing power to your meals. Crank up the heat! This vinegar will increase circulation in the body, which helps to ensure that nutrients reach important destinations all over our body; definitely a healthy choice.

I normally make my infused vinegars with apple cider vinegar—so looking forward to trying this one with red wine vinegar for a change. If you prefer other herbs (i.e. not a cilantro fan—substitute flat-leaf parsley, basil, oregano or thyme—or any of your favourite herbs). Thanks to Mountain Rose Herbs for this delicious idea.

MAKES 2 CUPS

1/2 cup cilantro, loosely packed
3 quarter-size slices gingerroot
1 small hot red pepper, fresh or dried
1 garlic clove, peeled
2 cups red wine vinegar

Put the cilantro, gingerroot, red pepper, and garlic in a large glass container with a lid. Cover with the vinegar and attach the lid. Set the container in a cool, dark place, shaking every day or two. Taste after a week and then filter if you like the taste (or let it steep longer until the flavour is to your liking). Pour into bottles, using a funnel and cap tightly. Label and date each bottle.

I am very fortunate to spend time each winter in Puerto Vallarta, Mexico. I have enjoyed getting to know some pretty amazing people during my more than fifteen visits. One of my favourite things to do each year is spend time in local kitchens, sharing cooking tips and learning more about local cuisine.

I have one friend, Graciela, with whom I trade recipes. Last year, I taught her how to make pesto with basil. She has shared so many ideas with me. One thing surprised me, though. It is my experience that the Mexican families in this area, at least, do not cook with a lot of heat. They use mild to medium chiles predominantly. Graciela explained that the children are not fond of spicy food, so moms make the dishes edible for all without the heat. There are always two to three kinds of bottled hot sauce on the table, however, to kick things up a bit! This makes total sense and everyone is happy. Another little tidbit from Graciela—when using fresh chiles, take the time to char (on the grill) or roast them in the oven before making any kind of condiment or salsa (sauce) to achieve maximum flavour. Toasting, roasting, grilling, etc. allows the skins to be removed and deepens the flavour. It's not difficult.

How to Roast or Grill Chile Peppers

Place the chile directly on the barbecue grill (preheat on high) or on a lightly greased cookie sheet in the oven set to broil.

It won't be long until the skin blackens and begins to bubble, 2 to 3 minutes.

Turn the chile over and allow to blister and blacken on the other side for a couple more minutes. Remove from the heat and place in a plastic bag or into a bowl, covering with plastic wrap. Allow to steam for about 5 to 6 minutes.

Place slightly cooled chile on a cutting board and peel the skin off the chile with your hands, if you can stand the heat, or a fork. I've used an old tea towel, which works fine. Compost the skins or discard.

Peeling and Seeding Chiles. Susan Belsinger

Homemade Sriracha-Style Hot Sauce

There's a hot sauce out there that is all the rage! Sriracha has become a household word, in recent years. I am sharing a recipe for DIY Sriracha-Style Hot Sauce from my friend Amanda Rose. I have changed it slightly. Amanda used red and orange Santa Fe peppers, as she wanted good but not excessive heat. Choose your own favourites and further adapt this recipe to make it your own. In light of the teachings from my friends in Mexico, I will try this recipe with roasted chiles, the next time I make it!

1 pound hot peppers, chosen for colour and heat
2 heads garlic
2 1/2 cups white wine vinegar
2 tablespoons sugar or honey
1 tablespoon sea salt

Wash the peppers and spread them out to dry. Cut off the stem ends of the peppers and discard. Slice the peppers in half lengthwise. Remove and discard the seeds and membranes.

Peel and mince the garlic cloves.

Pour the vinegar, sugar, and salt into a non-reactive container (I used a glass gallon jar for this). Mix until the sugar and salt have dissolved into the vinegar. Add the peppers and garlic to the vinegar mix. Cover and refrigerate overnight.

The next day, strain the garlic and chiles from the vinegar and reserve. Strain the vinegar a second time into a large saucepan. Cook the vinegar until it is reduced by 50%. Add the reserved, strained peppers and garlic to the reduced vinegar and continue cooking until the peppers and garlic are completely soft and cooked through. Blend the cooked sauce in a food processor. Be careful—the vinegar will be hot. Return the blended hot sauce to the pan and keep it at a low simmer before canning it. Follow the manufacturers' directions for canning, or bottle and keep in the refrigerator.

Charlene's Jalapeño Poppers with Bacon

My cousin, Charlene, made a very tasty hors d'oeuvre for a family party last Christmas. It was the *hit of our get-together, which was a fun-filled "appetizer pot luck". When these babies came out of the oven, there was a line up!*

Makes 24

12 jalapeño peppers
1 small tub (8 ounces) of herb and garlic cream cheese
1 cup grated sharp cheddar cheese
1 to 2 cloves garlic, minced
12 slices bacon

Preheat oven to 375ºF. Don a pair of kitchen gloves or beware! Slice the peppers in half lengthwise and remove the seeds and membrane. Set aside.

In a small bowl, mix the cream cheese, cheddar cheese, and minced garlic until well combined. Stuff the cheese and garlic mixture into the jalapeños.

Cut the bacon in half lengthwise. Wrap each pepper with bacon. Place the peppers cheese-side-up on a cookie sheet lined with parchment paper.

When all are assembled, place in middle rack of hot oven.

Bake for 40 minutes or until the bacon appears a bit crispy.

Firecracker Shrimp

Sometimes, it's as easy as a shake or two from our hot pepper shaker! Do you have a container of hot pepper flakes in your spice cupboard? My dear friend Michael Bouffard shared this quick picante shrimp appetizer with me last year, so I could re-create it at home.

Michael is the co-owner of Bravos, the best restaurant, in my foodie opinion, in Puerto Vallarta. http://www.bravospv.com This is a winning dish and simple to make; a perfect seafood appetizer and ready in less than 10 minutes. You may notice, there's no amount listed for the chile pepper flakes. That's up to you. This dish can offer a light kick or a blast—hence the name!

MAKES 1 DELICIOUS APPETIZER TO SERVE 2 OR 3

2 tablespoons each, butter and olive oil
8 to 10 shrimp
Chile pepper flakes
2 cloves garlic, chopped
Juice from 1/2 lemon

Heat butter and oil in a sauté pan. When hot, add the shrimp and the chile flakes. Stir to cover with the buttery oil and mix up the chile flakes. When the shrimp are half cooked, add the garlic.

Stir to allow the shrimp to cook evenly and keep the garlic from burning. Add the lemon juice when the shrimp are just done.

Carol Little R.H. is a traditional herbalist in Toronto, where she has a private practice working primarily with busy homemakers, professional women, businesswomen, and entrepreneurs. She writes 'easy to digest' posts weekly in her herb-infused blog @ www.studiobotanica.com. Carol is a past board member and current professional member of the Ontario Herbalists Association. She combines her love of travel and passion for all things green and loves to write about both. Carol has written for *Vitality Magazine* for many years. She writes a monthly column for the online *Natural Herbal Living Magazine*. She is a contributor to IHA's quarterly newsletter and contributes each year to the Herb of the Year™ publication.

Preparing peppers, Pat Crocker

Assorted hot peppers. Susan Belsinger

Chile Pepper Shrub

Susan Belsinger and Tina Marie Wilcox

SHRUB IS AN age-old beverage: a syrup made from fruit, vinegar, and sweetener, which is believed to be of Turkish origin. Its first recorded use was in the 1600s. The drink was carried across land and ocean by travelers and trade ships and kept scurvy away from sailors at sea. "Fruit vinegar" quenched the thirst of Europeans as well as farmers in colonial America.

Recipes for shrubs, also referred to as "switchel" and "beveridge," vary greatly and date as far back as pre-colonial times. Shrub has been secretly savored for centuries by herbalists across the continents, and is now a popular ingredient used by mixologists in both alcoholic and non-alcoholic libations. Shrubs can be made with sweetened fruit juice, fruit, vinegar, honey, or sugar. Nowadays, shrubs are being concocted with tropical fruits, vegetables, herbs, or combinations thereof.

Generally, shrubs are sipped from a cordial glass, poured over ice, or served with a bit of sparkling water. They are a wonderful remedy for congestion, sore throats, as well as an excellent tonic for the body. They tend to make us perspire when we drink them. We enjoy elderberry shrub, however, you may substitute other berries such as blueberries, raspberries, blackberries, currants, gooseberries, or a combination thereof. We also like the kick of chile pepper shrub; sometimes we flavor it with fruit shrub or even cocoa powder for the *mole* kind of effect. The following recipe is from *the creative herbal home*, Susan Belsinger and Tina Marie Wilcox, *herbspirit*, 2007.

Marion's Habanero Shrub

Our friend Marion Spear makes shrubs from all kinds of fruits and introduced us to shrub made with habaneros; it is killer—hers is quite pungent. The Herbin' League musical duo, Marion Spear and Tina Marie, belt down shots of Habanero Shrub when singing at outdoor festivals. It really clears the verb pipes.

We find this shrub an invigorating, delicious tonic and it helps keep germs at bay. It really helps with a sore throat, colds, and flus. We have made this with habaneros, fish peppers, and fatali (as in fatal)—and found all of them to work! Often we combine chile pepper shrub with equal amounts of elderberry shrub for a double whammy against cooties. For less heat, use fewer chiles. The recipe is easily multiplied; we make the vinegar infusion by the quart or half gallon and add honey to sweeten to taste. The original recipe calls for near equal amounts of infused vinegar to honey, however Susan prefers less honey, using about 2 to 3 cups honey to 1 quart vinegar. For the best medicine, use local honey. We give it as gifts to friends and family, who come back for more.

Besides sipping this shrub, we add it to cocktails, tomato juice, salsas, soups, and sauces and it adds a great kick to cabbage en escabeche, coleslaw, and wilted greens. It is excellent in salad dressings.

MAKES 2 PINTS

About 1/2 cup ripe, prepared blemish-free habanero peppers or other chile peppers
About 2 cups organic apple cider vinegar
Less than 2 cups honey

Wearing rubber gloves, wash and halve or quarter chile peppers. Put the chiles in a clean pint-size jar and pour in the vinegar. Cover tightly. Place jar in a cool place out of direct sunlight. We shake the jar daily to activate the infusion process.

In two to four weeks, taste the vinegar—sometimes we leave the chiles in the vinegar for up to three months. After the vinegar has been infused with the flavor and heat of the habaneros, and you are happy with the taste—strain out the chiles. In a 4-cup measuring cup or pitcher, combine the infused vinegar with the honey and stir well with a whisk. Pour the shrub into two pint jars or one quart jar, label, and store in a cool, dark place.

Homemade Pepper Products. Susan Belsinger

Herbal enthusiasts Susan Belsinger and Tina Marie Wilcox met in 1996 when Susan went to present two herb programs at the Ozark Folk Center, where Tina Marie is herbalist and head gardener. Having herbs, gardening, and the pursuit of good food in common, they hit it off, and that was the beginning of a long-distance friendship. Gardening from their respective homes, Susan in Maryland, and Tina Marie in Arkansas, they've exchanged a lot of seeds, plants, roots, and ideas over the years. They have been collaborating on presentations across the country and writing for national publications like *The Herb Companion*, *Herbs for Health* and *GRIT*, as well as the *Brooklyn Botanic Garden All-Regions Guides* together. They coauthored the *creative herbal home*, which celebrates living the herbal life.

Nick Pappas. Diann Nance

Pappas' Peppers Pizza Oil

Diann Nance

WHEN MOST ANYONE in Clarksville, Tennessee, thinks of chile peppers, they think of Nick Pappas and his pizza oil, as well as Nick's own infectious personality. When *Capsicum* was named Herb of the Year 2016™, my thoughts immediately turned to Nick and his pepper products and his popularity in the community. My interview with him revealed some information new to me. I'm going to use Nick's own words as he answered my questions.

"Once, while in France with my wife Michele, we ordered a pizza to go. In the box were a few packets of chile oil. I asked her what it was for, and she said it was for the pizza. They would drizzle a bit of the oil onto the pizza slice as they ate it. That spring I planted my first pepper plants in the garden and started to practice making chile oils. Michele found a recipe in her grandmother's old French cookbook. We made small batches and gave bottles to friends and family as gifts.

A few years later Michele got cancer and died. I wanted to perfect the process of making pizza oil and develop it as a real product with her picture on the label. That is when I met Karla Kean and Martha Pile, extension agents. They pointed me to the right people and programs. The University of Tennessee extension program is where I got certified to work in the commercial kitchen in the extension office. I met with the Department of Agriculture and got my product permit. Michele L'Henoret Pappas was my inspiration.

I use a large variety of peppers depending on availability and success in the garden. My original summer blend is made from fresh peppers from my garden—Tabasco® peppers, cayenne peppers, and red Caribbean peppers in extra-virgin olive oil. My winter blend is made from store-bought dried chile peppers—chile piquin, chile Arbol, and Thai chile peppers. My *Combustion Extreme Ghost Scorpion Oil* is made with 'Bhut Jolokia' (ghost peppers) and 'Trinidad Scorpion Butch T' peppers in extra-virgin olive oil.

I have developed several other products using chiles. Apple wood-smoked jalapeño powder is a very popular product. I have also created a variety of pepper jellies—blueberry jalapeño, strawberry jalapeño, cherry jalapeño—as well as a few other combinations of fruits and berries with jalapeño. I have also developed a technique of adding bitter chocolate (cacao) to hotter peppers like habanero and ghost and scorpion jellies. I am always thinking of new products.

Peppers are the spice of life—very healthful and flavorful. They are good for your heart and blood. Don't hurt yourself with peppers that are too hot for you, but peppers come in degrees of heat to suit anyone. The super hot peppers like the ghost and scorpion peppers will ward off unwanted pests in your garden. In India, gardeners make a paste from the 'Bhut Jolokia' ghost peppers and paint the fence posts around the garden to keep elephants out. Pepper plants make beautiful ornamental displays in the garden or flower bed."

When I asked Nick if he would share a recipe, he graciously agreed.

Blueberry Jalapeño Jelly

MAKES ABOUT 4 CUPS

1 pint whole blueberries
1 pound whole jalapeño peppers, stems removed
1 1/2 cups white vinegar
1/2 cup lemon juice
6 cups white sugar
2 packets of Ball® liquid fruit pectin

In a food processor, chop the berries and peppers in a medium rough chop. In a large non-reactive pan, combine the fruit and chiles and the vinegar and heat to a good boil. Set timer for 10 minutes. After 10 minutes, add lemon juice and sugar, stir well, then bring to a boil. Watch that the pan does not boil over. Remove from heat if necessary to prevent boil-over. Return to heat and repeat a few times.

Now you need a second pot ready with a fine wire mesh basket on top. Carefully pour the hot boiling mixture through the basket and strain out all of the seeds and other solids. Discard the solids in the basket. Add the pectin to the strained mixture and return to a hard boil stirring well. Remove from heat to cool slightly, then return to heat. Repeat a few times. Now it is ready to ladle into hot sterile jars. If you want, you can use a dry spoon to skim off any foam.

Seal the jars with lids and rings and process in water bath according to manufacturer's instructions.

> Nick left me with this final thought, "Whenever you get bummed out or depressed, bite into a hot chile pepper and you will soon forget your blues."

Diann Nance, born and raised on a farm in north central Texas, is presently living and growing herbs among the beautiful rolling hills of Tennessee. After a forty-year teaching career which included time spent in Texas, Taiwan, Germany, and finally Tennessee, she realized a long held dream of starting a plant-growing business. Diann's Greenhouse specializes in herbs, propagating over 150 varieties of culinary, medicinal, and aromatic plants. Her interest in herbs and their uses in our daily life can be attributed to her mother, who loved plants and sharing her knowledge. Diann continues this tradition by growing plants, conducting workshops, and demonstrating the uses of herbs. She is a Master Gardener, an active member of The Herb Society of America and the International Herb Association, and a curious learner about all plants. Diann's contact information, quarterly newsletter, and schedule of workshops can be found at www.diann'sgreenhouse.com.

Getting ready to plant. Susan Belsinger

The Amazing Medicinal Properties of Cayenne

Daniel Gagnon

COMMON NAME, LATIN NAME, AND FAMILY

Cayenne (*Capsicum annuum* var. *annuum*) [*Solanaceae*]

Bird pepper (*Capsicum annuum* var. *glabriusculum*) [*Solanaceae*]

Other common names: Capsicum, chile, chili, habanero, hot pepper, paprika, pimento, red pepper, and Tabasco pepper among many common names.

PART USED:

The fruit, also referred to as a pepper, is the part used in herbal medicine. The fruit is used in the dried powdered form. However, in New Mexico, we prefer our green chile either fresh or fresh frozen. According to serious chile aficionados, the flavor of green chile cannot be surpassed. The longer I live in Santa Fe, the more I agree with them.

THE CONSTITUENTS FOUND IN CAYENNE

Cayenne may contain up to 1.5% (usual range 0.1-1.0%) of pungent principles, of which the main one is capsaicin. Additional pungent principles include dihydrocapsaicin, nordihydrocapsaicin, homocapsaicin, and homodihydro-capsaicin. Other constituents present include carotenoids (capsanthin, capsorubin, carotene, lutein, etc.); fats (9-17%), proteins (12-15%), vitamins A, B1, B2, B3, B6, C, E, bioflavonoids, as well as a small amount of a volatile oil.

SAY HELLO TO CAPSAICIN

Spicy peppers contain a substance called capsaicin. This is what makes them hot. It's good to know that this substance is not water soluble. In other words, capsaicin will not wash off with water. After preparing peppers or using a capsaicin cream, it may take hours for the warmth, stinging, burning sensation to wear off. You should also be aware that after handling peppers, you should never touch your eyes, lips, mucous membranes (like the inside of your nose), or your skin as the capsaicin on your hands may transfer to these tissues. Then the sensation of warmth, stinging, and burning will affect these parts also. This is why I suggest that, if you are going to be preparing peppers or using a capsaicin cream, you should use gloves.

CAPSAICINOIDS, WHAT YOU DO TO ME

Concentrated in the veins of the fruit, the capsaicinoid compounds stimulate your nerve endings making your brain "think" that you are in pain. As a balancing measure, the brain responds by releasing substances called endorphins, which are similar in structure to morphine. When you eat cayenne, something similar to a mild euphoria results, creating a high. This release of endorphins may be the reason why peppers are mildly addictive. Ask any "pepperhead".

CAPSAICIN, THE HOT ONE

Capsaicin is the most pungent of the group of compounds called capsaicinoids that have been isolated from cayenne. Although it is barely soluble in water, it is very soluble in fats, oils, and alcohol. Two of the compounds, capsaicin and dihydrocapsaicin, make up 80 to 90% of the capsaicinoids found in peppers. Capsaicinoids are typically ranked according to their heat or pungency level. Scoville heat unit (SHU) ratings are the accepted way that peppers are rated. Peppers vary in heat, flavor, and color from crop to crop, variety, and from season to season. Keep in mind that when peppers are dehydrated they tend to increase in "heat" by a factor of about 10.

WHAT ARE SCOVILLE UNITS?

The search for ways of describing the hotness of peppers is quite old. Nahuatl, the language of the Aztecs, had six adjectives to describe the hotness of peppers; the order of increasing pungency are: *coco, cocopatic, cocopetz-patic, cocopetztic, copetzquauitl, and cocopalatic*. The modern description of the relative heat of cayenne is based on a system called the Scoville heat units. A Scoville unit is a measurement of capsaicin level in a particular pepper or variety, the relative heat index of each pepper. A mild cayenne rates at 40,000 units; a moderate cayenne averages around 80,000 units; while a hot cayenne tips at the scale at 120,000 or more units. The system gives a number to the pungency of peppers. Pungency is used by food scientists to refer to the spiciness, the hotness, and/or the degree of heat that a food possesses.

Whole pepper	
Scoville heat units (SHU)	Pepper type
0-100	most Bell/Sweet pepper varieties
500-1000	New Mexican peppers
1,000-1,500	Espanola peppers
1,000-2,000	Ancho & Pasilla peppers
1,000-2,500	Cascabel & Cherry peppers
2,500-5,000	Jalapeño & Mirasol peppers
5,000-15,000	Serrano peppers
15,000-30,000	de Arbol peppers
30,000–50,000	Cayenne & Tabasco peppers

Whole pepper

Scoville heat units (SHU)	Pepper type
50,000–100,000	Chiltepin peppers
100,000–350,000	Scotch Bonnet & Thai peppers
200,000–300,000	Habanero peppers
301,000	Chocolate Brown Habanero
577,000	'Red Savina' Habanero
835,000	'Naga Jolokia'
1,000,000 +	'Dorset Naga Jolokia'
1,000,000 +	'Bhut Jolokia' or Ghost Chile

As of August 2015, the current reigning Guinness World Record holder for the hottest pepper belongs to Smokin Ed's 'Carolina Reaper'. This super-hot pepper rated at an average of 1,569,300 SHU.

Isolated compounds from peppers

Scoville heat units (SHU)	Isolated capsaicinoid compounds type
2,000,000	Consumer-type pepper spray
5,300,000	Police-grade pepper spray
8,600,000	Homocapsaicin and homodihydrocapsaicin
9,100,000	Nordihydrocapsaicin
16,000,000	Dihydrocapsaicin
16,000,000	Pure capsaicin

www.chez-williams.com 2015

HOW SCOVILLE UNITS GOT THEIR NAME

In 1912, an American pharmacist named Wilbur L. Scoville devised a technique, the "Scoville Organoleptic Test," for measuring a pepper's bite. As an employee of Parke, Davis and Co., a Detroit pharmaceutical company, he had been assigned to solve a problem. One of Parke-Davis best-selling products, Heet®, a pain-relieving liniment used externally, was made with chile peppers. Scoville was looking for a scientific way to evaluate the heat of chiles to be added to the Heet® formulation in order to standardize the strength of the product. Scoville's second goal was to titrate the right amount of capsaicin in the formula to avoid an excessive skin burning sensation of the person using the company's product.

Scoville tried first to measure pungency by studying how pepper extract reacted with other chemicals but concluded that no test was sensitive enough to offer a rating with any degree of precision. He found that the tongue, on the other hand, was far more sensitive than most instruments of his period. The tongue is capable of detecting capsaicin, the main compound in cayenne, dissolved in a solution a million times its volume.

No laboratory test or instrument available during that time could detect such a low concentration. At first, his peers were skeptical that such a method would work. What could be more subjective than the tongue, they questioned. Scoville answered: "Physiological tests are tabooed in some quarters, yet when the tongue is sensitive to less than a millionth of a grain, it certainly has an advantage."

Scoville's method was simple: he soaked each different variety of pepper separately in alcohol. The soaking of the peppers in alcohol extracted the pungent compounds from the fruit. Then he took a precise measure of the extract and, to it, added sweetened water in incremental portions until the presence of pungency was barely detectable on his tongue. In the case of the Japan chile, he found it took sweetened water in volumes between 20,000 to 30,000 times of the pepper extract before the pungency was barely discernable. He thus rated the Japan chiles 20,000 to 30,000 Scoville units. Zanzibar chiles were rated 40,000 to 50,000, and Mombasa chiles 50,000 to 100,000.

CHALLENGES ASSOCIATED WITH THE SCOVILLE ORGANOLEPTIC TEST

One problem with Scoville's test is that no two tongues ever agreed completely, so that panelists' estimates had to be averaged (usually a panel of five testers). Another problem was that the number of tests a panelist could do in a day was limited. Because the tongue would temporarily get used to a given level of pungency, it had to be given a rest to cool down before resuming the task. In an eight-hour period, no more than 6 samples could be run through the panel. However, despite all these limitations, Scoville Organoleptic Test remained the standard to evaluate and rate the potency of cayenne for years after he developed his method.

THE TONGUE IS BEING REPLACED BY HPLC

Scoville's name has since been closely associated with the measure of pungency, but in the last few decades, the oral test is being replaced by a laboratory machine called a High Pressure Liquid Chromatograph (HPLC). The HPLC is more sensitive than the tongue. Many more samples can be tested within eight hours, and the instrument offers less of a concern for accuracy. The American Spice Trade Association (ASTA) established specific HPLC measurements that are expressed in ASTA units. However, Scoville's name has become so well established with the evaluation of peppers' potency that ASTA uses a conversion scale to express its units into familiar Scoville units.

WHAT CAYENNE CAN DO FOR YOU

Internally: Cayenne helps to equalize your blood pressure, lowers your cholesterol, specifically your LDL-HDL ratio, and enhances cholesterol excretion through the feces via bile. It decreases platelet aggregation, stops bleeding, and lessens inflammation by reducing the production of the inflammatory compound called thromboxane B2 and by interfering with the activation of another inflammatory compound named phospholipase A2. Cayenne stimulates digestive system mucous lining circulation thereby protecting the stomach and stimulating the healthy secretion of digestive juices. It has been used to treat mouth pain due to chemotherapy and radiation and to treat cluster headaches. Cayenne also thins the blood through a mechanism that is different from the one activated by aspirin.

Externally: Applied externally cayenne stops intolerable pain. Though at first it may create its own sensation of heat and burning, it eventually gives more relief than if the health issue were left untreated. It seems that it depletes the nervous system cells of their reserve of a neurotransmitter called substance P (P stands for pain). Once the reserves are depleted the pain sensation goes away. For some individuals, this is the only remedy that offers relief for their chronic pain. Cayenne is an excellent liniment in muscle or skin pain, such as muscle spasms in shoulders, arms, and spine. A topical application of cayenne cream or liniment may relieve the symptoms of osteoarthritis and rheumatism. It is also used to relieve herpes zoster, shingles, psoriasis, pruritus ani, diabetic neuralgia, postsurgical neuralgia, postmastectomy pain, and trigeminal neuralgia. The full analgesic effect is usually felt within three days of regular application. Capsaicin's analgesic effect is similar to the effect of eugenol, the main active constituent found in clove oil. Both induce a long-lasting local analgesic effect.

HOW CAYENNE CAN HELP

Cayenne has amazing medicinal properties and exerts a considerable positive influence on the health of the body. We'll examine how it:

Enhances blood circulation
Like ginger (*Zingiber officinalis*) and black pepper (*Piper nigrum*), cayenne increases the secretion of catecholamines. Catecholamines are neurotransmitters/hormones made by the adrenal glands. The best known is epinephrine (also known as adrenaline) made by the adrenal medulla and accounts, in part, for the warming effect felt after the ingestion of chili/chile/hot peppers/cayenne.

Even though cayenne is hot to the taste, it actually lowers body temperature. Researchers think that it does so by stimulating the cooling center of the hypothalamus. This action may explain why many tropical cultures like to eat cayenne peppers. These populations feel that spicy-hot foods help them deal with the high temperatures.

**Helps maintain healthy cholesterol levels
and serum triglycerides levels**
Used as a food, cayenne has been shown to lower cholesterol, specifically the LDL-HDL ratio. Cayenne decreases liver cholesterol levels in rats. It also enhances cholesterol excretion through the feces by stimulating bile excretion.

Research has shown that capsaicin significantly lowers serum triglyceride levels in male rats fed a diet containing 30% lard, as compared to the control group. When guinea pigs were fed a cholesterol-enriched, vitamin C deficient diet, and also consumed cayenne, they experienced significantly lower serum triglyceride concentration when compared with the control group fed a regular diet. Similarly, when cayenne was used to treat turkeys that were fed a cholesterol-rich diet, it was shown to significantly lower what is considered the bad cholesterol (very low density lipoprotein [VLDL]-cholesterol) levels and increase the good cholesterol (high density lipoprotein [HDL]-cholesterol) as compared to the control group.

Prevents platelet aggregation and increases breakdown of clots
Cayenne has a number of beneficial effects on the cardiovascular system. It possesses several antioxidant compounds that prevent damage to body tissues. Research has shown that cayenne initiates healthy cardiovascular responses such as hypotension, decreased heart rate, and vasodilation.

Studies have shown that cayenne reduces the likelihood of developing atherosclerosis by reducing blood cholesterol and triglyceride levels. Because cayenne prevents certain blood elements from sticking together (platelet aggregation) as well as increasing fibrinolytic activity (breakdown of clots), it has been associated with the prevention of thromboembolisms and strokes. Additionally, cultures which consume large amounts of cayenne pepper have been shown to have a much lower rate of cardiovascular diseases.

Stimulates and protects digestive mucous membranes
It is well known that large amounts of cayenne can be irritating to

mucous membranes of the digestive tract. On the other hand, small amounts actually activate production of saliva, increase secretion of digestive juices, and stimulate the production of protective mucus along the digestive tract.

In recent clinical studies, an extract of cayenne, capsaicin, was found to protect against ulcer-causing *Helicobacter pylori*. Test results show that doses similar to those achieved in the diet are sufficient to provide the anti-*Helicobacter pylori* action. Furthermore, research suggests that taking cayenne thirty minutes prior to taking aspirin may protect the stomach lining from serious gastric mucous membrane damage.

Acts as pain-desensitizing liniment for muscle or skin pain, osteoarthritis and rheumatism

When capsaicin is applied topically to the skin or mucous membranes, it first stimulates and then blocks small-diameter pain fiber by depleting them of the neurotransmitter substance P. When substance P is depleted, the pain also dissipated. A second benefit of depleting substance P is that the depletion stops the release of inflammatory substances in the joint tissues of osteoarthritis and rheumatoid arthritis sufferers.

A single dose of capsaicin activates pain, inflammation, and hypersensitivity. However, repeated (long-term) application of the same compound leads to desensitization as well as analgesic and anti-inflammatory activity. Scientists have explained that capsaicin-induced analgesia and desensitization occurs on the basis of neuropeptide release and depletion. However, exactly what the mechanism of action is has yet to be clearly elucidated.

Reduces inflammation, thermoregulation, and pain

C-fiber sensory neurons are nerve cells that transmit sensory information. When stimulated they can release inflammatory neuropeptides known as substance P and can cause a wide variety of responses including neurogenic inflammation, thermoregulation, and chemical-initiated pain. Capsaicin first activate, and then, at higher doses and over time, desensitize these neurons. The desensitization occurs by a process known as tachyphylaxis. As capsaicin is used over a period of time, the neurons habituate to the stimulation and a diminished response to successive application of capsaicin occurs; habituation provides the basis for the current therapeutic interest in capsaicin. Capsaicin is thought to stimulate C-fibers by activating vanilloid receptors. Vanilloid (VR1) receptors are abundant in the body's peripheral sensory fibers and respond to heat and acids. The intense sensation of pain and heat that is experienced after eating a hot chile is testimony to this C-fiber activation. But as experienced chile eaters will testify, they can tolerate hotter and hotter food over time due to tachyphylaxis.

Although the pain and burning from consumption of cayenne and capsaicin can be disturbing and, in some cases alarming, no actual harm results from its moderate consumption. The specific action on nervous system receptors creates an illusion of pain and burning. There is no tissue damage associated with these sensations. This is quite different from mustard oils, which are highly corrosive and produce sensations of pain and burning as well as actual blistering and tissue damage. On the other hand, capsaicin is a pronounced irritant, as seen by the incapacitating effect of capsicum sprays. Sometimes the ingestion of cayenne does seem to produce a lingering sensation of discomfort and this probably highlights the role of substance P in neurogenic (nervous system-mediated) inflammation. Once the process of neurogenic inflammation has been triggered, it can become self-perpetuating. Neurogenic inflammation has been implicated in a number of chronic functional disorders of uncertain etiology such as interstitial cystitis and irritable bowel inflammation.

The desensitization of C-fibers has value for pain relief in a number of chronically painful disorders. Controlled clinical trials of topical use of capsaicin cream have demonstrated symptom relief in osteoarthritis, neuropathy, and postherpetic neuralgia. Topical capsaicin is effective in painful skin disorders such as psoriasis and pruritus ani. In combination with feverfew (*Tanacetum parthenium*) it is useful for cluster headaches.

Banishes phantom pain and postmastectomy pain
Phantom pains are pains that feel like they are coming from a body part that's no longer there. For example, a person may have lost a leg months or years ago, but still feels tingling, cramping, hot, cold, and pain in the missing leg. Doctors once believed this post-amputation phenomenon was a psychological problem. Today, experts recognize that these sensations are real and originate in the spinal cord and brain. In combination with fresh skullcap (*Scutellaria lateriflora*) extract taken

internally, cayenne applied externally on the remaining portion of the limb or nearby tissues is effective against phantom limb pain. The same regiment is effective in postmastectomy pain.

Moves the mucus along
In the healthy respiratory tract, mucus travels easily through the respiratory system by way of hair-like structures called cilia. These cilia propel thin, healthy mucus from the lower parts of the lungs into the throat and downward from the sinuses to the throat. When suffering with a cold, however, mucus becomes thick and sticky, therefore very difficult for the tiny cilia to move. Expectorant drugs are commonly used to loosen mucus and get it moving again. Some over-the-counter (OTC) drugs contain an ingredient called guaifenesin. Guaifenesin is chemically derived from the herb guaiacum (*Guaiacum officinale* and/or *G. sanctum*), which has as similar chemical structure as capsaicin. Both work the same way: In the stomach, guaifenesin, as well as capsaicin, stimulate receptor cells which stimulate the vagus nerve. This stimulation sends a signal to the bronchial glands, asking them to secrete more water into the mucus. The extra water helps to produce thin mucus and thin mucus is easy to move along. So the next time you feel congested and want to reach for an OTC decongestant, consider a hot bowl of green chile stew instead. Chile contains a good amount of capsaicin, is cheaper, tastes better, and does exactly the same thing as the OTC but without the side effects of the drugs.

PREPARATION AND DOSAGE:

Internally: Cayenne peppers can be used liberally in the diet, as long as they do not create digestive problems. Liquid extract: Take five to ten drops in warm water as needed. Capsules: Use up to three 400 to 500 mg capsules a day. Tea: steep 1/4 to 1/2 teaspoon of cayenne powder in a cup of hot water for 10 to 15 minutes.

Externally: Creams containing 0.025 or 0.075% capsaicin can be applied directly on the affected areas up to four times a day.

WHAT TO DO WHEN CAYENNE'S HEAT IS TOO MUCH

In order to douse the heat when eating chile peppers, drink milk or eat sour cream, ice cream or yogurt. Dairy products are especially effective in breaking down the capsaicin oils, which are not soluble in water. Also eating foods that are high in fats tempers the heat of chile peppers. In New Mexico, chile is almost always served with *sopaipillas*, a Southwestern fry bread. The sopaipilla is usually drenched in honey and eaten to quench the mouth from especially fiery chili.

Contraindications: Cayenne is contraindicated in external use on injured skin or near eyes. Cayenne preparations irritate injured or broken skin even at very low concentration. It may cause a painful burning sensation.

Ingestion of cayenne may cause gastric irritation, heartburn, or gastroesophageal reflux disease (GERD) in sensitive individuals. It is often best for these individuals to abstain from using this herb.

SIDE EFFECTS:

Internally: Excessive amount of cayenne may cause gastrointestinal cramping, pain, burning of mucous membranes, and diarrhea.

Externally: Topically applied capsaicin may produce a local burning (in some cases severe burning, itching, and stinging) sensation; however, this effect will go away with time and rarely is severe enough to suggest that use of the cream should be discontinued.

Capsicum is a powerful local stimulant; its active principles are strongly irritant to the eyes and tender skin, producing an intense burning sensation, but, unlike other herbs like mustard, it will not produce blistering of the skin.

DRUG INTERACTIONS:

Cayenne has no known drug interactions.

REFERENCES:

Bone. K. and Mills, S. 2013. *Principles and Practice of Phytotherapy*. 2nd edition. London, England: Churchill Livingstone.

Brinker, F. 2001. *Herb Contraindications and Drug Interactions*. 3rd Edition. Sandy, OR: Eclectic Medical Publications.

Cuprian, A. Gozariu, M.. and Cuparencu, B. 1998. Effects of the intrathecal administration of capsaicin on the cardiac rhythm in anaesthetized rats, *J. Pharm Pharmacol*. 50 (suppl 9): 212.

Dib, B. 1987. Effects of intrathecal capsaicin on autonomic and behavioral heat loss responses in the rat. *Pharmacol Biochem Behav*. 28(1): 65-70.

Duke, J. 2000. *Handbook of Medicinal Herbs*. 2nd Edition. Boca Raton, FL: CRC Press.

Gagnon, D. 2000. *Liquid Herbal Drops in Everyday Use*. 4th ed. Santa Fe, NM: Botanical Research and Education Institute.

Gardner, Z. and McGuffin, M. editors. 2013. *Botanical Safety Handbook*. 2nd edition. Boca Raton, FL: CRC Press.

Iwasaki, Y., Morita, A., Isawasa, T., Kobata, K., Sekiwa, Y. and Morimitsu, Y. 2006. A nonpungent component of steamed ginger—{10}-shogaol—increases adrenaline secretion via the activation of TRPV1. *Nutr Neurosci*. 9: 169-178.

Jones, NL., Shabib, S., and Sherman, PM. 1997. Capsaicin as an inhibitor of the growth of the gastric pathogen *Helicobacter pylori*. *FEMS MicrobiologyLetters*. 146: 223-227.

Kang, JY., Yeoh, KG., Chia, HP., Lee, HP., Chia, YW., Guan, R. and Yap, I. 1995. Chili-protective factor against peptic ulcer? *Dig Dis Sci*. 40: 570-579.

Kang, JY., LaBrooy, SJ., Yap, I., Guan, R., Lim, KP., Math, MV., and Tay, HH. 1987. Racial differences in peptic ulcer frequency in Singapore. *J. Gastroenterol Hepatol*. 2: 239-244.

Kawada,T., Hagihara, KI., Iwai, K. 1986. Effects of capsaicin on lipid metabolism in rats fed a high fat diet. *Jn Nutrition*. 116: 1272-1278.

Kuhn, M. and D. Winston. 2001. *Herbal Therapy and Supplements*. Philadelphia, PA: Lippincott Williams and Wilkins.

Leung, A. and S. Foster. 1996. *Encyclopedia of Common Natural Ingredients used in Food, Drugs and Cosmetics*. 2nd Edition, New York, NY: John Wiley & Sons, Inc.

McGuffin, M. et al. 1997. *Botanical Safety Handbook*. Boca Raton, FL: CRC Press.

McGuffin, M., Kartesz, JF, Leung, AY, and Tucker, AO. 2000. *Herbs of Commerce*. 2nd edition. Silver Springs, MD: American Herbal Products Association.

Mills, S. and K. Bone. 2000. *Principles and Practice of Phytotherapy*. London, England: Churchill Livingstone.

Negulesco, JA., Young, RM., and Ki, P. 1985. Capsaicin lowers plasma cholesterol and triglycerides of lagomorphs. *Artery*. 12(5): 301-311.

Negulesco, JA., Noel, SA., Newman, HAI., Naber, EC., Bhat, HB., Witiak, DT. 1987. Effects of pure capsaicinoids (capsaicin and dihydrocapsaicin) on plasma lipid and lipoprotein concentrations of turkey poults. *Atherosclerosis*. 64(2-3): 85-90

Pizzorno, J, and M. Murray, 1999. *Textbook of Natural Medicine*, 2nd edition. London, England; Churchill Livingstone.

Pizzorno, J, and M. Murray, 2006. *Textbook of Natural Medicine*. 3rd edition. St Louis, MO; Churchill Livingstone Elsevier.

Scoville, W. 1912. Notes on Capsicums. *The Journal of the American Pharmaceutical Association*. 1: 453-454.

Skidmore-Roth, L. 2001, *Mosby's Handbook or Herbs and Natural Supplements*. St. Louis, MO: Mosby.

Skidmore-Roth, L. 2010. *Mosby's Handbook or Herbs and Natural Supplements*. 4th edition. St. Louis, MO: Mosby.

Visudhiphan, S. Poolsuppasit, S., Piboonnukarintr, O., and Tumliang, S. 1982. The relationship between high fibrinolytic activity and daily capsicum ingestion in Thais. *The American Journal of Clinical Nutrition*. 35: 1452-1458.

Watanabe T, Sakurada N, and Kobata K. 2001. Capsaicin-, resiniferatoxin-, and olvanil-induced adrenaline secretions in rats via the vanilloid receptor. *Biosci Biotechnol Biochem*. 65(11): 2443-2447.

http://www.chez-williams.com/Hot%20Sauce/chemistry_and_scoville_units.htm. [Accessed August 30, 2015].

http://www.sizes.com/units/scoville_unit.htm. [Accessed August 30, 2015].

Daniel Gagnon, Medical Herbalist, MS, RH (AHG) is a French-Canadian who relocated to Santa Fe in 1979. He has been a practicing Medical Herbalist since 1976. He is the author of *The Practical Guide to Herbal Medicines*, a book designed to provide herbal care options, and co-author of *Breathe Free*, a book on healing the respiratory system. He regularly teaches herbal therapeutics both nationally and internationally. Daniel is the owner of Herbs, Etc., an herbal medicine retail store and manufacturing facility. www.herbsetc.com Daniel can be reached at botandan@aol.com.

Holy Mole!

Arthur O. Tucker and Susan Belsinger

REDOLENT WITH CHILES, chocolate, garlic, and herbs, this sumptuous sauce called *mole* will have you shouting *Olé*!

Mole? Perhaps we should explain. Mole (mōh-lāy) is the national dish of Mexico: a tantalizing sauce made from sautéed onions and garlic combined with exotic spices and herbs, ground nuts (such as almonds, pumpkins seeds or sesame), chiles, and simmered with dark bittersweet chocolate.

Although there are countless variations of this hot sauce—from red to green to black—chiles and chocolate are at the heart of many of them. The combination of endorphin-producing chiles with chocolate creates a veritable Aztec ambrosia.

Mole is traditionally served with turkey or pork, but also pairs well with tortillas, chips, enchiladas, burritos, grilled vegetables, tamales, *huevos*, *chilequiles*, and more. Try it—you'll like it—it will have your taste-buds tap-dancing.

THE MYSTERIOUS HISTORY OF MOLES

The origin of *mole* is captivating and mysterious, much like the dish itself: an intriguing blend of Old and New World influences.

The word mole derives from the Aztec *molli*—a mixture of ingredients as a sauce. The Portuguese *molho* (pronounced mol-lu) also means sauce, and the Spanish *moler* means "to grind." The similarity of these terms suggests that mole quite possibly arose from the marriage of native Aztec and introduced Spanish cuisines.

Several historical references describe Aztec foods, including the spicy cocoa beverage *cacahuatl*. According to the sixteenth-century conquistador Bernal Díaz del Castillo, the Aztec emperor Montezuma faced his harem of 200 wives only after drinking 50 chalices of the stimulating drink!

Although chocolate was key to both *cacahuatl* and most moles, there never was a single recipe for *cacahuatl*, just as there are many different moles today. Fray Bernardino de Sahagún, the sixteenth-century Spanish missionary and author of the *General History of the Things of New Spain*, recorded a menu of Aztec chocolate drinks: "green cacao-pods, honeyed chocolate, flowered chocolate, flavored with green vanilla, bright red chocolate, *huitztecolli*-flower chocolate, flower-colored chocolate, black chocolate, white chocolate."

A closer look at these flavorings seems to support the connection between cacahuatl and moles:

Huitztecolli has been identified as the thick ear-like petals of the *Cympotealum penduliflorum* flower. Its complex flavor has been compared to a mix of black pepper, allspice, cinnamon, and nutmeg—flavors also found in many moles.

Vanilla (*Vanilla planifolia*) was known to the Aztecs as *tlilxochitl* or "black flower," a reference to the plant's fermented fruits. (Vanilla's flowers actually are greenish-yellow.) An important part of Aztec chocolate, vanilla also is used in some moles.

Mecaxochitl ("string flower") was reportedly used in Aztec chocolate, according to Francisco Hernandez, the Spanish physician who recorded the medicinal plants of Mexico in the late sixteenth century. The plant probably was *Piper amalgo*, a relative of black pepper (*P. nigrum*).

Chiles (*Capsicum annuum*) were added to Aztec chocolate to produce the drink *chilcacahuatl*. Moles often contain both chiles and chocolate.

According to the late Sophie Coe, author of *America's First Cuisines* (University of Texas Press, 1994) and *The True Story of Chocolate* (Thames and Hudson, 1996), the Aztecs also used the leaves of *acueyo* or *tlanpea* (*Piper auritum*) to add a sassafras flavor to chocolate. (Modern cooks who want to mimic this flavor should substitute anise; safrole, the chief constituent of *P. auritum*, has been linked to liver cancer.)

Coe notes that *Rosita de cacao* or *molinillo* (the flowers of *Quararibea fieldii* or *Q. funebris*), *huanita* or *izoquizochitl* (the flowers of *Bourreria huanita*) and *yollozochitl* (the flowers of *Magnolia mexicana*) all added floral notes to Aztec chocolate.

By examining these and other sources, we can trace the melding of native and introduced cuisines into something new: moles, a delicious and unique culinary marriage.

MOLES OF MEXICO

The recipes for mole are as varied and individual as its makers, with each region and cook boasting its own version. Chocolate is fundamental to the darker-hued moles, but is absent from *mole verde* and most *mole amarillo*, which are flavored subtly with herbs and spices.

The best known and most popular mole dishes are from Puebla and Oaxaca. *Mole poblano*, which originated in Puebla, is a rather elaborate preparation with chocolate, dried chiles, nuts, various spices, and sometimes raisins or plantains. Oaxaca, famed for its Seven Moles, is home to *mole negro* (made with *guajillo* chiles) and *mole amarillo* (prepared with *Chile amarillo*).

Veracruz and Guerrero are known for *mole verde*. Veracruz cooks make this fresh green mole sauce without any nuts or seeds, while the cooks of Guerrero insist that pumpkin seeds are essential.

Of course, we must not forget *guacamole*, the delicious avocado mole.

Today, no Mexican feast day—*Cinco de Mayo, el Dia de los Muertos*, a birthday or a wedding—is complete without at least one mole dish. You can buy prepared mole pastes and powders in Mexican markets, but they don't compare to the sumptuous moles you can make from scratch using quality ingredients. The fragrances in the kitchen when roasting the chiles, nuts, and seeds; the sautéing of the sauce redolent with alliums and chiles; and the final simmering of the spices, chocolate, and other ingredients are all part of the art and pleasure of creating mole.

Here are four of our favorite mole recipes to whet your appetite.

COOK'S NOTES

Whichever recipe you follow, choose quality ingredients for the best flavor. Follow these tips when buying and preparing mole ingredients.

Chiles. Any dried chile can be used, but the most common are *ancho* or *mulato, guajillo, pasilla, Amarillo,* and sometimes *chipotle.*

To prepare dried chiles, split them open and remove the seeds (wear rubber gloves). Then heat them quickly on a *comal* or skillet for 30 to 60 seconds—until they begin to release their fragrance—flip them, and toast the other side. Do not allow them to darken or they will taste burned. Place the toasted chiles in a bowl and cover them with water for at least 30 minutes, or until they soften. Pour off and discard the water, then puree the chiles along with broth in a blender. (A processor does not work as well for this.)

Broth. Chicken broth is commonly used, but vegetable broth or water can be substituted.

Oil and/or lard. Most older recipes call for fresh lard but we recommend using olive, sunflower, or safflower oil, which are more healthful and easier to find.

Nuts and seeds. Nuts, including almonds, peanuts, pecans, and hazelnuts, are used to thicken and enrich the flavor of moles. *Pepitas,* or hulled pumpkin seeds, are popular in *mole verde* and *pipián* sauces. To prepare nuts and seeds, toast them lightly (either in a skillet or in an oven) over medium-low heat for 5 to 10 minutes. After toasting, grind them in a blender or spice grinder.

Chocolate. Look for a Mexican blend that combines chocolate, sugar, ground almonds and cinnamon into a pressed cake. The cakes are often sold under the brand name *Ibarra* in Hispanic markets and some grocery stores. If you can't find Mexican chocolate, use a good-quality 60 to 70 percent chocolate along with a few teaspoons of sugar if the mole seems too bitter.

Herbs and spices. Garlic is used in nearly all mole recipes. Oregano, cilantro, thyme, marjoram, parsley, *epazote,* and *hoja santa* also are common mole ingredients.

- *Epazote* (*Chenopodium ambrosioides*) has an inimitable resinous flavor and can be grown and dried easily.

- *Hoja santa* (*Piper auritum*) is more difficult to find in the U.S. Tarragon or anise, which have the sassafras-like flavor of hoja santa, could be substituted.

- If the mole recipe includes oregano, try to use Mexican oregano (usually *Lippia* spp.) rather than Greek or Turkish oregano (*Origanum* spp.), if possible.

- Favored spices are cinnamon—preferably the Mexican *canela*—coriander seeds, cloves, allspice, vanilla, and black pepper.

Masa harina. Masa harina, flour made from dried corn soaked in water with lime (calcium oxide), is used to thicken and sweeten sauces and stews. Be sure to dissolve it in a little bit of broth or water before adding it to the hot sauce.

Cacahuatl Chili

Art's cacahuatl-inspired chili is a Tex-Mex chili in a rich mole sauce. To make it vegetarian, substitute about a quart of mixed vegetables, such as kidney beans, sweet potatoes or orange squash, corn, green pepper, and/or carrots sautéed in olive oil for the beef.

You can adjust the amount of heat by increasing or decreasing the cayenne pepper. Most chili powders are a blend of peppers, along with spices such as cumin, but you could make your own blend from the chile peppers.

YIELDS ABOUT 1 1/2 QUARTS (6 TO 8 SERVINGS)

2 pounds ground beef
8-ounce can tomato sauce plus 4 cans water
1/3 cup chili powder
1 1/2 teaspoons paprika
1 1/2 teaspoons red (cayenne) pepper
3 3/4 teaspoons dried onion
1/4 teaspoon dried garlic
2 1/2 teaspoons ground cumin
1/2 teaspoon Mexican oregano
2 teaspoons raisins
1/4 teaspoon French tarragon
1/8 teaspoon ground cinnamon
1/4 teaspoon ground black pepper
3 tablespoons dark chocolate (bits or shavings)
1/4 cup toasted sesame seeds
1/4 cup toasted slivered almonds
1/4 teaspoon pure vanilla extract
2 tablespoons masa harina, optional

Sear the meat in a 2-quart Dutch oven or stew pot until browned, and then pour off the fat. Add tomato sauce and water.

Grind spices, raisins, chocolate, seeds, and nuts to a coarse state in a blender. Add this spice mixture and the vanilla to the pot and stir to blend.

Cover kettle and simmer 1 hour and 15 minutes or until meat is tender, stirring occasionally. Skim off any fat.

To thicken, mix masa harina with some water to form a thick, but flowable mixture; stir into the chili. Simmer another 15 to 20 minutes, then taste and adjust seasoning.

Long hot peppers. Susan Belsinger

Mole Rojo

This mildly spicy mole requires a little more work than some recipes, but it's worth the effort. You can't eat food like this in many places other than Mexico.

We use a 60 to 70 percent organic, bittersweet chocolate and add a little cinnamon and sugar. If you use Mexican chocolate, omit the cinnamon and sugar and use 4 ounces chocolate instead.

Mole rojo makes a delicious sauce for black bean and cheese enchiladas, grilled meats, seafood, or vegetables, and makes extraordinary huevos rancheros. For a superb stew, add cooked vegetables, cooked fowl, or meat to the finished sauce and simmer gently for 10 to 15 minutes.

MAKES ABOUT 5 CUPS

4 dried ancho chiles
4 dried guajillo chiles
4 dried chile colorado OR mulato chiles
1 dried habanero OR 2 or 3 dried red serrano chiles
About 5 cups vegetable broth
1 cup sliced almonds
1/3 cup sesame seeds
6 tablespoons olive, sunflower, or safflower oil
1 medium onion, chopped (about 1 1/2 cups)
3-inch cinnamon stick
6 garlic cloves, peeled
1 slice wholegrain bread, cubed (about 1 1/2 cups)
1 1/2 teaspoons dried epazote leaves, crumbled
1 1/2 teaspoons oregano leaves, crumbled
1 teaspoon salt
1/4 teaspoon freshly ground black pepper
1/4 cup masa harina
3 1/2 ounces 60 to 70 percent dark chocolate, broken into pieces
1/2 teaspoon canela or cinnamon
2 teaspoons sugar or honey

Prepare chiles: Follow directions for handling the chiles under "Cook's Notes" above. After you drain the soaking liquid from the chiles, place half of them in the blender with 1/2 cup broth and puree. Place a strainer over a bowl and pour the chile puree into it. Repeat the pureeing process with the remaining chiles and another 1/2 cup broth, and then pour puree into strainer.

Add another 1/2 cup stock to blender to remove residual puree then pour into the strainer. Using a spoon, press puree through strainer, extracting as much as possible. Discard what is left in the strainer and set puree aside.

Toast nuts and seeds: In a medium-size skillet over medium-low heat, toast almonds about 4 minutes, shaking occasionally. Add sesame seeds to the pan, shaking and stirring, for a few more minutes. When seeds start to pop, remove nuts and seeds to a plate to cool.

Cook onion and seasonings: In a sauté pan or skillet, heat 3 tablespoons oil over medium heat. Add onion and cinnamon stick, stir, and cook 5 minutes. Add garlic cloves and bread cubes and sauté 3 minutes, stirring occasionally. Add epazote, oregano, salt, and black pepper; stir another minute or two.

As onion mixture cooks, transfer almonds and sesame seeds to blender and add 1 1/2 cups broth. Blend until smooth. Add nut puree to chile puree.

Puree onion mixture: Remove cinnamon stick from sautéed onion mixture. Blend half of mixture with 3/4 cup broth until smooth, scraping down sides of blender if necessary. Add onion puree to chile and nut purees. Repeat with remaining onion mixture and another 3/4 cup broth. Add to other purees and stir well to combine.

Heat purees: Heat remaining 3 tablespoons oil in sauté pan (from the onions) over medium-low. Carefully add combined purees; do not overheat or puree will splatter. Stir and partially cover. Cook at a bare simmer, stirring occasionally, about 10 minutes.

Finish: Put masa in a small bowl. Rinse blender with final 1/2 cup of broth and pour it into masa, stirring with a fork until smooth. Add masa to mole and stir well. Add chocolate, canela, and sugar or honey, stirring to melt chocolate. Cook another 10 minutes. Taste for seasoning and add additional salt to taste.

The longer the sauce cooks, the thicker it will become. If you do not like it too thick, add a bit more broth. For stew, add vegetables and/or meat and simmer 15 to 20 minutes more.

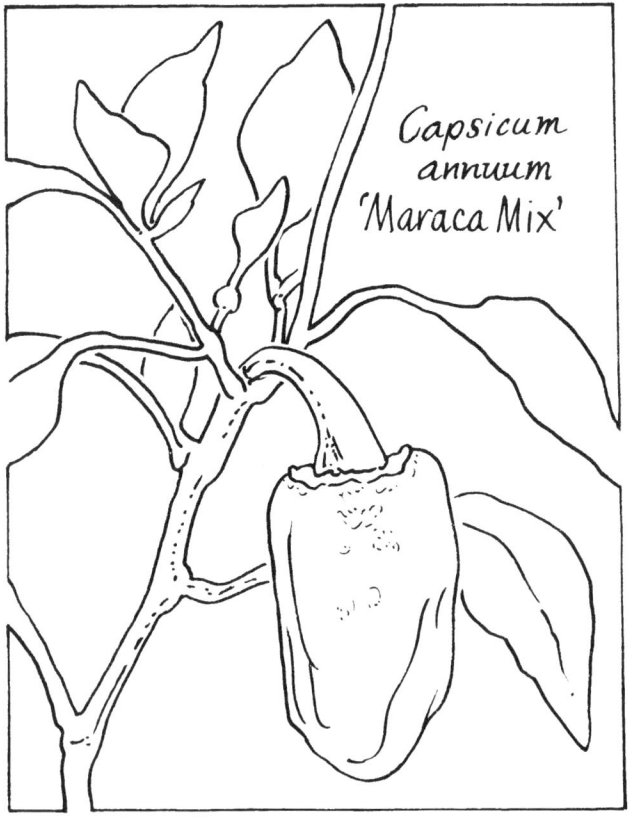

Capsicum Maraca from Pat Kenny

Mole Verde

Green moles, like this one, tend to be more rustic than red moles, which usually are strained for a smooth texture. This one is thick and mildly hot. For a hotter sauce, add 1 or 2 stemmed and seeded serrano or jalapeño peppers when pureeing the other ingredients.

For a delicious appetizer or vegetable side, slice roasted potatoes and place them on a baking sheet. Spoon some Mole Verde over them, then sprinkle with grated cheddar cheese. Place in a hot oven or under the broiler and heat until golden-brown.

Try this mole on cheese enchiladas (with strips of poblano or diced roasted potatoes in them), sweet potato enchiladas, breakfast eggs or burritos, or on grilled veggies, tofu, chicken, or fish. For a tasty stew, add vegetables or cooked meat to sauce and heat together.

MAKES A GENEROUS 1 1/2 QUARTS

1 cup raw pepitas (pumpkin seeds), toasted
4 large fresh poblano peppers, roasted, peeled, seeded, and cut into strips
3/4 pound tomatillos, roasted, husks removed, rinsed, and drained
1 cup chopped onion
7 garlic cloves, peeled
1 cup fresh cilantro
1 tablespoon chopped fresh epazote OR 1 generous teaspoon dried leaves, crumbled
3 tablespoons olive, sunflower, or safflower oil
About 1 1/2 cups vegetable broth (plus extra, if necessary)
3 tablespoons masa harina
About 1/2 teaspoon salt
Freshly ground black pepper

Use the blender to make this mole in two batches. First, grind all of the toasted pumpkin seeds in the blender, stopping to stir, as needed. If necessary, add 1/4 to 1/2 cup of vegetable broth. Scrape ground seeds into a bowl and set aside.

Combine half of the fresh ingredients in the blender: 2 poblanos, half the tomatillos, 1/2 cup onion, 3 or 4 garlic cloves, 1/2 cup cilantro, and half the epazote. Add 1/2 cup vegetable broth and puree, scraping the sides as necessary. Add puree to pumpkin seeds. Repeat the process with the other half of the ingredients, then add puree to the ground seeds and stir.

In a sauté pan, heat oil over medium heat. Carefully add puree (if it is hot it will sizzle), stir, then partially cover the pan. When sauce begins to simmer, reduce heat to medium-low and cook gently for 10 minutes, stirring occasionally.

Add 1/4 to 1/2 cup broth to blender. Put masa harina in a small bowl, and then pour broth and residue from blender over the masa. Stir with a fork until masa is smooth. Add masa to sauce, season with salt and pepper, and stir well. Partially cover pan and cook another 5 minutes or so. Taste for seasoning; adjust salt and pepper. If sauce seems too thick, add more broth.

Holy Mole Ice Cream

This ice cream requires a bit of prep time, but its incredible flavor is worth the effort. This recipe first appeared in The Chile Pepper Book *by Carolyn Dille and Susan Belsinger (Interweave Press, 1994).*

MAKES ABOUT 1 QUART

2 ounces fleshy dried chiles, such as ancho or mulato
1/2 vanilla bean, split lengthwise
4-inch cinnamon stick
3 whole cloves
2 cups half-and-half
1 cup whipping cream
1 cup sugar
5 ounces bittersweet chocolate

Wearing rubber gloves, stem chiles, cut them in half lengthwise, and remove seeds.

Place chiles, vanilla bean, cinnamon, and cloves in a heavy-bottomed saucepan. Add creams and scald over low heat. Remove from heat and let mixture steep 2 hours.

Strain cream to remove chiles and spices. Remove vanilla bean and reserve it; discard cinnamon and cloves. Place chiles and scalded cream into a blender and puree.

Strain mixture through a sieve, pressing on the leftover chile puree to remove all of the essence, into a clean heavy-bottomed saucepan. Scrape seeds from the vanilla bean into the scalded cream. Add sugar and chocolate. Cook over low heat, stirring, until sugar and chocolate dissolve.

Transfer mixture to a stainless bowl. Chill thoroughly, in the refrigerator overnight, or in an ice water bath.

Pour mixture into an ice cream maker and follow manufacturer's instructions.

References

Allende, Isabel. *Aphrodite: A Memoir of the Senses*. New York: Harper Flamingo, 1998.

Andrews, Jean. *Peppers: The Domesticated Capsicums*. Austin: University of Texas Press, 1984.

_____. *Red Hot Peppers*. New York: Macmillan, 1993.

Belsinger, Susan, and Tucker, Arthur. 2008. "Mole Sauce: The National Dish of Mexico." *Herb Companion*. http://www.motherearthliving.com/cooking-methods/mole-magica.aspx

Coe, Sophie D., and Michael D. *The True History of Chocolate*. New York: Thames and Hudson Ltd., 1996.

Dille, Carolyn, and, Belsinger, Susan. *New Southwestern Cooking*. New York: Macmillan, 1985.

_____. *The Chile Pepper Book: A fiesta of fiery, flavorful recipes*. Loveland, CO: Interweave Press, 1994.

Foster, Nelson, and Cordell, Linda S. *Chiles to Chocolate*. Tucson: the University of Arizona Press, 1992.

Frydenborg, Kay. *Chocolate: Sweet Science & Dark Secrets*. New York: Houghton Mifflin, 2015.

Naj, Amal. *Peppers: A Story of Hot Pursuits*. New York: Alfred A. Knopf, 1992.

Young, Gordon. 1984. "Chocolate: Food of the Gods". *National Geographic* 166 (5):664-687.

See Bio, pages 3 and 170

Mango habanero salsa, Susan Belsinger

Fueling the Flames of Capsicum Confusion

Pat Crocker

IT COULD BE said that the great search from the fifteenth century onwards for the shortest route to the East was because of a little black berry, *Piper nigrum*. Pepper! And it might also be argued that the race to get to the source of pepper was the spark that led Columbus to the New World.

When Spanish navigators discovered the hot and fiery chile pepper, abundant and adored by Caribbean natives, they called it *pimiento*, the Spanish word for pepper. Whether or not they thought the chile pod was actually the coveted *Piper nigrum*, by calling it pepper, they began a history of misidentification and confusion about *Capsicum* plants that continues to this day.

Although native to North America, seeds of the capsicum peppers were introduced to Europe by Columbus and were growing in Spanish gardens by about 1500. Soon the hot new plant was ablaze in dishes from India and Southeast Asia to parts of Africa.

CHILE CHAOS

Ranging from fiery hot to sweet and mild, chiles are a study in contradiction. Well known by chefs for their ability to cause severe burns to the skin and eyes (always wear gloves when handling hot chiles!), paradoxically, the offending capsaicin is the main ingredient in skin creams used to soothe the excruciating pain of arthritis and shingles. Consider this: chiles are often shunned by those who believe that they cause or irritate ulcers, yet in Mexico, a long-standing remedy for stomach problems has been to consume a whole serrano or jalapeño chile pepper.

And the confusion doesn't stop there. Chiles are a hotbed of conflicting species, varieties, and heat. The names change from region to region; just attempting to sort out the American/Spanish/Mexican nomenclature is a huge challenge. Typically the fresh and dried version of the same chiles bear different names, which are different again when the chile is smoked, or green or ripe. Botanically they are classified as berries; horticulturally, they are fruits. We use them fresh as vegetables but when dried, they're a spice.

CHILE VS CHILI

> *(In) the Nahuatl language of the Aztecs… chil refers both to the red pepper and the colour red.*
> –Art Tucker and Thomas De Baggio,
> *The Encyclopedia of Herbs*, 2009.

The original Spanish and the current Mexican word for peppers is chile (from that Nahuatl word) and I prefer to use *c h i l e* as the spelling for the plant and the pod.

C h i l i (*corruption,* chilli) refers to an all-bean or bean and meat dish (Chili con Carne) or to a type of sweet hot sauce used as a condiment (Chili Sauce). However, you would not be altogether incorrect in using chili as the spelling of the plant or pod, since it is the Anglicized version of chile. Even though Chile is also the name of a South American country, in my recipes, chile peppers are spelled with an e, not an i.

HOT CHILES: THE CULINARY FIREBRANDS

Why do chile-heads brave the searing, red-hot flames of chile peppers? Capsaicin irritates the pain receptors on the tongue that ignite the pain center in the brain, triggering a release of morphine-like natural painkillers called endorphins. The endorphins try to douse the fire by setting the body awash in a sense of well-being, and the chile lovers ride the wave of euphoria throughout the rest of the meal. You could say that they are addicted to the pain-pleasure from the chile high.

But that's not the only reason people are all fired up over chiles. In addition to their distinctive aroma and taste, one quarter of a cup (50 mL) of the fresh, diced scorching orbs yields 4,031 IU of vitamin A, which becomes even more concentrated as the pod turns red and dries. Simply eating one teaspoon (5 mL) of red chili sauce supplies the body with the recommended daily dietary allowance for vitamin A.

The same quarter cup of chopped fresh chile pepper delivers 91 mg of vitamin C (as compared to 66 mg in one orange). And while the vitamin C diminishes by more than half in the dried red pods, the effect is still more than a flash in the pan.

Chile peppers help people with bronchitis and related problems by irritating the bronchial tubes and sinuses, causing the secretion of fluid that thins the constricting mucus and helps move it out of the body. Capsaicin also blocks pain messages from the brain, making it an effective pain reliever. With its clot-dissolving properties, capsaicin may also help prevent heart attacks if taken on a consistent basis.

Factor in the medicinal tonic, warming, stimulating, circulatory, mucus-expelling properties, the calcium, iron, magnesium, phosphorus, and potassium, all in all, using chile peppers to ignite the taste and heat of foods is a very good thing for one's overall health.

A HOT CHILE PEPPER PRIMER

There are five cultivated species of the *Capsicum* genus and hundreds of varieties with a wide range of potency and heat. The Scoville scale is a standard measure of the heat that is generated by the capsaicin in a chile pepper. The number of Scoville Heat Units (SHU) range from zero–the rating for a sweet red bell pepper–to over 200,000 for a habanero and upwards to over a million for new varieties of hot chiles. The rating reflects the number of times the capsaicin in a chile pepper would have to be diluted before being undetected. Here are just some varieties of hot chile peppers, listed from mild to hot.

From left to right: New Mexican, Poblano/Ancho, Jalapeño. Pat Crocker

New Mexican, formerly called 'Anaheim'—long green, mild chiles available fresh, canned, roasted; often left on the bush to turn red. Mild, tingly-hot (around 1,000 on the Scoville scale), it is widely used in many classic Mexican dishes, a good choice for novice chile users.

Poblano/Ancho, Poblano is the name of the fresh version of this broad, heart-shaped flat pepper, the widest of all hot chiles. Poblano means 'people' and these chiles are relatively mild and so they make a great jumping off point for training your palate to accept some heat. Called ancho when dried, it acquires a nutty taste and raisin-like appearance and is the most commonly used variety in Mexico. The terms 'mulato' (brown) and 'negro' (black) refer to different varieties of poblano chile.

Jalapeño. At between 2,000 to 8,000 on the Scoville Heat Unit scale, jalapeño peppers lend a meaty texture and rich flavour to dishes. Their thick flesh makes them an excellent roasting chile. They are called chipotles when smoked and dried.

Serrano. Meaning 'from the mountains', serrano peppers are more flavourful than jalapeño and often pickled or used fresh in salsa, stews and moles.

Cayenne. Grown commercially in New Mexico, Africa, India, Japan, and Mexico, the most common form of cayenne is dried (powdered or flakes) and it is the chile pepper that herbalists use most in preparations and as a crisis herb for treating inflammation. Scoville measure: 25,000 to 50,000.

From left to right: Serrano. Cayenne. Cherrybomb. Pat Crocker

Cherrybomb. They may look like small round red (or green) bell peppers, but cherry bomb peppers are extremely hot, between 100,000 and 250,000 on the Scoville Heat Unit.

ThaiHots. Grown and used in Thailand and throughout Asia, Thai hots are hot, but still half as hot as habanero.

Habanero, also known as Scotch Bonnet and rated at 200,000 to 300,000 Scoville Units, habanero packs a punch in hot pepper sauce and Caribbean jerk sauces, where it imparts a unique, fruity, apricot-like aroma.

Trinidad Congo, is a ribbed, habanero-type pepper and very hot.

From left to right: ThaiHots, Habanero, Trinidad Congo. Pat Crocker

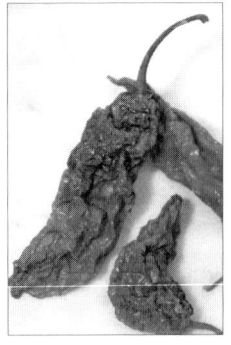

Ghost. Pat Crocker

Ghost. Also known as 'Naga Jolokia', with a Scoville Heat Unit of over 1,000,000, Ghost pepper, shown dried, shares the spotlight with 'Naga Morich' and a few other habanero-type varieties as one of the hottest peppers in the world. Too hot for me, just a tiny piece would be enough to set off a Three-Alarm Barbeque Sauce.

HANDLING HOT CHILE PEPPERS

The active components that fire up chiles are the *capsaicinoids*, which are concentrated in the placenta, the thin white membrane surrounding a spongy white center found in the middle of the pepper, to which the seeds are attached. These irritating elements transfer easily from the chiles to your hands, the basket or harvest container, the knife, and the cutting surface–anything that they come in contact with. To avoid painful burning of your eyes, lips, and other mucous areas, use disposable gloves to harvest and prepare hot chiles for recipes.

In their *Big Book of Herbs* (see Resources), Arthur Tucker and Thomas DeBaggio recommend that if you get capsaicin on your hands, wash with a small amount of chlorine bleach or ammonia because these household products change the irritants into water-soluble salts. Capsaicin is also alcohol-soluble, so for burning in the mouth, they claim, "cheap vodka makes a good mouthwash."

Tucker and DeBaggio go on to clear up the misinformation about what parts of the chile pepper are hottest. Some sources claim that the seeds are the hottest part and this is not quite the case. Tucker and DeBaggio note, "The pure seeds themselves contain none or up to 10 percent of the total capsaicinoids; the heat on the seeds primarily arises from contamination from the placenta." According to these experts, it is the thin inner membrane (called the placenta) on the inside of the chile pepper that holds the highest concentration of the fiery elements and anything that touches this heat center will be tainted with the heat from the capsaicinoid essences.

HOW TO ROAST BELL AND CHILE PEPPERS

Roasting peppers not only provides an easy method of peeling peppers, it intensifies their nutty flavors, caramelizes their sugars, and makes them soft and tender. Choose thick-walled fresh peppers for roasting. Roasted peppers may be canned or frozen to preserve them for future use.

1. Wash and dry peppers. If roasting bell peppers, cut in half lengthwise and remove stem, membrane and seeds. If using chile peppers, leave whole with stem intact. Arrange on a lightly oiled, rimmed baking sheet, cut side down. Brush lightly or drizzle with olive oil.

2. Roast on the top rack in an oven set to broil (or 500° F/260° C) for 10 to 12 minutes, or until skins blacken and blister. You will need to turn whole chile peppers once or twice during roasting.

3. Cover the roasted peppers with a clean kitchen towel or place them in a paper bag and let cool. If you are planning to freeze the roasted peppers, cool and seal in a freezer bag without removing the skin, which will slip off easily upon thawing. Skin should rub away or pull off easily. Cut off stem end on chile peppers and remove seeds if desired, but leave chile peppers whole. Slice bell peppers, quarter or leave halves.

Roast pepper until skins blacken and blister

Harissa

Popular in Morocco, Tunisia, and Algeria, harissa is a fiery sauce used almost in the same way that North Americans use ketchup. It is used separately as a dip for grilled vegetables or couscous, stirred into soups and stews, or used as a hot sauce in other dips and sauces.

MAKES 1/2 CUP

12 dried red chile peppers
3/4 cup boiling water
1 tablespoon whole coriander seeds
2 teaspoons whole cumin seeds
1 teaspoon whole fennel seeds
1/2 teaspoon whole fenugreek seeds, optional
2 cloves garlic
1/2 teaspoon salt
1/2 cup extra-virgin olive oil

Trim stems off chiles and discard along with some of the seeds. Using kitchen scissors, cut chiles into small pieces. Place in a small bowl and pour boiling water over. Soak for about 30 minutes until soft. Drain.

Meanwhile, in a small dry heavy skillet, toast coriander, cumin, fennel, and fenugreek seeds, if using, over medium heat for about 3 minutes or until fragrant and light brown. Remove from heat and let cool.

Using a mortar and pestle or small food processor, pound or process the garlic with the salt. Add toasted spices and drained chiles and pound or process until smooth. Add olive oil slowly and grind or process until the sauce is well mixed. Harissa should be the consistency of mayonnaise.

Store harissa in a small clean jar with lid in the refrigerator for up to 3 weeks.

Pulled Chicken and Beans

MAKES 6 TO 8 SERVINGS

2 tablespoons extra-virgin olive or coconut oil
1 onion, chopped
1 poblano or bell pepper, chopped
4 cloves garlic, finely chopped
1 tablespoon ground cumin
1 can (28 ounce) diced tomatoes and juices
2 cups chicken broth
4 boneless, skinless chicken breasts
1 can (15 ounce) navy beans, drained and rinsed
2 cups roasted red pepper slices (see roasting directions above, or canned)
1/4 cup chopped fresh cilantro or parsley
1 tablespoon freshly squeezed lime juice
1/4 to 1/2 teaspoon chile powder, or to taste
Sea salt and pepper

In a large soup pot, heat oil over medium heat. Sauté onion for 5 minutes. Add pepper, garlic, and cumin and cook, stirring frequently for 3 minutes or until vegetables are soft.

Add tomatoes and juices and broth and bring to a boil. Add chicken breasts, cover, reduce heat to medium-low and simmer for 20 minutes or until a thermometer registers 165° F. Lift out breasts and slice very thinly. Return to the pot.

Add beans, red pepper, cilantro, lime juice, and chile powder, and bring to a simmer to heat through.

Serve immediately or cool, and refrigerate for 2 to 3 days. Reheat to serve.

Turkish-Stuffed Baked Eggplant

Imam *is the Persian word for "holy man." The Middle Eastern name of this dish,* imam bayildi, *literally means "the holy man fainted," implying that he was so enraptured he collapsed after taking a whiff of the fragrant spices in the baked dish.*

MAKES 4 SERVINGS

2 medium eggplants
3 tablespoons olive oil
1 onion, coarsely chopped
1 cup thinly sliced fennel bulb or celery
1/2 cup chopped fresh hot chile peppers
3 cloves garlic, minced
2 large tomatoes, seeded and diced
1 teaspoon ground coriander seed
1/2 teaspoon ground cinnamon
1/2 teaspoon ground cumin
1/2 teaspoon ground turmeric
1/2 teaspoon salt

Preheat oven to 375°F. Trim ends from eggplants and discard. Fill a large saucepan to the halfway point with water and bring to a boil over high heat. Add eggplants and cook for 7 minutes. Remove and rinse under cold water to stop the cooking. When cool, cut each in half lengthwise. Scoop out the flesh leaving a 1/4-inch thick shell. Arrange shells, cut side up on prepared baking sheet. Coarsely chop and reserve flesh.

Meanwhile, in a large skillet, heat oil over medium heat. Add onion and sauté for 10 minutes or until soft. Stir in fennel or celery, chile pepper and garlic and sauté for 5 minutes. Stir in tomatoes, coriander, cinnamon, cumin, turmeric, salt, and reserved eggplant. Cook, stirring, for 3 minutes or until vegetables are tender.

Spoon stuffing equally into each eggplant shell. Place eggplants on a lightly oiled baking sheet. Cover with foil and bake in preheated oven 30 minutes. Serve immediately or let cool and serve at room temperature.

Hot Veggie-Oatmeal Crumble

A tasty and complete meal, this casserole travels well and makes a great potluck dish. As an added bonus it can be made ahead up to two days before baking.

SERVES 4 TO 6

1 cup vegetable stock
1/2 cup brown rice, rinsed
1 cup chopped onion
1 cup chopped red bell pepper
1/2 cup white wine
1 can (28 ounce) tomatoes, drained, reserving juice
1 1/2 cups cauliflower florets
1 1/2 cups broccoli florets
1 cup ricotta cheese, divided
1 cup chopped spinach, divided
1 1/2 cups Savory Oatmeal Topping (see recipe below)

In a medium saucepan, bring stock to a boil over high heat. Stir in rice. Cover, reduce heat and simmer gently for 35 minutes or until rice is tender. Drain if any liquid remains.

Meanwhile, in a large saucepan, combine onion, bell pepper, and wine. Simmer over medium-high heat for 7 minutes or until vegetables are soft. Add tomatoes, cauliflower, and broccoli. Increase heat to high and bring to a boil. Reduce heat and simmer gently for 7 minutes or until florets are tender-crisp, adding some of the reserved tomato juice if mixture gets too dry.

Preheat oven to 350°F. In bottom of 8-inch lightly oiled baking dish, combine rice and half of the ricotta and spinach. Spread evenly over bottom of dish. Spoon vegetables over rice. Spread remaining half of ricotta and spinach over vegetables. Scatter Savory Oatmeal Topping evenly over top. Bake in preheated oven for 20 minutes or until vegetables are bubbly and topping is browned.

Tip: Casserole can be prepared through Step 4, covered and refrigerated for up to 2 days. Bring to room temperature before baking.

Savory Oatmeal Topping

MAKES 1 1/2 CUPS

1/2 cup large flake rolled oats or spelt flakes
1/2 cup chopped nuts (almonds, peanuts, filberts, or other)
1/3 cup shredded mozzarella
1/4 cup chopped fresh parsley
1 to 2 tablespoons extra-virgin olive or coconut oil

In a small bowl, combine oats, nuts, cheese, and parsley. Stir in oil, a small amount at a time, mixing until it resembles a coarse crumb.

Pat Crocker is a chile-head. She loves to sweat it out at dinnertime. Culinary Herbalist, photographer, writer, lecturer and author of several award-winning books, Pat's latest book, *Kitchen Herbal*, is now available. Look for Pat's other books including *Coconut 24/7, Flex Appeal, Preserving, The Healing Herbs Cookbook, The Vegetarian Cook's Bible, The Juicing Bible* and *The Smoothies Bible*, which are available at bookstores throughout Canada and the United States. Holy Mole! www.patcrocker.com

What's Really Hot?

Jim Long

IN 2007, THE Guinness World Records organization certified the 'Bhut Jolokia' pepper as the hottest pepper in the world. New Mexico State University performed extensive testing, as did several universities in Sri Lanka and India, as well, and all aided in the process of official verification. The next year, if you searched for the words, "Bhut Jolokia" or "ghost pepper" on Google, my garden blog would show up at the top in the search engine rankings. I wasn't the only one in the U.S. growing the pepper, I was just one of the first who was writing about it in my blogs and encouraging others to grow it. I've been growing the chile pepper every year since and using it in hot sauces and cooking.

About three years ago, the 'Bhut Jolokia' dropped in ranking from the world's hottest to the second-to-the-hottest pepper on earth. It was replaced by the 'Trinidad Moruga Scorpion' pepper. What's the difference between the two? In terms of Scoville Heat Units (the officially recognized measurement of pepper heat), the 'Bhut Jolokia' weighs in at one million to 1.2 million heat units. By contrast, the 'Trinidad Moruga Scorpion' comes in at a whopping 1.2 million to 2 million heat units, depending on growing conditions. Though most people recognize a jalapeño is hot (tipping the scales somewhere between 2,500 to 10,000 heat units—depending upon growing conditions and where it's grown), the Bhut and Scorpion peppers are exponentially hotter.

The 'Bhut Jolokia', also known as ghost pepper and 'Naga Jolokia', comes from Sri Lanka. The word *jolokia* is Hindi for pepper. The word *bhut* translates to ghost, referring to the heat that could turn you into a ghost. Similarly, the word *naga* translates to hornet in English, referring again to the heat because the taste of the raw pepper on your tongue is much like the sensation of being stung on the tongue by a hornet!

Why do people even grow such hot peppers? The closer you are to the equator, the more you need to sweat to keep cool, and hot peppers in the daily diet aid in that. People who eat hot peppers become accustomed to the heat and want more. Capsaicin, the active component in hot peppers, has been shown to produce an "endorphin rush," a reaction from the brain when it releases pain-relieving endorphins. The feeling that results from eating hot peppers, then, can become a bit addictive. Those of us who love the heat of peppers—we're called pepperheads—are pleasantly addicted to that release of endorphins.

But why do people keep trying to beat the world's records for the hottest peppers? Two primary reasons top the list:

(1) bragging rights and (2) money.

There is intense competition among men—and it IS a male thing, I've never known women involved in this heat contest—to come up with the hottest of the hot. Think of it as drag racing, who can build the fastest, flashiest car to race. In the pepper world, men compete to have the hottest, officially proven, top of the charts peppers.

The money angle enters the picture once your hot pepper has been verified by all the judging organizations involved, since then you can give an official name to the pepper, license growers to sell it, and collect a royalty. Ghost pepper seed recently was selling for between $10 and $25 for five seeds, and I knew people who were very happy to buy it for that price. You can be sure the 'Moruga Trinidad Scorpion' (a cross between the 'Bhut Jolokia' and a variety of 'Trinidad Scorpion') will be knocked off its pedestal in the future by another, even hotter pepper. At this very moment there are pepperheads growing and testing even more crosses and hybrids of these already-hot peppers!

Jim Long is a professional gardener and author of more than two dozen books on herbs, gardening, and historical subjects. He writes for a variety of gardening and herb magazines and has appeared on numerous HGTV and Discovery Channel programs as well as the P. Allen Smith Gardens show. Jim is a frequent speaker at State Master Gardener conferences, festivals, and garden shows nationwide. He sells his herb products and books through his website: <u>www.LongCreekHerbs.com</u>.

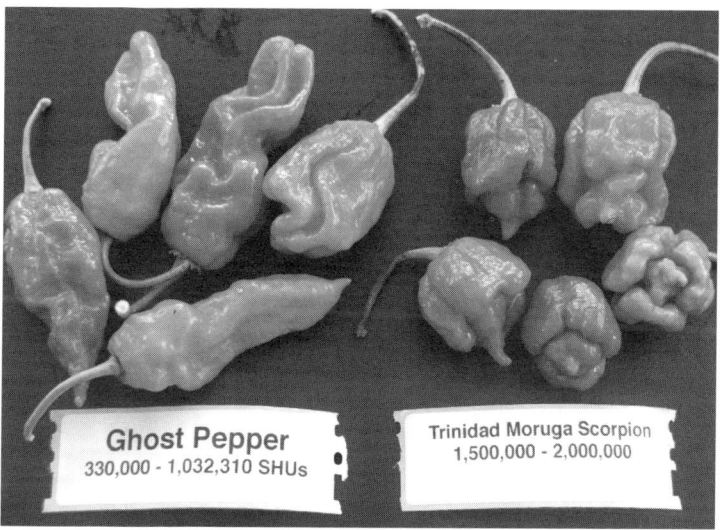

Ghost and Scorpion peppers, Jim Long

Hot peppers in the greenhouse, Karen O'Brien

Fire in the Garden

Charles E. Voigt

WHEN THE AUTHOR was a young 4-H vegetable gardener, hot peppers were something exotic, not something in every garden or kitchen. Hungarian Wax, a hot banana pepper, was about the only one commonly available in east-central Illinois. Since then, waves of immigrants have brought a broad range of cuisines to the United States, with accompanying hot pepper diversity. That, coupled with Americans eating out much more than they did in the 1950s, has exposed people to the zing that hot peppers can bring to eating. Some have embraced it wholeheartedly, while others approach with more caution.

A LITTLE PEPPER HISTORY

Why is the confusing name "pepper" used? When Christopher Columbus "discovered" peppers, or chiles, (*Capsicum* species) on a Caribbean island in 1492, he was searching for true pepper, *Piper nigrum*. Since the burning sensation each produced was similar, and he was eager to justify his conclusion that he had reached India, or the Spice Islands, he dubbed them "peppers." In fact, Native Americans probably began using and domesticating these plants at least 6,000 to 10,000 years earlier, in or near what is today Bolivia.

After Columbus returned to Spain carrying *Capsicum* seeds and dried pods, it took only twenty years for this plant to become popular all over Europe and Asia, and as far away as Indonesia and the Spice Islands which Columbus originally sought to find. Dubbed "the poor man's spice", it was quickly adopted where it traveled, to the extent that people all over the world soon thought they had always had chile peppers in their lands. Chile pepper has become the most frequently used seasoning and condiment in the world. It is a spice for all levels of society, cheap enough for the least affluent consumer, and complex enough for royal palates.

HOT OR NOT?

The unacclimated human palate can detect the presence of capsaicin, the chemical which produces the pepper's heat, at levels as small as one part per million. Capsaicin is really a group of related chemical compounds which produce the burning sensation, but which do not actually affect temperature. Each of these seven capsaicinoids has a slightly different mode of action, which is why different peppers affect taste in different ways. Some bite the front of the tongue, while others "sneak up" farther back.

The heat index of a chile pepper is measured in "Scoville Units," using a method developed by Wilbur Scoville in 1912. It is based on sequential dilutions until it can no longer be detected. This pungency is measured in multiples of 100 Scoville units (SHU) ranging from the sweet bell pepper at zero on the scale, to the extremely hot habanero at 200,000 to 300,000 SHU. Newer discoveries and breeding have resulted in concentrations of over two million SHU in individual fruits. Pure capsaicin is rated at 16 million SHU, so these peppers are one-eighth capsaicin, by weight, a staggering concentration.

The white placentas, which are the ribs or membranes within the pepper fruits, contain up to 80% of the capsaicin in the peppers. Seeds themselves do not produce the chemical, but pick it up by being attached to the membrane within the pepper fruit. Neither cooking nor freezing diminishes the pungency, but removing the veins and seeds is reasonably successful in lowering the heat. Chilehead purists would surely call this a crime against peppers.

Water stress on pepper plants can increase pungency, while an overabundance of moisture may lower the overall heat. Cooler than normal weather can also lower the heat, while hot temperatures and bright sunlight produce the highest levels of capsaicin. For this reason, parts of the desert southwestern United States have the reputation of producing the most fiery pepper pods. While this may be true to some extent, some really pungent peppers can be grown almost anywhere in the United States.

Capsaicin is not water soluble, so water and water-based drinks will not douse the heat induced by eating hot peppers. Since they are soluble in alcohol, drinks high in ethanol can help move the chemical out of the mouth. Casein in milk can also surround the molecules and carry them on their way, so dairy products, the fattier the better, may help. The fat in these dairy products is effective in surrounding and defusing the heat-generating compounds. Finally, absorbent materials like crusty bread, crackers, and chips may help soak up the heat and clear the palate.

Fresh chiles are high in vitamin C, containing twice as much as citrus fruits. They are also high in vitamin A, folic acid, potassium, and vitamin E. Dried, they lose most of their vitamin C, but the vitamin A content increases drastically.

Eating foods spiced with hot varieties of *Capsicum* can be addictive. The painful heat sensation actually causes the body to produce endorphins, the body's natural pain killers. These endorphins bring on a mild state of euphoria. Like other stimulants, the body gradually becomes acclimated to lower levels of capsaicin, and requires higher and higher amounts for the same endorphin buzz. This is why those addicted to this sensation need hotter and hotter peppers to keep the buzz coming.

Hot peppers should be handled with care, especially the profoundly hot varieties. They should be chopped or processed in a well-ventilated area. If your eyes, nose, mouth, or any other moist body orifice come into contact with capsaicin, intense and lasting pain may result. After handling, hands should be washed thoroughly in soapy water, scrubbing with a brush. The most ferociously hot varieties can actually irritate and blister the skin. Plastic or rubber gloves or other protective wear may be advisable, especially when working with large quantities. Eye protection might also be helpful.

To neutralize the burning on hands or other strictly external body parts, a mixture of one part household bleach to five parts water can be used. Hands should be washed in the solution and rinsed thoroughly. This bleach solution should ***never*** be used on eyes or other moist orifices.

The best that can be done for eyes and other moist burning orifices is to flush with plain cold water. This will sting like crazy for a while, but should not cause permanent damage. This is the theory behind the concentrated pepper sprays used today in place of the more dangerous mace. Concentrated capsaicin can be as debilitating as mace, usually with much less chance of permanent damage.

One of the main reasons for developing the Scoville Scale was to standardize capsaicin for treatments for chronic pain. These "deep heating rubs" give their warming chemical heat, the pain of which overloads the body's pain sensors, causing them to cease sending pain messages for a time, giving temporary relief.

CULTIVATION AND CARE

Though perennial in their native habitat, peppers are grown as annuals in the temperate regions of the world, including most of the United States. By starting the seeds indoors or in greenhouses, the shorter warm growing seasons of much of the lower forty-eight states can accommodate ripening of all but the most stubbornly tropical types. Depending on species, seeds should be sown from six to ten weeks before conditions are expected to be favorable for transplanting outdoors. *Capsicum chinense* germinates especially slowly and the young seedlings also develop slowly, so this species will need longer than most others. Ideal greenhouse conditions will speed growth, while less than perfect windowsills will mature plants more slowly.

If space allows, seeds can be sown in individual cell packs, one or two seeds per cell. A relatively fine-textured, pre-sterilized, commercial soilless medium works well. Cover seeds 1/4- to 1/2-inch deep. Bottom heat of about 75°F will speed germination and plant development. Once germination and emergence are complete, these seedlings can be singulated, either by thinning or transplanting extras to their own cells. If space is limited, seeds can be started in a small container, then transplanted into individual cells or small pots once the first true leaf develops.

Daytime temperatures in the 70 to 75°F range are near ideal for growing the seedlings. Night temperatures can be 5 to 10°F cooler. If on a windowsill, containers may need to be rotated regularly to even out growth. If natural light is inadequate, seedlings will stretch out, with weak, slender stems. Artificial lights, usually cool white fluorescent tubes, can be hung about four inches above the tops of the seedlings. These should not be on twenty-four hours a day. Plants need some dark time to respire.

As plants near the size to move to the garden, they should be acclimated for a week or more, gradually introducing them to full sunlight, wind, and outdoor conditions. This is called "hardening off." The process allows the plants to form a thicker wax layer on the leaves, which will help them to withstand full infrared radiation, wind, and temperature fluctuations. Peppers will be greatly stunted if moved to the garden too soon and then subjected to cold temperatures. These stunted plants' development may be retarded for some time after temperatures warm. Later transplants, which are not chilled, may actually surpass those that are.

If plants get too tall, they may be planted deeper than they originally grew. Nightshades have the ability to form adventitious roots on the buried stem section, giving a larger, stronger root system. Dig planting holes, fill with water, and add a starter fertilizer solution high in phosphorus to get roots established quickly. Roots need to be feathered out if they are circling the cell or pot, then placed in the mud at the bottom of the hole, covered with dry soil, and not watered from above for a day or two. This will minimize evaporation and allow the plants to get established, unless extremely hot or windy conditions prevail.

Fertility for peppers should be well balanced. While high nitrogen is often said to cause lots of leaves, at the expense of fruit, this is not necessarily the case. High nitrogen will make larger plants, which may become brittle and need to be staked. A good garden fertilizer with balanced quantities of the three major nutrients, nitrogen, phosphorus, and potassium, should yield good results, unless the soil is unusually poor. Compost tea or other organic sources can also be used. Some types tend to grow wide-spreading upper branches, which may need some support as a heavy fruit load develops. Others will do well with no assistance. In particular, sweet bell peppers, but also most other types, may not set fruit above 95°F. The blossoms will simply abort.

Spacing will vary greatly with the variety of pepper that is being grown.

Some may be only a foot or so tall, while others may grow to be small shrubs three to four feet high in a single season. Variety descriptions should provide an approximate mature size, which should be taken into account when planting. Commercially, double rows may be grown, with plants spaced fifteen to eighteen inches apart and offset from each other. On raised beds, plants may be spaced about their mature size apart in all directions. Plants too thickly planted may be more prone to disease development, because of decreased air circulation.

If all goes well, blossoms should begin to appear soon after transplanting. Any fruits that have set before transplanting should be removed to promote vegetative growth first. If temperatures are favorable, fruit should soon follow blossoms. Once the plants have sufficient leaf surface, these should develop normally. After fruit are set, the New Mexico state question, "Green or Red?" must be answered. Heat may be more pronounced in green chiles because the sugars in ripe fruit temper it a little. Also, ripening fruit will take more energy, so the overall yield may be somewhat less. Many chiles are so prolific this will not matter. Fruit should be cut with garden shears or pruners. Pulling them free may severely damage the plant. Whole branches may break off.

PEPPER PROBLEMS

Diseases may sometimes be a problem with any pepper variety. Some of the rarest ones may come with seed-borne diseases afflicting them. More reliable seed sources should have done seed treatments to minimize these diseases. Some common problems include bacterial spot, anthracnose, and various viruses. Tobacco mosaic virus can be transferred from tobacco products to the hands of users, and from there to pepper or tomato plants, so hands should be washed thoroughly after use and before touching plants.

Like tomatoes, peppers are sometimes subject to blossom end rot, a problem of calcium mobility within the plant. While calcium may be adequate in the soil, it may not always be available to the farthest regions of the plant, i.e. the growing tips and the blossom ends of fruit. Calcium travels with water in the plant, and anything that slows or stops water movement through the plant stops the delivery of calcium. High heat and drought are major causes, and some varieties are much more susceptible than others. Even water supply, mulches to provide even soil temperature and moisture, and good siting can help. In severe situations, a dilute spray of calcium chloride may help to stop the problem. Once a fruit is damaged, it cannot be "fixed", however. Only new fruit can be saved.

Insects that can attack peppers include aphids, cutworms, corn earworms, European corn borers, tobacco hornworms, flea beetles, and spider mites. Cutworms attack newly set transplants, curling around the base of the stem and severing it in one night. In small patches, cutworms can be deterred by placing cutworm collars around the seedlings. These are merely barriers that the caterpillars can't climb. Any slippery circular container will do. *Bacillus thuringiensis* will help control young caterpillars. Hand picking works pretty well for tobacco hornworms, and parasitic wasps may eventually kill them, too. Insecticidal soap may be effective against aphids and spider mites. A high pressure water stream can sometimes wash away both aphids and mites.

PEPPER PRESERVATION

How can peppers be preserved? Thin-walled varieties can be air-dried. Thicker-walled types, such as jalapeño, may need assistance, such as smoking, which turns them into chipotle. Dried poblanos are called anchos. Small home dryers can be used, outdoor sunshine in dry climates can work, and older gas ovens with pilot lights work well, with the door ajar and just the pilot burning. When dried to crispness, these can be stored in glass jars.

A PEPPER PRIMER

There are five domesticated species of *Capsicum*. By far the most common species grown in the United States is *Capsicum annuum*, which is technically incorrect, since they are natively perennial plants. There are more cultivars of this species in the world than all the other four combined. Sizes, shapes, and other characteristics vary widely. The most common flower color is white, but purple flowers also occur. Fruit color most commonly starts green and goes to red when ripe, but other colors also abound. These include many of the most common and best-known pepper varieties, such as jalapeño, poblano/ancho, serrano, cayenne, pepperoncini, Anaheim/NuMex, and sweet bell peppers. Most of the ornamental varieties are also of this species.

Probably the second most numerous are cultivars of the species *Capsicum chinense*, another misnomer because these originate in South America, not China. Their fruits may have been thought to resemble Chinese lanterns. Some of the world's hottest varieties are from this species. It is especially popular in the Yucatan. Fruit come in a variety of colors with tropical, fruity flavors. They have multiple flowers per node, a constriction where the pedicel meets the fruit, and crinkled leaves. There is one cultivar, called 'Aji Dulce', which has the flavor of habanero, but little or no heat. Madalene Hill called this one "Orchid Pepper." Flowers are usually small and white, with a fruity scent. The heat of this species may be the most affected by environmental factors. Cultivars in this species include habanero, Scotch bonnet, 'Datil', 'Fatali', and 'Billy Go'.

One variety of the species, *Capsicum frutescens*, is more widely grown than all the others. In fact there are relatively few cultivars of this species. Plants are compact, making them good container specimens. Peppers grow upright rather than pendulous and are usually red, orange, or yellow. Tabasco is in this species, and is a trademarked name of the McIlhenny Spice Company in Louisiana. Tabasco peppers have been used and described since before the Spanish arrival. Other cultivars are Zimbabwe bird pepper, Cambodian 'Angkor Sunrise', and the Brazilian 'Malagueta'.

Capsicum baccatum (little berry) is grown mainly in South America, where it is known simply as "Aji." Flowers are characterized by diffuse yellow or green spots on the base of the petals. Plants are tall for peppers, up to about 5 feet. Fruit vary in size from small berries for wild varieties to over a foot in length for cultivated varieties. They are often brightly colored and quite flavorful. Cultivars include 'Aji Amarillo', 'Aji Colorado', 'Aji Andean', and 'Lemon Drop'.

Capsicum pubescens is the rarest of the five species. The name means "hairy" and the leaves are quite pubescent and furry. Seeds are unusually shaped and black or dark brown in color. None of the other species have these seed colors. They grow mostly in the mountainous regions of Central and South America. They are adapted to temperate climates and are more cold-tolerant than other species. A few do not produce well at high temperatures. Fruits are unusually thick-walled, shaped like small oval apples, and come in red, yellow, and orange. Flowers are typically purple. Under proper conditions, these can grow to nine feet or more in height. Their capsaicinoid profile is very different, giving them very different flavor and heat from more common species. Cultivars include Peruvian 'Rocoto', Bolivian 'Locato', and Mexican 'Manzano'.

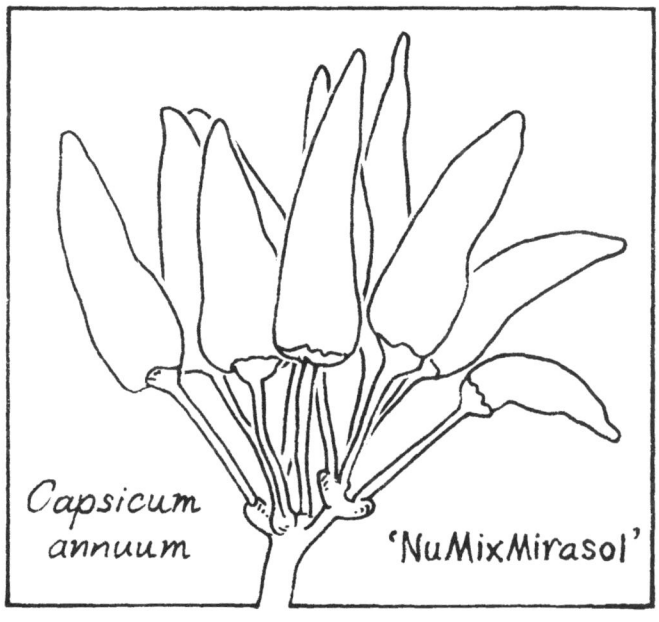

Capsicum annuum 'Nu Mix Mirasol', Pat Kenny

Breeding of hotter and hotter peppers has become an obsession among "chileheads." Interspecific hybrids like 'Bhut Jolokia' have been made. 'Bhut Jolokia' was the first pepper to top one million Scoville Units. It is a cross between *C. chinense* and *C. frutescens*. Others in this hotter than hot category include 'Infinity Chili', 'Naga Viper', 'Trinidad Moruga Scorpion', and 'Carolina Reaper'. Individual fruits of the latter have topped two million Scoville Units. Pure capsaicin is rated at sixteen million Scoville Units, so one eighth of these peppers is made up of capsaicin. One can only wonder how much higher this concentration can go. Cautious enjoyment is encouraged.

Charles Voigt has been on the faculty at the University of Illinois, Urbana-Champaign, since 1988. His appointment is 75% Extension and 25% Research, with emphasis on culture and management of vegetable and herb crops. In addition, since Fall, 2002, each semester he has taught a home horticulture class for non-horticulture majors. Growing up on a farm near Bonfield, Illinois, he received his Bachelor of Science Degree in Horticulture from the University of Illinois, Urbana-Champaign (UIUC), in 1972, moving on to Michigan State University to teach courses covering all areas of horticulture. He was active from until 1988 on the family farm as a field crop and vegetable grower, as well as working as a landscaper. In 2000, he completed his Master of Science degree in Horticulture, also at UIUC. Since returning to his alma mater, he has worked with variety trials and cultural studies of vegetables and herbs. Charles has been active in planning educational sessions for the Illinois Specialty Crops, Agritourism, and Organic Conference, as well as other state and local meetings. In 1989, when the Illinois Herb Association was being organized, Charles volunteered to be the University's adviser to that organization. He has been a member of the International Herb Association since 1991, serving on the Program Committee for many years, and as chair of the Horticulture Committee from 1997 to date, working on the choices for Herb of the Year™. Chuck is a member of The Herb Society of America, and has served as chair of their Promising Plants Committee. He is also a member of the Garden Writers Association.

Capsicum Cuisine

Skye Suter

TODAY WE LIVE in one big connected world and are the beneficiaries of "capsicum cuisine" from every corner of the world. As I was researching new facts about peppers, I began to comprehend the enormous scope of the capsicum family. Although I was previously unaware of their sizeable presence, I now recognize and appreciate the huge impact they have had on humans. Peppers have many uses, some medicinal but mostly culinary. Members of the capsicum family can be found around the world in the culinary traditions of most cultures on this little planet.

I found the most wonderful sourcebook, *The Pepper Trail: History and Recipes from Around the World*, written by Dr. Jean Andrews. She was known as "The Pepper Lady" (a name she trademarked) and she wrote several books on capsicums. In this book she explores the historical path of capsicums as they made their way around the world, and follows that up with a lot of recipes. With its origins in the new world, the capsicum in all its forms made its way around the globe.

Here in North America, we have adapted pepper into our cuisine from our southern neighbors as well as from Europe, Asia, and Africa. In its native habitat of Latin America (including the Caribbean, Mesoamerica, Mexico, Central America, and all of South America) capsicum reigns supreme in every type of dish from tortilla fillings, guacamole, rice, and potatoes, even beverages. South American and Mexican influences have given rise to the popularity of Mexican style or "Tex-Mex" dishes throughout North America.

European "capsicum cuisine" was influenced by the countries surrounding the Mediterranean as well as adjoining continents that connected Europe to the ancient spice trails. These included Africa and the Middle East as well as India and China.

From Spain we get *romesco*, a pimento and ancho chile-based dip and *padron peppers*, a staple tapas offering of roasted fingerling-style peppers. From Italy, a modest sandwich made with roasted peppers preserved in oil and served on a crusty loaf of well-done Italian bread is one of the simple and delicious pleasures of life. Africa has its famous *pepe soup*, a soup made from a meat, fish, or vegetable base that is heavily spiced with hot peppers. From North Africa into the Middle East, spicy *harissa* sauces made from chiles are famous as well as *muhamara*, a hot pepper dip. India is noted for its copiously spiced cuisine that includes chiles in most dishes. *Achaar*, or Indian pickle, is made from limes or mangos. Indian hot mint chutney made from fiery chile peppers can be especially head-clearing. Chinese vegetable or meat based stir-fry dishes often contain *Sichuan* chile peppers which offer a hot and delicious dining experience.

Capsicums have gone through a complex naming history that has given reign to mass confusion. Throughout history, capsicum has been called all manner of names. Pepper is the English namesake for a mixed lot of plants that share the capsicum genus. For that reason I use the word capsicum and pepper interchangeably in this article.

The allspice (*Pimenta dioica*), a tree from the myrtle family, was called "pimiento" by Columbus and thereafter the Spanish, all because he thought he was in the East Indian Archipelago. From pimiento the Spanish added a layer of confusion by calling the already named allspice/pimiento "pepper." In Mexico the Nahuatl word for capsicum was chilli. The Spanish also adopted and adapted from the Mexican chilli and weighed in with "chile", subtracting one 'l'. The word chili referred to the pungent and sweet qualities of the capsicum. And what about black pepper (*Piper nigrum*)? Neither black pepper nor allspice has any true relationship to capsicum. In other cultures peppers go by other names, for example in Thai it is "prik" and in Hindi it is "mirch." I think we can draw connections from one word to another and make some sense out of this confusing name game linked to capsicum history.

The endless variety of pepper types have many different names that refer to their many characteristics, including heat, color, and form. Distinguishing adjectives used to characterize peppers and for identification include large, small, sweet, hot, off-the-charts hot, mild, dried, wrinkled, plump, smooth, long and skinny, round and plump, green, pale, bright, pinkish-red, deep red, yellow, every shade of orange and purple (also called black) and more descriptive terms.

There are about twenty-six species of capsicum of which five have been domesticated. Most capsicums found around the world are *Capsicum annuum*. The other four domesticated species are *C. chinense., C. baccatum , C. frutescens,* and *C.pubescens.*

Due to the popularity of hot peppers today, everyone has heard of the Scoville scale, which measures the heat of a pepper. The Scoville Organoleptic Test that was developed in 1912 measured the amount of capsaicin in hot peppers. Heat ranges from the mildest bell peppers, which have no heat to speak of, to the top of the fiery scale with names like 'Ghost' peppers and 'Trinidad Moruga Scorpion.'

Habaneros and Scotch Bonnets are both high on the Scoville scale. They also have a similar look. The habanero has a lantern shape while the Scotch Bonnet is slightly different, having no neck and being inverted at the apex giving it the look of a tam o' shanter. Guajillo and mirasol are the same chile. Mirasol is the fresh item while guajillo is the dry version. The name guajillo means "little gourd" and is so named because its seeds rattle like a dry gourd. There are several peppers that have a different name when fresh or dried. Jalapeños are a familiar name but they are called chipotles when smoked. When chipotles are jarred with vinegar, they are called *en adobo*. Poblanos are the fresh version of anchos and mulatos which are the dried versions at different times of maturity.

Pepperoncini comes from the Italian word for chile, "peperone." In the U.S. pimentos are grown in the south and in California. The original Spanish spelling was pimiento, but was dropped by pimento growers. Indian peppers or chiles are long and slim. Green ones are "hari," while red ones are "lal."

The "finger pepper" group of capsicums go by names like "ginnie peppers," "chilli peppers," or "cayenne peppers," and vary from 3- to 12-inches long. The "finger pepper" moniker obviously references our hand digits; however, I don't think our fingers come in 12-inch lengths.

Bell peppers have that familiar wide shape; most types can sit upright like a box or container. Green bell peppers are neither sweet nor hot. I suppose that is what makes them perfect for stuffing. The other colors of bell peppers, orange, yellow, red, and purple are sweet, some more than others.

Products made from peppers are also available to us in large variety. We get cayenne pepper, chile oil, ground pepper, chili/chile powder, chili/chile sauce, chutney, crushed red pepper, curry powder, fish sauce, five spice powder, garam masala, harissa, hoisin sauce, nam prik, paprika, pepper jelly, pepper sauce, pickled and processed products, pimento, red pepper powder and flakes, salsa picante or Mexican hot sauce, satay sauce, sambal, sofrito, and whole peppers dried or fresh. There is a whole world of peppers waiting to be experienced by amateur and hard core explorers of capsicum.

PLEASING PODS OF PEPPERS

While mulling over these wonderful pods I came to understand the roles capsicums take on in our kitchen. Did you know that numerous recipes employ more than one form of pepper? Some form of capsicum seems to find its way into a meal at our house, practically on a daily basis. And on some days peppers have made their way into every meal of the day.

A weekend egg and bacon breakfast will often include potatoes. Home fries at our house appear on the plate as little half-inch cubes of potato sautéed in butter, olive oil, and paprika.

Lunch is often an Indian-inspired chickpea concoction or *raita*. Raita is a yogurt-based dish sprinkled with pepper flakes and sometimes ground cayenne. The chickpea dishes I use often contain a whole dried chile or fresh green chile for seasoning.

Dinner fare around here could be anything from a bouillabaisse to fish tacos. Bouillabaisse is a crowd pleaser with a side of fresh-from-the-bakery Italian bread for dipping. Our favorite herbs such as parsley, saffron, bell peppers, and pepper flakes make this dish stand out in our mealtime repertoire.

Fish tacos make an ideal meal for showing off the capsicum family. Sriracha or hot pepper sauce made from chiles, fish batter colored with paprika, bell peppers in many colors, fresh poblanos or jalapeños, pepper flakes, and cayenne added to the salad—these form the basis for the meal. All of the above contribute to making fish tacos a piece of pepper heaven. Though this dish has a lot of preparation, much of it can be made ahead, leaving the cook able to assemble the dish quickly for everyday dining.

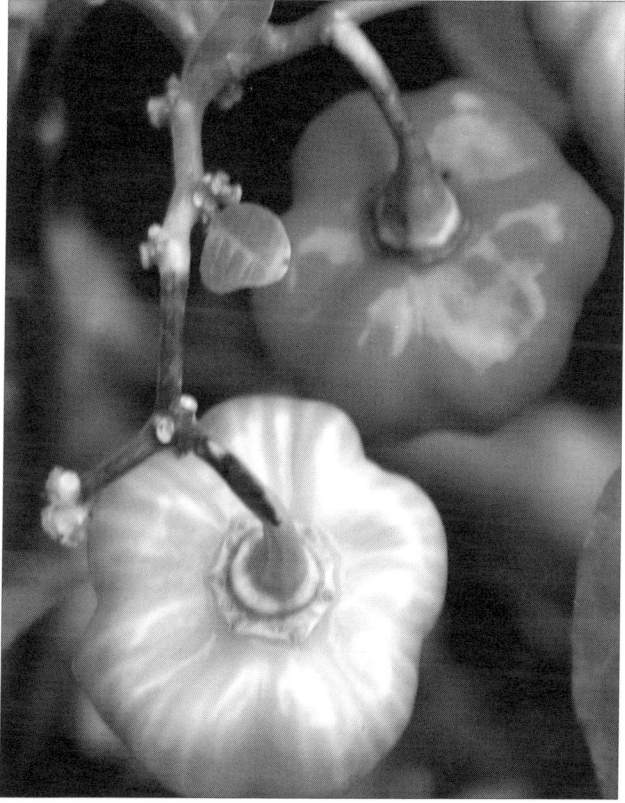

Ripening peppers, Karen O'Brien

Fish Tacos with Two Kinds of Slaw

Fish tacos with all the fixin's is a favorite summertime meal around our house. We enjoy the self-serve element of assembling tacos at the table. It allows each individual to portion out desired amounts and pick and choose from a diverse array of add-ins. Two or three morsels of batter-fried fish can be plunked down on the tortilla, then add hot sauce and a spoonful or two of the salads and any vegetables. Sour cream, rice and beans, or whatever else you wish can be added, too.

Assemble salads ahead of time so the flavors will have time to blend. (The day before is usually best.) When preparing the meal, the tortillas can be heated through at the same time the fish is being fried. (Set tortillas aside to keep warm.) At this time also prepare any other sides such as avocados or tomatoes.

Recipes for Batter Fried Fish, Taco Slaw, and Spicy Sweet Jicama Salad are following.

SERVES 4

2 pounds Batter Fried Fish
16 soft corn tortillas , heated individually in a dry cast iron pan.
2 cups Taco Slaw
2 cups Spicy Sweet Jicama Salad
Sriracha or other chili sauce
2 avocados sliced, optional (squeeze juice of one lemon or lime over them to keep them from darkening).
1 cup sliced cherry tomatoes, optional. (Slice tomatoes in half and season with sea salt.)
Baby greens, optional
2 tablespoons fresh minced chives, optional

Batter Fried Fish

SERVES 4

4 large eggs
1 cup all-purpose white flour
1 cup cornstarch
1 teaspoon paprika
5 to 6 ounces of beer (reserve the rest of the bottle to add if needed)
2 pounds of haddock, Cod or other firm fleshed fish
Vegetable oil, or other oil for high heat

Separate the yolks from the whites and discard the yolks, or save for other use. In a medium to large bowl, whip the egg whites with a whisk until soft peaks. Add flour, cornstarch, paprika, and the beer. Whisk to blend ingredients together. Batter should be of a thin consistency yet thick enough to stick to fish pieces. Pour oil into large frying pan; about 1/2 inch deep. Heat oil to medium high. Test for proper heating by dripping a small amount of batter into the oil. If batter starts to bubble, the oil is ready for the fish. Cut fish into 1 to 1 1/2-inch cubes and put into batter to coat. Gently put cubes into the hot oil, turning with a slotted spoon as needed. Fry until batter is golden, about 5 minutes or so. Remove fish to a wire rack or paper towel to drain off some of the oil. Serve hot.

Fish Taco Slaw

This recipe is adapted from a recipe I found in Bon Appetit Magazine.

SERVES 8 TO 10

1 medium head green or red cabbage, thinly sliced
1 medium bunch cilantro, chopped (reserve about 1/2 cup unchopped to serve as garnish on table. Parsley can be substituted for cilantro).
3/4 cup sour cream, or 1/2 cup softened cream cheese and 1/4 cup grated Jack cheese with peppers
1/2 cup mayonnaise
2 to 3 teaspoons lime or lemon juice
1 teaspoon lime zest (lemon zest can be substituted)
1/2 teaspoon ground cayenne pepper
Sea salt and fresh ground black pepper

Slice cabbage by hand or run through food processor to achieve thin slices. Set aside. In a large bowl, combine the chopped cilantro, sour cream (or cream cheese/cheese combination), mayonnaise, lime or lemon juice and zest, cayenne pepper, and the salt and pepper to taste. Whisk till well blended. Fold in the cabbage and refrigerate until ready to use. I find using my hands blends everything together better than a spoon.

Spicy Sweet Jicama Salad

This recipe draws on elements from 3 or 4 different recipes and ingredients of my liking. It makes more than you'll need for the Fish Tacos, but leftovers are wonderful later and hold up well in the refrigerator.

MAKES 8 TO 10 SERVINGS

1 large jicama, peeled and julienned (substituting 1/2 head of shredded cabbage plus 2 to 3 raw turnips, peeled and julienned will give a similar texture and flavor)
3 medium-size bell peppers, seeded and julienned—for extra color, use one red, one orange, and one yellow or purple.
1 cup seedless globe grapes, halved

Dressing
1 teaspoon cumin seed plus 2 teaspoons toasted cumin seed
1 teaspoon coriander seeds
1 handful fresh cilantro, about 2 to 3 tablespoons, without stems, minced (parsley may be substituted)
1 teaspoon chile flakes
2 fresh jalapeño peppers, seeded and julienned
1 tablespoon honey
1 teaspoon fresh oregano, minced or 1/3 teaspoon dried oregano
1 teaspoon fresh thyme or 1/3 teaspoon dried thyme
Zest and juice from 1 large lemon
1 small to medium shallot, minced
1/4 cup red wine vinegar or apple cider vinegar
3/4 cup good quality extra virgin olive oil
Coarse sea salt and freshly ground black pepper

Prepare the jicama, bell peppers and grapes, then toss together in a bowl and set aside. Combine all ingredients for dressing: cumin, coriander, cilantro, chile flakes, jalapeño peppers, honey, oregano, thyme, lemon zest, lemon juice, shallot, vinegar, olive oil, and salt and pepper to taste. Whisk them all together in a large serving bowl. Add salad ingredients to the bowl and toss both together. Taste for seasoning, adding a little more vinegar, oil, salt, honey, or other ingredient to correct flavor to your liking. Refrigerate for a minimum of one hour. For a more flavorful salad, make it a day ahead to infuse the sweet and hot seasonings.

REFERENCES

Andrews, Dr. Jean. *The Pepper Trail: History and Recipes from Around the World.* University of North Texas Press, 1999

Alfia Muzio. "Perfect Fish Tacos." *Bon Appetit.* August 2014. Last accessed August 2015 at http://www.bonappetit.com/recipe/perfect-fish-tacos.

McMullan, Mark & Livsey, Julian. "The Capsicum Genus." the Chiliman.org. Last accessed, August 2015 at http://www.thechileman.org/guide_species.php.

Helmenstine PhD, Anne. "Scoville Scale Organoleptic Test." About Education. About.com. Last accessed August 2015 at http://chemistry.about.com/od/foodcookingchemistry/a/Scoville-Scale.htm.

Skye Suter has been involved with illustration and plants for most of her life. She worked as an editorial art director at a newspaper where she also wrote and illustrated a garden column and wrote art reviews. After a stint at home to raise the kids, she worked at a botanical garden for another ten years in administrative capacities, education, graphic design, and more. Currently she writes, illustrates, and relates to herbs in every aspect of life. She is in her sixth year as president of the Staten Island Herb Society. Skye is also involved with local arts groups and nature organizations. She has a new e-newsletter out about herbs and related subjects. If you are interested in receiving this free newsletter write to her at theherballeaf@gmail.com to get your name on the list.

Capsicum
Experiencing Peppers
Donna Frawley

MY FIRST MEMORY of peppers occurred when we were on vacation with my grandparents. My grandfather, Louie, was a very kind, gentle man who ate green peppers as most would eat an apple. He took big bites right out of the green flesh. I loved my grandpa and anything he did, I wanted to do, so I ate green bell peppers just like him and enjoyed every bite. Back in the 50s and 60s I never remember any colored peppers that are now available today. I only remember green peppers. Maybe it was our lack of patience to leave them on the plant until they turned red, orange, yellow, or purple. At any rate, I loved peppers from an early age. My introduction to hot peppers like jalapeño, cayenne, habanero, and poblano is a more recent experience. I was making some crock-cured pickles with hot banana peppers combined with cucumbers. I accidentally dropped my knife in the brine and once I retrieved it, my hand was on fire for eighteen hours. In my experience, eating hot peppers is like an addiction. The more you eat the hotter the next batch has to be. I would consider myself a baby in the eating of hot peppers, though. We put them in our chili, salsa, and I dry cayenne peppers to put in one of the mixes that I sell. Over the years we have experimented using peppers in a number of ways: stuffed peppers, pickled peppers, many types of salsa, catsup, etc. And I am always willing to try something new.

Our peppers are grown in full sun with cages around them to keep the rabbits away when the plants are young and to help support the plants later on when they are heavily laden with fruit. I like to harvest the cayenne peppers when they are deep red. Some years that means taking a flashlight and harvesting them at night when we hear there will be a possible frost that will ruin the peppers.

Pickled Hot Peppers

I like to mix the colors of peppers in the jars so they look as attractive as they taste. As with all hot peppers, if your hands are sensitive to the heat, wear rubber gloves when working with them.

MAKES 4 PINTS

1 pound (about 8 cups) red, green, and yellow hot peppers
4 heads fresh dill, more if you like
4 cloves garlic, peeled
3 cups distilled white vinegar
1 cup water
2 tablespoons pickling salt
1 tablespoon sugar
1/4 teaspoon crushed dried red chile pepper flakes

You will need 4, wide-mouth pint jars with lids and rings, sterilized and hot. Wash peppers and drain. With a sharp knife, make 2 small slits in each pepper so the brine will penetrate and the peppers will be submerged and not float. Put 1 or 2 heads of dill and 1 clove of garlic in each of 4 hot, wide-mouth pint jar. Pack peppers into jar, leaving 1/2 inch headspace. In saucepan, combine vinegar, water, salt, sugar, and dried pepper flakes; bring to boiling. Reduce heat and simmer 5 minutes. Pour hot liquid over peppers, leaving 1/2 inch headspace. Adjust lids. Process 10 minutes in boiling water canner.

Calypso Peach Salsa

My daughter, Samantha, and I entered our local "Chili and Salsa Taste Off" with this recipe and received first place. It has a wonderful flavor and depending on how many jalapeño peppers you put in, it can range from "Chicken Little" to "Cowabunga Dude."

1 1/2 cups coarsely chopped peaches
1 cup coarsely chopped honeydew
1 cup coarsely chopped fresh pineapple
1/2 cup chopped red bell pepper
1 or 2 medium jalapeño pepper, seeded and finely chopped
2 tablespoons minced fresh cilantro
1 lime, juiced, about 2 tablespoons juice
2 teaspoons sugar
1/4 teaspoon salt
Tortilla chips

A food processor is handy to chop the peaches, honeydew, pineapple, and red bell peppers. Alternately, you can chop them by hand for more uniform pieces. Combine fruit and red pepper in a bowl and stir in the jalapeño, cilantro, lime juice, sugar, and salt. Let stand at least 1 hour. Serve with tortilla chips. (The thicker brands of chips are sturdier and work really well with this hearty salsa).

Piccalilli

This original recipe came from The Matron's Household Manual—To Young Housekeepers, published in 1875. I thought you would enjoy the non-standardized recipe from that era!

"Chop 1 peck of green tomatoes, add 1 pint of salt, cover with water, and let it stand twenty-four hours. Squeeze out this juice, put in fresh water, and drain off. Chop one head of cabbage, then chop all together fine. Put in kettle, cover with equal quantities of water and vinegar, bring to a scald, and drain off. Add the skin of 12 peppers, 1 table spoonful of cloves, 1 of allspice, 1/2 pint of mustard seed, 6 onions, 1 pint of molasses, 1/2 pint of grated horseradish. Put in jar and cover with cold vinegar."

Today the recipe would look like this:

MAKES ABOUT 10 QUARTS

8 quarts green tomatoes
2 cups salt
Water enough to cover
1 medium head cabbage, chopped
3 cups water
3 cups vinegar
1 tablespoon whole cloves
1 tablespoon whole allspice berries
12 green or red bell peppers, seeded and chopped
1 cup mustard seed
6 onions, chopped
2 cups molasses
1 cup grated horseradish

Coarsely chop tomatoes, put in large non-reactive container. Add salt and cover with water. Let sit for 24 hours. Pour off liquid. Cover again with water to rinse and then drain. Very finely chop tomatoes and cabbage together. Put in kettle and cover with water and vinegar. If the vegetables are not covered with liquid, add more water and vinegar in equal proportions. Put cloves and allspice in a fabric bag and add to vegetables. Add the peppers, mustard seed, onions, molasses, and horseradish. Stir together. Bring to scalding and cook until tender, about 10 to 15 minutes. Pack in sterilized pint or half-pint jars leaving 1/2 inch headspace. Adjust lids and process in hot water bath for 10 minutes for half-pints and 15 minutes for pints.

Assorted Bell Peppers. Susan Belsinger.

Tomato Catsup

This takes some time, but is well worth it. It makes a great dip for cooked shrimp.

MAKES 6 TO 8 PINTS

6 quarts sliced tomatoes
4 red peppers
5 large onions
1 stalk celery
1 cup cider vinegar
1 1/2 cups sugar
2 tablespoons salt
1/4 cup whole mixed pickling spices

In a non-reactive pan, simmer sliced tomatoes until soft, about 30 minutes. Turn into colander and drain off juice. Put peppers, onion, and celery though food chopper or food processor. Add the chopped vegetables to tomato pulp. Simmer 1 hour. Push through fine sieve, leaving skin and seeds behind. Add vinegar, sugar, salt, and spices (tied in a bag). Simmer 1 1/2 to 2 hours or until thick. Turn into hot sterilized pint jars leaving 1/2 inch headspace, adjust lids and seal in hot water bath for 10 minutes.

Donna Frawley started her business Frawley's Fine Herbary in 1983. She began by selling at her local Farmers' Market and that fall opened a home-based business which continues today. Donna majored in Home Economics and worked at a private country club in Minnesota. She used that interest and skill to develop 60 culinary herb mixes, several blends, 8 herb flavored vinegars, and 8 herbal teas. She carries over 100 bulk culinary herbs and spices plus fresh herbs that are sold at Midland, Michigan's local Farmers' Market from May through October and a local specialty store during the growing season. She has authored three books, *The Herbal Breads Cookbook*, *Our Favorite Recipes*, and *Edible Flowers Book*, has a DVD "Cooking With Herbs", writes a monthly herb column in her local newspaper, and has written for the Herb Companion Magazine. Donna teaches cooking classes and speaks on many culinary herb topics through her shop and has talked to many outside groups over the years. She is a regular instructor at Whiting Forest where she has taught over 28 classes. Donna is a member of the Valley Herb Society, the Great Lakes Herb Business Association, the Michigan Herb Associates, and the International Herb Association (IHA).

Pepper line. Jim Long

Pepper Espalier. Skye Suter

Aji Eschabeche
Aji Cristal
Rooster Spur
Thai
Aji Lima
Black Beauty Bell
Cayenne

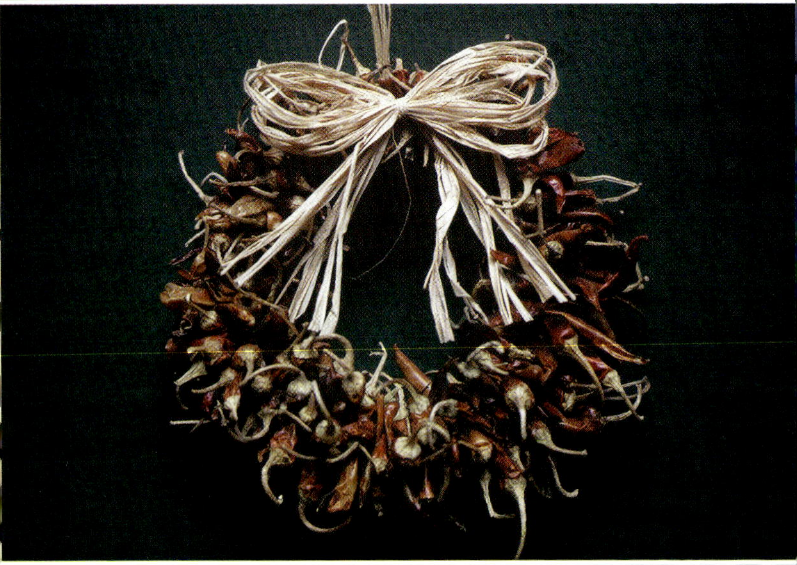

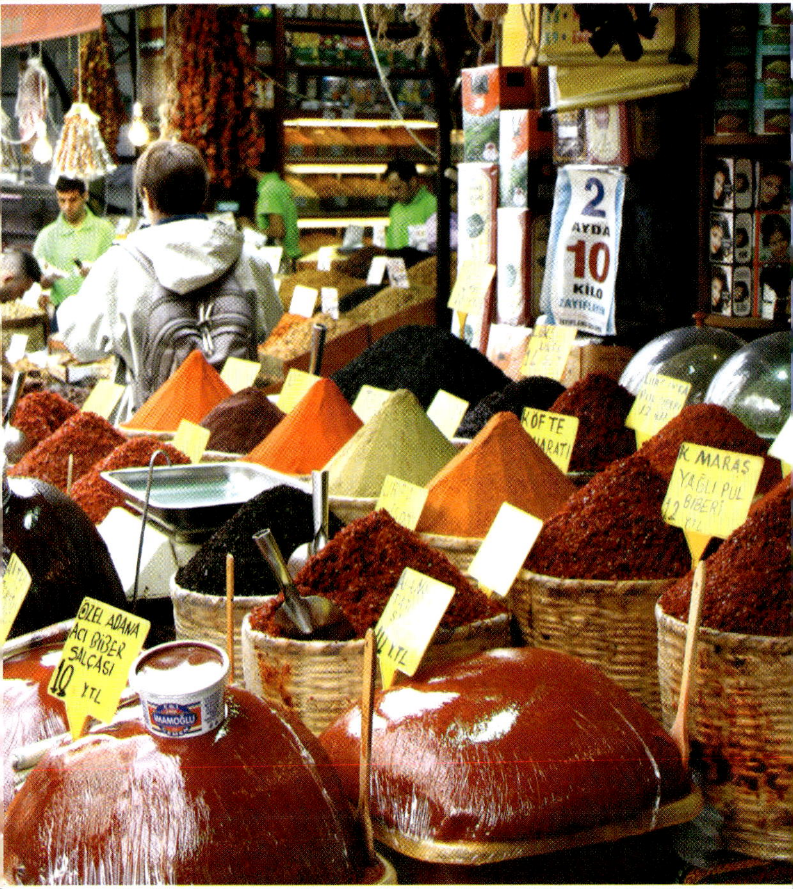
2
AYDA
10
KİLO
KÖFTE
K. MARAŞ
YAĞLI PUL
BİBERİ
12 YTL
ÖZEL ADANA
ACI BİBER
SALÇASI
10 YTL
İMAMOĞLU

Smoked Peppers
A How-To Primer

Kathleen Connole

THESE RECIPES WERE developed almost by accident, when my adventurous cooking husband decided to smoke some fresh peppers along with some trout that he had caught. They were so tasty that we kept finding more uses for them, and discovered that when added to a pot of beans, the dish would smell and taste just like good old ham 'n beans, without the ham (which we do not eat any more!) The store-bought *chipotle en adobo* inspired a search for a recipe to make our own.

The smoker used for this recipe is a simple, rectangular box style with a lid, large enough to have the fire on one side of the bottom—and the food above—but on the other side of the grate. The heat source (charcoal) is at the bottom; there is a vent for controlling the fire.

This is an indirect smoking technique: The hardwood charcoal is started on one side of smoker. Once charcoal is going good, or covered with white hot ash, wood pieces are placed on top of the charcoal. Peppers are slowly cooked alongside this indirect heat and smoke.

For smoking one batch of peppers, you'll need:

15 to 30 of pieces hardwood charcoal (briquette-size)
Wood chips of choice for smoking (hickory, cherry, or apple all would be good) wood chips can be soaked before adding or keep them moist by misting them frequently so they do not burn.
For 30 medium fresh jalapeños (washed and dried), use about 15 pieces of charcoal, or, for 15 large fresh sweet red bell peppers (washed and dried), use about 30 charcoal pieces.

Place peppers on grate beside fire once it is going and wood chips have been added. Cover, and check every 30 minutes. Keep fire low enough to smoke but not flame; add more charcoal and wood as needed, and mist to keep flames down. (Do not allow wood to actually catch fire.)

Peppers are done when tender; skins will wrinkle and easily slip off. Time depends upon the size and type of peppers—approximately 1 to 2 hours for jalapeños and up to 4 hours for sweet red bells.

Remove peppers from grill and cool until they can be handled. Remove skins and stems, pack into clean jars. Store in refrigerator or freeze. They will keep for several weeks in refrigerator.

Use smoked peppers in any recipe in which a smoky flavor would be appealing.

Some suggested uses: Add to chile sauce for enchiladas, vinaigrettes, soups and stews, pinto or black bean dishes, roasted vegetables, sweet potatoes, sautéed greens, and sandwich spreads such as pimento cheese spread. They give a nice smoky flavor without using ham, so are great for vegetarian dishes.

Smoked Jalapeños in Adobo Sauce

These are like the chipotles en adobo that you buy in a can—only better. Make your own chipotle mayonnaise by chopping some of these and adding them to mayonnaise.

MAKES ABOUT 2 PINTS

1 onion, diced
2 tablespoons olive oil
4 cloves garlic, minced
30 fresh smoked jalapeños, skins and stems removed
1/2 cup ketchup (good quality – no high fructose corn syrup!)
1/2 cup tamari soy sauce
2/3 cup apple cider vinegar
1 cup water

Sauté onion in olive oil, using a large, heavy bottomed saucepan over medium heat, until transparent; add garlic and cook a few more minutes. Add peppers and ketchup, soy sauce, vinegar and water. Cover and simmer over low heat, stirring occasionally, until sauce reduces to desired thickness. (Placing the pan lid slightly ajar keeps the hot pepper fumes from escaping, yet allows enough moisture to escape for the sauce to cook down.)

Pack into clean jars and keep refrigerated, or freeze. This will keep in refrigerator for several weeks.

Kathleen Connole is a member of the Herb Department at the Ozark Folk Center State Park in Mountain View, Arkansas. She received her degree in Plant Science from the University of Missouri – Columbia, and worked as a greenhouse grower and container garden designer in Kansas City, Missouri. When Kathleen relocated to Marion County, Arkansas in 2005, her desire to learn more about the culture and uses of herbs resulted in her attending Tina Marie Wilcox's Ozark Folk School. Soon after that she joined the Folk Center's herb team as horticulturist for the park. Kathleen's current passion is studying and sharing the natural history of the plants of the Heritage Herb Garden collection.

Sweet pepper. Gail Miller

A Chile by Any Other Name Would Taste as Hot?

Art Tucker

RED PEPPER, CHILE

Capsicum (kăp-sĭ-kŭm)

Family: Solanaceae

Growth form: shrubby perennials from 20 inches to almost 10 feet (0.5-3 m) tall

Hardiness: hardy only in frost-free locations

Light: full sun

Water: moist but not constantly wet

Soil: friable and porous, pH range 4.3 to 8.7, average 6.1 (*C. frutescens*)

Propagation: seeds in spring, 4,500 seeds per ounce (160/6) (*C. annuum*)

Culinary use: myriad

Craft use: wreaths, ristras

Landscape use: annual border, vegetable garden

Cultivated red peppers originated in South America about 7500 b.c., and Europeans were first exposed to them with Columbus's arrival in

1492. By 1494, Dr. Diego Alvarez Chanca, physician to Columbus's fleet, wrote back to Spain of the agí used by the natives in Hispaniola (Dominican Republic and Haiti). When the Spanish arrived in Mexico, they picked up the native name chilli, from the Nahuatl language of the Aztecs; in Nahuatl, chil refers both to the red pepper and the color red. Today chile is the word used in Mexico with a descriptive adjective, as chile poblanos.

Chiles spread very rapidly to Europe, Africa, and the Far East and were immediately accepted, unlike the tomato, also a member of the Solanaceae, which was imported with dire warnings of potential toxicity. In the Far East today, "chillie" or "chilly" is used for the pungent types, while the larger, milder peppers are called "capsicums." Americans seem to use all names and spellings, including "pimento," the anglicized version of the Spanish word for pepper. The American Spice Trade Association (ASTA) defines "red pepper" as any ground product of hot peppers, while "chili peppers" are any large, mild peppers that go into chili powder. Sharon Hudgins has provided further discussion of the etymology and use of the names pepper and chile.

The genus *Capsicum* includes about twenty-two species, but only five are cultivated, with *C. annuum* comprising most of the domesticated germplasm. The Greek *kapto*, to bite, fittingly gave the inspiration for this genus after the pungency of the fruits.

Chile flavor varies with the cultivar, processing, and climate; cultivar and processing aside, generally the hotter the climate, the hotter the pepper. Peppers ripening between 86°F and 95°F (30 to 35°C) have twice the fire as those which develop between 59°F and 72°F (15 to 22°C).

Capsaicinoids, the active components of hot peppers, transfer easily to your hands when you touch hot peppers; this can become a painful experience if you touch your eyes, mouth, genitalia, or other mucous membranes. Capsaicinoids have particular affinities with plastic contact lenses, and no amount of washing seems to remove them completely. Capsaicin, one of the capsaicinoids, is the effective burning agent used in personal protection sprays and animal repellents. Unless you really enjoy pain, the best precaution is to wear disposable plastic gloves, especially when chopping or seeding chiles. If you get hot pepper on your hands, washing with a small amount of chlorine bleach or ammonia will stop the burning sensation; the chlorine or ammonia changes capsaicin into water-soluble salts. For burning in the mouth, cheap vodka can be used as a mouthwash; the capsaicin is alcohol-soluble. Alternatively, the casein in dairy products will break the bond of capsaicin with the pain receptors in the mouth.

The burning sensation caused by hot peppers is commonly referred to as "heat" and is measured in Scoville Heat Units (SHU). This method was developed in 1912 by Wilbur L. Scoville, a pharmacologist with Parke Davis, a drug company that used capsaicin in its muscle salve, Heet™. Because of the inadequate chemical tests of the time, five human heat samplers tasted and analyzed a solution made from exact weights of chiles. The pungency was recorded in multiples of 100 units. Pure capsaicin and dihydrocapsaicin are rated at sixteen million Scoville Heat Units; the analogues of capsaicin have lower ratings: 9.3 million for nordihydrocapsaicin, 8.1 million for homodihydrocapsaicin, and 6.9 million for homocapsaicin. Recently, the cultivar 'Bhut Jolokia' (primarily *C. chinense*, perhaps with some introgression from *C. frutescens*) was introduced at 855,000 SHUs, the hottest known pepper, beating out *C. chinense* 'Red Savina' at 577,000 SHUs.

A relative heat scale rates heat from 0 to 10. The 'Habañero,' perhaps the hottest, commonly available pepper, rates a 10, with 200,000-300,000 Scoville Heat Units. At the other end of the scale, a bell pepper has 0 Scoville Heat Units and a rating of 0.

Within the past few decades, high-pressure liquid chromatography (HPLC) has been used to measure the Scoville Heat Units and relate them to actual capsaicinoid content. The ppm of capsaicinoids can be approximated by dividing SHU by 15. The American Spice Trade Assocation (ASTA) uses ASTA Heat Units based upon the ppm of capsaicinoids.

Some peppers are arranged on the relative heat scale in Table 1.

0 = 'Bell'	6 = 'Sante Fe Grande'
1 = 'Anaheim Mild'	7 = 'Jalapeño'
2 = 'Anaheim'	8 = 'Cayenne'
3 = 'New Mexico 6-4'	9 = 'Scotch Bonnet'
4 = 'Ancho'	10 = 'Habanero'
5 = 'Floral Gem'	10+= 'Bhut Jolokia'

Table 1. An average relative heat scale of some pepper types, from mildest (0) to hottest (10+).

The distribution of the fiery principles within chiles is uneven, but they appear to be concentrated on the partitions, or placenta, of the fruit. The pure seeds themselves contain none or up to 10 percent of the total capsaicinoids; the heat on the seeds primarily arises from contamination from the placenta. Conical, thinner walled fruits generally are more pungent than rounder, thicker fruits.

Don't feed hot peppers to dogs and/or cats. They can be lethal for some breeds.

Julia Child claims that chiles produce "palate death." According to research performed by Harry Lawless, Paul Rozin, and Joel Shenker at the University of Pennsylvania, regular users of chiles rate the intensity of orally-induced irritation from capsaicin as markedly lower than non-users. Despite this difference, the partial masking of the magnitude of olfactory or gustatory sensations by capsaicin is about equal in the two groups. This research also indicated that decrements in flavor identification under capsaicin are greater in chile non-eaters.

On the other hand, Beverly Cowart of the Monell Chemical Senses Center found that "Even for individuals who are rarely exposed to hot species, and who find the irritant sensations they produce intense and quite unpleasant, the ability to appreciate basic tastes in the presence of such irritation seems remarkably unaffected." At the most, Julia Child may be partially correct for non-chileheads, and certainly for Hell-fire cultivars like 'Bhut Jolokia.'

Capsaicin has been characterized by Young-Joon Surh and Sang Sup Lee as a "double-edged sword," and studies on the toxicity, mutagenic, and carcinogenic/co-carcinogenic/anticarcinogenic activities of capsaicin have yielded conflicting results, mostly depending upon the dose. Most studies have indicated that low consumption of chiles is beneficial but high consumption of chiles may be deleterious. Indeed, while it may be macho to consume the hottest peppers possible, clinical studies have shown that oral administration of capsaicinoids can damage the gastrointestinal tract to produce ulcers, act as a laxative, or even be fatal in massive doses. The dose of orally administered capsaicin that will kill 50% of the mice ranges from 97 to 294 mg/kg. Capsaicin in the amount of 0.232-0.706 ounces would have about the same effect on 150-pound humans. Assuming a median capsaicinoid content of 0.5 percent of dry weight and an approximate capsaicin content of 50 percent of the total capsaicinoids, that would be 93 to 282 ounces of dried chiles.

Remember, though, that other capsaicinoinds accompany capsaicin, and while their toxicological effects have not been well estimated, a better guess at the fatal level of dried chiles would be 47 to 141 ounces. While only a fool would eat 2.9 to 8.8 pounds of dried hot chiles, remember that people have done more bizarre things to join fraternities or beat world records.

Chile consumption may create risk for gastric cancer, yet it also protects against aspirin-induced injury of the gastroduodenal mucosa in humans and exhibits a protective factor against peptic ulcers. Conflicting experiments have shown that capsaicin may either aggravate ethanol-induced damage of the gastric muscosa of rats or exert strong gastroprotective activity against damage induced by ethanol in rats. Orally administered capsaicin also exhibits chemoprotective activity against some chemical carcinogens and mutagens, but one study in Chile (no pun intended) found that gallbladder carcinoma was correlated with the high intake of both green and red chiles.

Capsaicin has been used to deaden nerve pain in the treatment of rheumatoid arthritis, osteoarthritis, and peripheral neuropathies. Capsaicin is a bronchoconstrictor and produces hypothermia. It displays both antiarrhythmic as well as anti-ischemic effects in isolated heart preparations similar to those of a calcium-channel antagonist. Capsaicin prevents chemically induced skin inflammation and can act as an anesthetic; it effectively treats pruritic psoriasis. Researchers at Kyoto University have reported that capsaicin enhances lipid metabolism (and thus decreases adipose tissue weight) by promoting the secretion of catecholamine from the adrenal medulla of the brain, although capsaicin may also damage acetylcholine chloride receptors on the adrenal medulla. A topical application of 0.075% capsaicin may be of value in diaetic neuropathy and intractable pain and particularly in postherpetic neuralgia.

Capsaicin is an antioxidant and prevents decomposition of fats in cooking, giving two reasons for including hot peppers in fatty foods. The discovery of vitamin C was made in paprika, and later studies have confirmed that red peppers are rich in vitamins. Capsanthin, the leading carotenoid, is also antioxidant. The fruits of red peppers are considered GRAS at 1 to 910 ppm, the oleoresin at 0.5 to 900 ppm, and the extract at 12 to 1,200 ppm.

Repeated application of capsaicin may relieve idiopathic rhinitis. Alkamides from the fruits of red pepper are antimicrobial as are the carbohydrates of red pepper seeds.

Peppers are self-pollinating but insects can cause considerable crossing. Steven Tanksley at New Mexico State University found that the natural cross-pollination was 42 percent with the rates for individual plants as high as 91 percent. If you grow more than one type, be sure to clothe separate cultivars with mosquito netting or, even better, a spun polyester cloth (Reemay®) to prevent cross-pollination if you plan to save seeds from year to year. Some breeders separate their plots by 1/8 mile just to make sure.

Real chileheads plan their chile plots the fall before. Choose a sunny, well-drained site, pH 5.5 to 6.5, and work in soil amendments and fertilizers as you would for a general vegetable garden soil (as determined by a soil test at least two months before planting). A medium-textured sandy loam or loam is best. To minimize problems of diseases, choose a site where no Solanaceous plants (peppers, tomatoes, eggplants, or potatoes) have been grown at least for the past three years. Avoid intermixing peppers with other Solanaceous vegetables and rotate frequently to avoid the spread of diseases. Also avoid soils where the herbicides Karmex, Tenoran, Cotoran, or Lorox were previously used; these chemicals kill peppers.

The average yield of peppers is one pound per plant. One ounce of seeds, or 4,500 seeds, will provide enough for about an acre. Treated seeds are less susceptible to disease, particularly bacterial spot. Besides Thiram or Captan, which will control fungi, seeds may be treated with 1 part Clorox® to 4 parts water at the rate of 1 gallon per pound of seed. Wash seed in the solution for forty minutes, stirring often. Discard Clorox® solution as it becomes dirty. Spread seed to air-dry promptly.

Peppers are best grown from transplants because they require a long growing season, and gardeners usually purchase plants or grow their own indoors in a greenhouse to gain the maximum yield. Start seeds indoors in a flat or other shallow container filled with pasteurized, soilless mix. Sow seeds 1/4 to 1/2 inch deep. Keep evenly moist at 72 to 82°F (22 to 28°C). Temperature stress increases the time of germination, so a constant temperature of 81°F (27°C) is best. Slight scarification by placing the seeds in a plastic bag and gently rolling with a rolling pin will also reduce germination time. Oxygen will enhance germination, while light will not.

According to research conducted at the Louisiana Agricultural Experiment Station at Baton Rouge, germination may be enhanced by soaking the seed in 1,000 ppm gibberellic acid for forty-eight hours and priming in 2.75 percent potassium nitrate for 144 hours. Germination will take up to two weeks, with the hybrids germinating faster than the open-pollinated selections. Pregermination in a gel is used commercially.

After seedlings are up, place in the sun. Fluorescent lights (cool white) should be used if the seedlings become spindly, with the lights about 4 inches above the leaf tips for twelve to fourteen hours per day. Grow seedlings at 70 to 80°F (21 to 27°C) during the day and 63 to 70°F (17 to 21°C) during the night.

When the first set of true leaves appear, seedlings may be transplanted into 2.5 to 3 inch pots filled with a loose, pasteurized soil; stems may be covered to the first set of true leaves. Continue growing the potted plants under lights. At transplant time, choose stocky plants with good root systems for the garden; leggy plants must be clipped to perform as well (or better) than stocky ones. A transplant should have no flowers or fruit but six to eight true leaves and be less than 10 inches tall. Harden plants for about 10 days before transplanting directly into the ground; acclimate the plants by setting them outside for longer and longer each day.

Plant one or two weeks after all danger of frost is past or when the soil temperature at the transplanting depth reads above 55°F (13°C) for three consecutive days. A properly hardened plant rarely wilts, but if in doubt, choose a cloudy day or cover the transplants with cloches to reduce wilting. Plant in full sun at 12- to 24-inch intervals (depending upon the mature size of the cultivar) in raised rows 36 inches apart; furrows next to the raised row will aid in irrigation and help to prevent root rot. Feed lightly; a 5-10-5 water-soluble fertilizer has been recommended by one grower.

Staggered double rows are also recommended to use space more efficiently, with 12 to 18 inches between plants but 12 to 15 inches between individual rows and 36 inches between each set of double rows. Plants may need staking and will result in more attractive fruit. Plants will generally bear fruit in 65 to 80 days, depending upon the variety. Avoid fertilizers high in nitrogen, which will produce lush foliage at the expense of the fruits. If plants have poor color or stunted growth, additional fertilizer may be needed. Soil should be evenly moist, and if rainfall does not provide about 1 inch per week (65 gallons/100 square feet), additional watering may be required. Straw and rotted sawdust mulches will help to conserve moisture and reduce weeds.

Even for the quick-maturing sweet peppers, at least three months of warm weather are required for good yields and four or five months for most other cultivars. Peppers are very sensitive to temperature changes. Blossom drop occurs below 70°F (21°C) and above 90°F (32°C), and fruit sets poorly when day temperatures exceed 85°F (29°C). Fruits set at temperatures above 81°F (27°C) are likely to be small or poorly shaped because of heat injury, and above 95°F (35°C) few fruits will set, even if the air is very dry. Thus, uniform temperatures of 70 to 85°F (21 to 29°C) are recommended in the literature for maximum yields of sweet peppers. The smaller-fruited chiles are more tolerant of temperature extremes, but they need a longer growing season than sweet peppers.

Pepper color changes from green to red or yellow, but fire starts to peak when the peppers assume full size. Harvest peppers by cutting, not pulling. Chiles may be roasted and peeled, frozen, dried, and/or pickled;

drying on the plant is probably the most primitive method. In Mexico, the peppers are gathered when completely mature and immediately spread on *paseras*, raised soil beds oriented to receive maximum sun and slanted so that the rain water will run off. The peppers are spread over a layer of straw or dry grass to allow air circulation and water drainage. Fruit is turned daily and will take twenty to thirty days to dry completely.

In a modified pasera recommended by Jean Andrews, inclined platforms are covered with sheets of clear plastic and weighted with stones. This method requires less turning and results in better color, according to Andrews. The fruit may also be spread on other clean, flat, dry surfaces or strung as ristras. Commercial drying requires gentle heat. In Mexico, 'Jalapeño' chiles are typically dried by smoking, resulting in a new product, chilpotle. Smoked peppers without seeds, capones (the "castrated ones"), command higher prices.

Pepper seeds will germinate best after a period of dormancy. Storage conditions before planting also influence germination. After cleaning, seed should be dried to 5 percent moisture or lower and stored in refrigerated, sealed, moisture-proof containers; a small bag of dried silica gel in a sealed jar works well for the home gardener. Seeds stored for six months will germinate better than freshly gathered seeds.

Aphids spread viral diseases (curly top virus, pepper mottle virus, alfalfa mosaic virus, cucumber mosaic virus, and tomato spotted wilt) and must be controlled. Researchers at Louisiana State University have found that an aluminum-foil mulch repels aphids and aluminum-painted polyethylene mulch produces significantly greater yields as compared to that obtained from herbicide or hand-cultivated treatments, but I suppose that white sand may have similar properties.

To partially control anthracnose, which causes circular sunken brown spots on fruits, remove any plant debris and water only in the early morning. Mottled or twisted plants should be removed immediately and sent them to the nearest landfill; they are infected with viruses. Do not smoke tobacco near peppers, and wash hands exposed to tobacco to avoid the spread of tobacco mosaic virus. Chile wilt, caused by *Phytophthora capsici*, results from poorly drained soils and/or heavy rainfall. Verticillium wilt also is soil-borne and best avoided by crop rotation. A host of other diseases include blossom-end rot, *Phytophthora* pod rot, *Fusarium* pod rot, black mold, *Rhizoctonia* root rot, bacterial spot, and *Cercospora* leaf spot. Cutworms, tomato hornworms, and tomato fruitworms are some of the major insect pests. Root-knot nematodes may cause serious yield losses and increase root rots. Peppers are also susceptible to sunscald, salt injury, and wind injury.

COMMON RED PEPPER

Capsicum annuum (kăp-sĭ-kŭm ăn-ū-ŭm)

French: piment commun, poivron, poivre (piment) de Guinée, poivre rouge

German: Paprika, Roter Pfeffer

Dutch: spaanse peper

Italian: peperone, peperoncino, pepe di caienna

Spanish: pimiento, paprica, pimentón

Portuguese: pimento, pimentão

Swedish: spansk peppar

Russian: perets ovoshchnoy, struchkovy pyerets

Chinese: hsiung-ya-li-chiao

Japanese: papurika

Arabic: filfil ahmar

The var. *annuum* of this species, meaning "annual" (a misnomer, since they can be grown in the greenhouse for the winter), includes most of the familiar peppers, and they are classified into at least five groups. The most prominent is the Longum Group, alias capsicum pepper, chili pepper, and paprika. Mexico, China, India, and Pakistan provide most of the imported capsicum peppers.

The use of ground sweet peppers as a product called paprika reputedly dates to an Ottoman invasion of Hungary in the sixteenth century. A young Hungarian girl was forced into the harem of the pasha of Buda, and she saw how the palace gardeners grew red peppers. When Hungarians stormed the palace, she was freed and fled back to her village with the peppers. These peppers, originally from the Americas via India, became "paprika" in Hungarian and gave rise to a whole series of parikashes, or dishes incorporating paprika. Today, Kalocsa, Hungary, hosts a Paprika Museum and an annual Paprika Festival in October. Paprika even has its own popular folkloric figure in Hungary called Jancsi Paprika, often represented by a puppet embodying a Hungarian version of Sancho Panza.

In the Old World, the traditional peppers became milder, some still with a distinctive bite, others sweet. Despite Hungarian initiative in the development and spread of paprika, Spain provides most of the paprika imported into the United States, with Hungary and France second and third. Paprika today strictly refers to the ground product, not a pepper cultivar. Paprika can be made from any variety of *C. annuum* that is relatively low in heat but not devoid of it, and with brilliant red color. In the western United States, 'NuMex R. Naky' and 'NuMex Conquistador,' two "mild" hot peppers, are grown for processing into paprika. Other peppers recommended for paprika are 'Hungarian', 'Kalosca' (especially recommended for home growers), 'Paprika Supreme' and 'Papri Mild II'.

With new cultivars being introduced every year, it would be impossible to list all cultivars of *C. annuum*, and some, such as 'Chilhuacle Negro', which is used to prepare the black molé sauces of Oaxaca, are quite obscure. Some of the more popular cultivars readily available in the United States are listed below. I have omitted the vegetable types with 0 heat, such as 'Banana,' 'Bell,' 'Cubanelle,' and 'Pimento.'

Cultivar: 'Anaheim' or 'New Mexican' / 'New Mexico'

Synonyms: 'Chile Colorado,' 'California Green Chile,' 'Long Green/Red Chile'

Origin: released in 1903 by H. L. Musser; developed by Emilio Ortega in 1896

Relatives: 'Aconcagua,' 'Anaheim M,' 'Anaheim TMR,' 'Anaheim TMR 23,' 'Anaheim TMR 24,' 'California Chili,' 'Chimayó,' 'Diablo Grande,' 'Dixon,' 'El Paso,' 'Española Improved,' 'Fresno,' 'Fresno Chile Grande,' 'New Mexico No. 6-4,' 'New Mexico No. 9,' 'Nu-Mex Big Jim,' 'NuMex Conquistador,' 'NuMex Eclipse,' 'NuMex Joe E. Parker,' 'Nu-Mex R. Naky,' 'NuMex Sunrise,' 'NuMex Sunset,' 'Rio Grande,' 'Sandi-,' 'Sweet-Cal,' 'Tam Chile'

Availability: canned, fresh, or dried

Uses: stews, sauces, ristras, stuffed for rellenos

Color: green or red

Heat rating: 2-3

Cultivar: 'Ancho'

Synonyms: 'Poblano' (a generic name), 'Chile Poblano,' 'Chile Para Rellenar,' 'Chile Joto,' 'Pasilla' (an incorrect designation)

Origin: ancient

Relatives: 'Ancho Esmeralde,' 'Ancho Flor de Pabellon,' 'Ancho Verdeno,' 'Ancho 102,' 'Chile de Chorro,' 'Miahuateco,' 'Mulato Roque,' 'Mulato V-2'

Availability: fresh (Poblano) or dried (Ancho)

Uses: stuffed for relleños, used in sauces including molé sauce

Color: brick red to dark mahogany

Heat rating: 3 to 5

Cultivar: 'Cayenne'

Synonyms: 'Ginnie'

Origin: pre-Columbian

Relatives: 'Cayenne Larger,' 'Cayenne Pickling,' 'Come d'Orient,' 'Dwarf Chili,' 'Du Chili,' 'Hades Hot,' 'Hot Portugal,' 'Japanese Fuschin,' 'Jaune Long,' 'Large Red Chili,' 'Large Thick Cayenne,' 'Long Cayenne,' 'Long Narrow Cayenne,' 'Long Red,' 'Long Thin,' 'Mammoth Cayenne,' 'New Giant Cayenne,' 'New Quality,' 'Prolific,' 'Rainbow,' 'Red Chili,' 'Red Dawn,' 'Ring of Fire,' 'Rouge Long Ordinaire,' 'Super Cayenne,' 'Trompe d'Elephant,' 'True Red Chili'

Availability: bottled sauces, dried, and powdered

Uses: sauces, soups

Color: bright red

Heat rating: 8

Cultivar: 'Cherry'

Synonyms: 'Hungarian Cherry'

Origin: pre-Columbian

Relatives: 'Bird Cherry,' 'Bird's Eye,' 'Bolita,' 'Cascabel,' 'Cerise,' 'Cherry Jubilee,' 'Cherry Sweet,' 'Cherrytime,' 'Christmas Cherry' (not Jerusalem cherry, *Solanum pseudocapsicum* L.), 'Creole,' 'Holiday Cheer,' 'Hot Apple,' 'Japanese Miniature,' 'Large Red Hot,' 'Red Cherry Hot,' 'Red Giant,' 'Super Sweet,' 'Tom Thumb'

Availability: pickled

Uses: salads

Color: deep red

Heat rating: 1 to 5

Cultivar: 'De Arbol'

Origin: Mexico, related to 'Cayenne'

Relatives: 'NuMex Sunburst,' 'NuMex Sunflare,' 'NuMex Sunglo'

Availability: dried

Uses: sauces, soups, stews, wreaths, ristras

Color: bright red

Heat rating: 7.5

Cultivar: 'Fips'

Synonyms: 'Fiesta'

Origin: pre-1965 House of Venay, Germany

Availability: potted plants

Uses: primarily ornamental, but also salsas, soups, stir-fries

Color: yellow to red

Heat rating: 6 to 8

Cultivar: 'Floral Gem'

Origin: 1921

Relatives: 'Floral Gem Jumbo,' 'Floral Grande'

Availability: pickled (Torrido Chili Peppers or Trappey's of Louisiana)

Uses: salads, gravies, beans, meat dishes

Color: used when yellow

Heat: 5

Cultivar: 'Fresno'

Synonyms: 'Chile Caribe,' 'Chile Cera'

Origin: 1952, Clarence Brown Seed Co.

Relatives: 'Cascabella'

Availability: fresh

Uses: salsas, ceviches, seasoning, sauces, pickling (*en escabeche*)

Color: red, but used primarily when green

Heat rating: 6.5

Cultivar: 'Jalapeño'

Origin: pre-Columbian, named for town of Jalapa in state of Veracruz, Mexico

Relatives: 'Early Jalapeño,' 'Espinalteco,' 'Jalapa,' 'Jalapeño M. Americano,' 'Jarocho,' 'Meco,' 'Mitla,' 'Morita,' 'Mucho Naco,' 'Papaloapan,' 'Peludo,' 'Rayada,' 'San Andres,' '76014 Jumbo-Jal,' 'Tam Jalapeño,' 'Tam Mild Jalapeño-1,' Típico'

Availability: pickled (*en escabeche*), canned (*mora, morita*), fresh, smoked (*chilpotle*)

Uses: salsas, sauces, ristras

Color: green or red

Heat rating: 5.5

Cultivar: 'Mirasol'

Synonyms: 'Guajillo,' 'Cascabel'

Origin: Mexico

Relatives: 'De Comida,' 'La Blanca 74,' 'Loreto 74,' 'NuMex Mirasol,' 'Real Mirasol'

Availability: dried

Uses: salsas, sauces, soups, stews

Color: deep orange-red with brown tones

Heat rating: 2 to 5

Cultivar: 'Pasilla' (not the 'Ancho' types offered in California)

Synonyms: 'Chile Negro,' 'Chilaca'

Origin: Mexico

Relatives: 'Apasceo,' 'Pabellón 1,' 'Salvatierra'

Availability: dried, dried and powdered

Uses: molé sauce, seafood

Color: dark raisin brown when dried

Heat rating: 3 to 5

Cultivar: 'Peter'

Synonyms: 'Penis'

Origin: unknown

Uses: primarily an ornamental conversation piece but can be used in salsas if Freudian significance is desired (Caution: if you make and sell a "penis pepper jelly," as one of our friends did, make sure that you have a warning label "not for topical application")

Color: bright red

Heat rating: 7.5

Cultivar: 'Santa Fe Grande'

Synonyms: 'Güero' (a generic term for yellow peppers)

Origin: Mexico

Relatives: 'Caloro,' 'Caribe,' 'Hybrid Gold Spike'

Availability: fresh

Uses: yellow molé sauces, pickled (*en escabeche*), hot vinegars

Color: pale yellow

Heat: 6

Cultivar: 'Serrano'

Origin: mountain ridges (*serranias*) north of Puebla and Hidalgo, Mexico

Relatives: 'Altamira,' 'Cotaxtla Cónico,' 'Cotaxtla Gordo,' 'Cotaxtla Típico,' 'Cuauhtemoc,' 'Huasteco-74,' 'Panuco,' 'Super Chili,' 'Tam Hidalgo,' 'Tampiqueño 74,' 'Veracruz S69'

Availability: fresh, dried

Uses: sauces (*salsa verde, pico de gallo*), pickled (*en escabeche*)

Color: orange-red

Heat: 6 to 7.5

Cultivar: 'Tomato'

Synonyms: 'Squash'

Origin: pre-Columbian Mexico

Relatives: 'Canada Cheese,' 'Early Sweet Pimento,' 'Red Cheese Pimento,' 'Sunnybrook,' 'Tomato Pimento,' 'Yellow Cheese Pimento'

Availability: dried, fresh

Uses: dried and powdered as paprika (but rather bland), salads

Color: red

Heat rating: 0

The var. *aviculare* is the chiltecpin pepper, alias the chiltepin, chilipiquin, or tepín (Nahuatl chilli + tepectl, flea chile). Many other synonyms are also used, but the most common name is "bird pepper" because birds eat the tiny round fruits with impunity and spread it in their droppings. It is considered the wild form of *C. annuum* and distinguished primarily by fruit size. It may be used for salsas, soups, stews, and flavored vinegars; its heat rating is 8. Improved cultivars are the 'Hermosilla Select,' 'NuMex Bailey Piquin,' 'NuMex Centennial,' 'NuMex Twilight,' 'NuMex Piquin,' 'Pequín' ('Piquin'), 'Texas,' and 'Tuxtla.'

Within the last decade or so a number of peppers from southeast Asia and Africa have revisited North American shores; these often incorporate various flavors along with varying degrees of heat. These so-called "exotic" or as-yet unclassified peppers vary from the size of a chiltepin pepper to cayenne types and include 'Barbere,' 'Calistan,' 'Pili-Pili,' 'Thai Hot,' and 'Yatsafusa.' I know that by 1542 three races of peppers were being grown in India, yet today the pepper cultivars of Africa and Asia remain relatively unknown. More remains out there for the pepper explorers.

Important Chemistry
The red peppers are rich in carotenoids (3 to 66 g/kg), primarily capsanthin (23 to 69 percent of total pigment), crytocapsin (trace to 19 percent of total pigment), and beta-carotene (4 to 13 percent of total pigment). Measured as provitamin A content, the red cultivars have 928 to 5,232 IU/g (0.06 to 3.13 mg/g) fresh weight (the optimum amount of vitamin A1 for an adult is about 5,000 IU daily).

Of the other fat-soluble vitamins, vitamin D2 varies from 80 to 240 IU/g (0.004 to 0.012 mg/g) dried weight of paprika (400 IU of vitamin D daily is recommended for babies, children, adolescents, and pregnant and lactating women). Vitamin E varies from 160 to 880 IU/g (0.16 to 0.88 mg/g) dried weight of paprika. Of the water-soluble vitamins, vitamin C (ascorbic acid) content varies from 1.60 to 58.80 IU/g (0.08 to 2.94 mg/g) fresh weight (1,500 IU of vitamin C daily is recommended for adults).

Chile heat is due to capsaicin and its vanillyl-acyl amide analogues with the degree of pungency related to the length of the acid side-chain. The heat of *C. annuum* is primarily due to 33 to 95 percent capsaicin of the total capsaicinoid content accompanied by trace to 51 percent dihydrocapsaicin and 7 to 22 percent nordihydrocapsaicin. Total capsaicinoid content will vary from 0 to 1.3 percent by dry weight. The var. *aviculare*, the bird pepper, has 54 to 62 percent capsaicin and 22 to 32 percent dihydrocapsaicin.

The characteristic odor of peppers is primarily due to pyrazines. The essential oil of 'Bell' peppers, for example, has 16 percent 2-methoxy-3-isobutylpyrazine, alkylmethoxypyrazine, and nona-(E,E)-2,5-dien-4-one; 10 percent limonene; and 11 percent (E)-beta-ocimene. The six primary comounds of chile aroma are hexanal, 2-isobutyl-3-methoxypyrazine, 2,3-butanedione, 3-carene, trans-2-hexenal, and linalool, producing a green grassy aroma.

AJÍ, BROWN'S PEPPER, PIRIS

Capsicum baccatum (kăp-sĭ-kŭm bă-kā-tŭm)

Baccatum means fleshy, or having berries with a pulpy texture. This species is difficult to distinguish from *C. annuum* in the fruiting stage, as it has many of the same fruit forms. The var. *baccatum* is probably the wild progenitor of the cultivated var. *pendulum*. Two cultivars are derived from var. *pendulum*, 'Kellu-Uchu' ('Aji Amarillo,' 'Cusqueño') and 'Puca-Uchu'; both of these little-known South American peppers are used locally in soups and stews and have a heat rating of 7 to 8. 'Kellu-Uchu' is widely used in Peru to accompany many dishes but particularly the potatoes of the region. Attempts to grow 'Kellu-Uchu' in Texas resulted in a 5-foot shrub that barely matured before winter; thus this pepper is best consumed as imported fresh or dried fruits.

Important Chemistry
The fruits of *C. baccatum* var. *pendulum* have 32 to 67 percent capsaicin and 27 to 53 percent dihydrocapsaicin of the total capsaicinoid content, which is 0.1 to 0.2 percent of the dried fruit. The fruits of *C. baccatum* var. *baccatum* have 61 to 72 percent capsaicin and 29 to 28 percent dihydrocapsaicin.

CHINESE PEPPER

Capsicum chinense (kăp-sĭ-kŭm chī-něn-sē)

Capsicum chinense was named by Baron von Nikolaus Joseph Jacquin, but why he chose the epithet chinense for this South American plant has never been adequately explained. The distinction between this species and *C. frutescens* are slight and perhaps they should be combined into one species, *C. frutescens*. The many unnamed cultivars (in red, orange, and brown) also have extreme variations in fruit shape and size, merging one into the other; 'Scotch Bonnet' is milder and more squashed in appearance compared with 'Habañero' but otherwise differs little.

These "Chinese" peppers are the hottest known. Recently, 'Bhut Jolokia' (primarily *C. chinense*, perhaps with some introgression from *C. frutescens*) was introduced at 1,041,427 SHUs. However, this claim has fallen by the wayside, and in 2015 an even hotter one, 'Moruga Scorpion' was introduced at 2,009,230 SHUs. The more commonly available 'Habañero' separates the children from the real chileheads! The germination of the seeds of these cultivars, however, is longer than types from *C. annuum*, as is the length of growing season required for full fruit maturation, and so cultivation of these peppers also serves to separate the dabblers from the devotées.

Cultivar: 'Bhut Jolokia'

Origin: Assam, northeastern India

Relatives: 'Red Savina'

Availability: fresh

Uses: one pepper can supply a family of chileheads for a week!

Color: bright red when fully ripe

Heat rating: 10+

Cultivar: 'Habanero'

Origin: probably Cuba

Availability: fresh, dried, bottled

Uses: salsas, chutneys, seafood marinades, pickled (*en escabeche*)

Color: dark green to orange, orange-red, or red when fully ripe

Heat rating: 10

Cultivar: 'Rocotillo'

Synonyms: 'Red Squash,' 'Rocoto' (not the true rocoto pepper)

Availability: fresh, pickled

Uses: ceviches, pickled (*en escabeche*), tasty as a hot snack

Color: green, orange-yellow, or red

Heat: 7 to 8

Cultivar: 'Scotch Bonnet'

Origin: Caribbean

Relatives: 'Jamaican Hot,' 'Ají Dulce' (a low heat/sweet cultivar)

Availability: fresh, sauces

Uses: Jamaican jerk sauce, Caribbean curries

Color: pale yellow-green, orange, or red

Heat: 9 to 10

Important Chemistry
The fruits of *C. chinense* have 65 to 75 percent capsaicin and 21 to 32

percent dihydrocapsaicin of the total capsaicinoid content, which is 0.3 to 1.2 percent of the dried fruit.

TABASCO PEPPER

Capsicum frutescens (kăp-sĭ-kŭm frū-tĕs-ĕnz)

French: piment enragé

German: Beissbeere

Dutch: spaanse peper

Italian: peperone

Spanish: chile, malagueta

Portuguese: pimentao picante

Swedish: spansk peppar

Russian: struchkovy pyerets

Chinese: hung-fan-chiao

Japanese: tôgarashi

Arabic: filfil

Capsicum frutescens (frutescens means bushy) has given us the 'Tabasco' pepper with a heat rating of 8 to 9. "Tabasco," in reference to a pepper, first appeared in print on January 26, 1850, in a letter to the editors of the New Orleans Daily Delta. The name Tabasco, however, was used as early as 1519 by Hernán Cortez; it was ultimately derived from the Nahuatl tapacho-co, place of coral (or oyster) shell. During two centuries of Spanish dominion in Louisiana, goods passed from the inland port of Tabasco (currently San Juan Bautista) in Mexico to New Orleans. New Orleans also played an important role in the war with Mexico (1846-1847), and Com. Matthew Galbraith Perry, who directed the second seizure of Tabasco with 420 marines, shipped his ill men back to New Orleans.

Currently this pepper is used to make a hot sauce manufactured by the McIlhenny Company of Avery Island, Louisiana, and the name Tabasco™ is the firm's exclusive trademark for the sauce. An additional cultivar, 'Greenleaf Tabasco,' is resistant to tobacco etch virus with heavy yields. Another cultivar derived from *C. frutescens* is 'Uvilla Grande,' but this is primarily an ornamental.

Important Chemistry
The heat of *C. frutescens* is primarily due to 50 to 79 percent capsaicin of the total capsaicinoid content accompanied by 21 to 50 percent dihydrocapsaicin. The fragrant components isolated by lyophilization include 38 percent isohexyl-isocaproate, 22 percent 4-methyl-1-pentyl-2-methyl-butyrate, and 13 percent 3-methyl-1-pentyl-3-methyl-butyrate.

ROCOTO

Capsicum pubescens (kăp-sĭ-kŭm pū-běs-ĕnz)

Spanish: rocoto, chile manzana

The rocoto pepper is distinguished by its large violet flowers held erect above the foliage and its hairy leaves (pubescens means downy). The seeds are also unique, wrinkled and blackish-brown. The rocoto grows at higher elevations than any other pepper and may become a shrub reaching above 6 feet. Fruits are yellow-green, orange, red, or lemon-yellow in at least fourteen different shapes; heat ratings are 8 to 9. The rocoto probably originated in Peru in pre-Columbian times but was introduced into Central America and Mexico in the twentieth century. Named landraces include 'Chiapas,' Huatusco I, 'Huatusco II, 'Perú,' 'Puebla,' and 'Zongolica.'

Important Chemistry: The fruits of *C. pubescens* have 44 to 54 percent dihydrocapsaicin, 25 to 39 percent capsaicin, and 4 to 15 percent nor-dihydrocapsaicin of the total capsaicinoid content, which is 0.1 to 0.4 percent of the dried fruits.

Red ripe rocotillos on the vine ready to harvest. Susan Belsinger

BOTANICAL KEY AND DESCRIPTION

Key:

1. Seeds dark, flower purple   *C. pubescens*

1a. Seeds straw-colored, flower white or greenish white (rarely purple) 2

2. Flower with diffuse yellow spots at bases of lobes   *C. baccatum*

2a. Flower without diffuse yellow spots at bases of lobes 3

3. Flower purple 4

4. Flower solitary *C. annuum*

4a. Flowers 2 or more at each node   *C. chinense*

3a. Flower white or greenish-white 5

5. Calyx of mature fruit with ringed constriction at junction with flower stalk   *C. chinense*

5a. Calyx of mature fruit without ringed constriction at junction with flower stalk   6

6. Flowers solitary   7

6a. Flowers 2 or more at each node   8

7. Flower milky white, flower stalks often declining at pollen release
C. annuum

7a. Flower greenish-white, flower stalks erect at pollen release
C. frutescens

8. Flower milky white   *C. annuum*

8a. Flower greenish-white   9

9. Flower stalks erect at pollen release, flower lobes usually slightly turned backward   *C. frutescens*

9a. Flower stalks declining at pollen release, flower lobes straight
C. chinense

C. annuum L., Sp. pl. 188. 1753.

The two varieties of this pepper are distinguished primarily by fruit size.

var. *annuum*

Native country: The common red pepper originated in Mesoamerica but is now cultivated worldwide.

General habit: The common red pepper is a much-branched, smooth, shrubby, perennial herb or subshrub 45 to 100 cm tall typically grown as an annual.

Leaves: Leaves are lance-shaped, 1.5 to 13 x 0.5 to 7.5 cm, stalked. Base is pinched, base is wedge-shaped or tapered.

Flowers: Flowers are solitary at each node, flower stalks declining at pollen release. Corolla is milky white (occasionally purple) without diffuse spots at the base of the lobes. Corolla lobes are usually straight. The calyx of the mature fruit has no ringed constriction at the junction of the flower stalk (though sometimes irregularly wrinkled).

Fruits/Seeds: Fruit is an indehiscent, many-seeded berry extremely variable in size, shape, and color. Seeds are straw-colored.

var. *aviculare* (Dierb.) D'Arcy & Eshbaugh, Phytologia 25:260. 1973 [C. *annuum* l. var. *glabrisculum* (Dunal in DC.) Heiser & Pickersgill].

Native country: The bird pepper or chiltecpin originated in southern Mexico or northern Columbia but is distributed today in southeastern and southwestern United States into northern Peru.

General habit: The chiltecpin is a short-lived perennial herb or small shrub to 2 m, smooth or rarely slightly hairy.

Leaves: Leaves are lance-shaped.

Flowers: Flowers are solitary, rarely two to three pairs. The flower stalk is slender, enlarging just beneath the fruit. The corolla is white, rarely greenish; anthers are violet to blue.

Fruits/Seeds: The fruit is green suffused with dark purple to black when immature, red when mature, erect, small, globose or egg-shaped, 5 to 10 mm in diameter, rarely exceeding 15 mm in length. Seeds are cream to yellow.

C. *baccatum* L., Mant. pl. 47. 1767.

Two varieties of this pepper are known. The primary difference is in the position of the fruit, mostly erect in var. *baccatum* and mostly pendant in var. *pendulum*. Another difference between the two varieties is the length of the filaments, 1.2 to 3.1 mm in var. *baccatum* and 2.6 to 4.2 mm in var. *pendulum*.

var. *baccatum*

Native country: The var. *baccatum* has a center of distribution in Bolivia and northern Argentina.

General habit: The var. *baccatum* is a much-branched, smooth (sometimes slightly hairy), shrubby, perennial herb, 0.5 to 3.0 m tall.

Leaves: Leaves are lance-shaped.

Flowers: Flowers are white to off-white with a pair of yellowish to tan to greenish spots at the base of each lobe.

Fruits/Seeds: Fruit is an erect, indehiscent, many-seeded berry. Seeds are straw-colored.

var. *pendulum* (Willd.) Eshbaugh, Taxon 17:51-52. 1968.

Native country: The var. *pendulum* is native from the lowlands to middle elevations in South America with its primary center in Peru and Bolivia.

General habit: The var. *pendulum* is a much-branched, smooth, shrubby, perennial herb, 1 to 1.5 m tall.

Leaves: Leaves are lance-shaped.

Flowers: Flowers are solitary at each node. Flower stalks are erect or declining at pollen release. Flower is white or greenish-white with diffuse yellow spots at the base of the flower lobes on either side of the midvein. The flower lobes are usually slightly turned backwards. The calyx of the mature fruit has no ringed constriction (though sometimes irreguarly wrinkled).

Fruits/Seeds: Fruit is a pendant, indehiscent, many-seeded berry. Seeds are straw-colored.

C. chinense Jacq., Hort. Bot. Vindobon. 3:38. t. 67. 1776.

Native country: The Chinese pepper is widespread in northern South

America, southern Central America, and the West Indies; domestication probably occurred in South America.

General habit: The Chinese pepper is a much-branched, smooth (rarely with dense, short hairs), shrubby, perennial herb, 45 to 75 cm tall.

Leaves: Leaves are egg-shaped to egg-lance-shaped, to 10.5 cm broad, smooth or wrinkled.

Flowers: Flowers are two or more at each node (occasionally solitary). Flower stalks are erect or declining at pollen release. Flower is greenish-white (occasionally milky white or purple) without diffuse spots at the base of the lobes. The flower lobes are usually straight. The calyx of the mature fruit usually has a ringed constriction at the junction with the fruit stalk.

Fruits/Seeds: Fruit is an indehiscent, many-seeded berry, 1.0 to 12.0 cm long, varying from spherical to elongate, smooth or variously wrinkled. Seeds are straw-colored.

C. frutescens L., Sp. pl. 189. 1753.

Native country: The Tabasco pepper probably originated in the western Amazon River basin of lowland Colombia and Peru.

General habit: The Tabasco pepper is a much-branched, smooth (to slightly hairy), shrubby, short-lived perennial herb 0.5 to 1.5 m high, living for two or three years.

Leaves: Leaves are widest at the center with equal ends.

Flowers: Flowers are solitary at each node (occasionally two or more). Flower stalks are erect at pollen release but flowers are nodding. Flower is greenish-white without diffuse spots at the base of the lobes. The corolla lobes are often slightly turned backwards. Calyx of mature fruit has no ringed constriction at the junction with the fruit stalk, though often irregularly wrinkled.

Fruits/Seeds: Fruit is an indehiscent, many-seeded berry typically 0.7 to 3.0 x 0.3 to 1.0 cm, but larger fruited forms occur. Seeds are straw-colored.

C. pubescens Ruiz. & Pav., Flora peruv. prodr. 2:30. 1799.

Native country: The rocoto pepper is native to relatively high elevations in Andean South America.

General habit: The rocoto pepper is a much-branched, hairy, shrubby, perennial herb.

Leaves: Leaves are lance-shaped, hairy.

Flowers: Flowers are solitary at each node. Flower stalks are erect at pollen release but flowers are nodding. Flower is purple (occasionally with white margins to lobes and/or white tube), without diffuse spots at the base of the lobes. The lobes are usually straight. Calyx of mature fruit has no ringed constriction at the junction with the fruit stalk.

Fruits/Seeds: Fruit is an indehiscent, many-seeded berry. Fruit flesh is thick and firm. Seeds are wrinkled and blackish-brown.

FOR FURTHER READING:

The red or capsicum peppers or chiles deserve a whole book, and indeed several already exist. I recommend, in particular, Jean Andrews' *Peppers: The Domesticated Capsicums*. This book suits the coffee table, kitchen, bedside, library, botany laboratory, classroom, and so on—it is a perfect synthesis of science, history, art, and humor. All chileheads must have it!

Other good chile books include Mark Miller's *The Great Chile Book*, which has excellent color photographs and a compact size. Dave DeWitt and Nancy Gerlach's *The Whole Chile Pepper Book* gives additional information on cultivation and culinary uses. J. W. Purseglove, E. G. Brown, C. L. Green, and S. R. J. Robbins have provided an excellent survey of commercial cultivation, processing, and standards of chiles in volume one of their *Spices*; I have not expanded upon these commercial features here and advise you instead to read their comprehensive treatment. Amal Naj's *Peppers: A Story of Hot Pursuits* features interviews with people working on peppers interwoven with a very readable fabric of pepper history and uses. Finally, for the chilehead and pungent-herb connoisseur, I recommend the magazine *Chile Pepper*.

Bibliography

Abdel-Salam, O. M. E., et al. 1997. Capsaicin and the stomach. A review of the experimental and clinical data. *J. Physiology* 91: 151-171.

Almela, L., et al. 1991. Carotenoid composition of new cultivars of red pepper for paprika. *J. Agric. Food Chem.* 39: 1606-1609.

Andrews, J. 1984. *Peppers: The Domesticated Capsicums*. Austin: Univ. Texas Press.

_____. 1998. The Pepper Lady's Pocket Pepper Primer. Austin: Univ. Texas Press.

Anonymous. 2004. Capsicum peppers. Rev. Nat. Prod. (Wolters Kluwer Health).

Asai, A., et al. 1999. Antioxidative effects of turmeric, rosemary and capsicum extracts on membrane phospholipid peroxidation and liver lipid metabolism in mice. *Biosci. Biotechnol. Biochem.* 63: 2118-2122.

Bajaj, K. L., et al. 1980. Varietal variations in some important chemical constituents in chili (*Capsicum annuum* L.) fruits. *Veg. Sci.* 7: 48-54.

Balaban, C. D., et al. 1999. Time course of burn to repeated applications to capsaicin. *Physiol. Behav.* 66: 109-112.

Baranyai, M., et al. 1982. Determination, by HPLC, of carotenoids in paprika products. *Acta Aliment.* 11: 309-323.

Ben-Chaim, A., and I. Paran. 2000. Genetic analysis of quantitative traits in pepper (*Capsicum annuum*). *J. Amer. Soc. Hort. Sci.* 125: 66-70.

_____, et al. 2006. QTL Analysis for capsaicinoid content in Capsicum. *Theor. Appl. Genet.* 113: 1481-1490.

Bevacqua, R. F., and D. M. VanLeeuwen. 2003. Planting date effects on stand establishment and yield of chile pepper. *HortScience* 38: 357-360.

Black, L. L., and L. H. Rolston. 1972. Aphids repelled and virus diseases reduced in peppers planted on aluminum foil mulch. *Phytopathology* 62: 747.

Bosland, P. W. 1992. Chiles: A diverse crop. *HortTechnology* 2: 6-10.

_____. 1992. *Capsicum: A comprehensive bibliography*. Chile Inst., Las Cruces, New Mexico.

_____. 1994. Chiles: History, cultivation, and uses. *In Spices, Herbs and Edible Fungi*. Ed. G. Charalambous. Amsterdam: Elsevier. 347-366.

_____, and J. B. Baral. 2007. 'Bhut Jolokia'—The world's hottest known chile pepper is a putative naturally occuring interspecific hybrid. *HortScience* 42: 222-224.

_____, et al. 1992. Growing chiles in New Mexico. *New Mexico State Univ. Coop. Extens. Serv. Guide* H-230.

_____, et al. 1992. Capsicum pepper varieties and classification. *New Mexico State Univ. Coop. Extens. Serv. Circ.* 530.

Boswell, V. R., et al. 1964. Pepper production. *Agric. Inform. Bull.* U.S.D.A. No. 276.

Breithaupt, D. E., and W. Schwack. 2000. Determination of free and bound carotenoids in paprika (*Capsicum annuum* L.) by LC/MS. *Eur. Food Res. Technol.* 211: 52-55.

Brzozowski, T., et al. 1992. Studies on gastroprotection induced by capsaicin and papaverine. *J. Physiol. Pharmacol.* 43: 309-322.

Buttery, R. G., et al. 1969. Characterization of some volatile constituents of bell peppers. *J. Agric. Food Chem.* 17: 1322-1327.

Carobi, C. 1996. A quantitative investigation of the effects of neonatal capsaicin treatment on vagal afferent neurons in the rat. *Cell Tissue Res.* 283: 305-311.

Carter, A. K., and C. S. Vavrina. 2001. High temperature inhibits germination of Jalapeño and cayenne pepper. *HortScience* 36: 724-725.

Cisneros-Pineda, O., et al. 2007. Capsaicinoids quantification in chili peppers cultivated in the state of Yucatan, Mexico. *Food Chem.* 104: 1755-1760.

Cordell, G. A., and O. E. Araujo. 1993. Capsaicin: Identification, nomenclature, and pharmacotherapy. *Ann. Pharmacotherapy* 27:330-336.

Cowart, B. J. 1987. Oral chemical irritation: does it reduce perceived taste intensity? *Chem. Senses* 12: 467-479.

Cremer, D. R., and K. Eichner. 2000. Formation of volatile compounds during heating of spice paprika (*Capsicum annuum*) powder. *J. Agric. Food Chem.* 48: 2454-2460.

D'Alonzo, A. J., et al. 1995. In vitro effects of capsaicin: antiarrhythmic and anti-ischemic activity. *European J. Pharmacol.* 272: 269-278.

Daood, H. G., et al. 1996. Antioxidant vitamin content of spice red pepper (paprika) as affected by technological and varietal factors. *Food Chem.* 55: 365-372.

_____, et al. 2006. Antioxidant content of bio and conventional spice red pepper (Capsicum annuum L.) as determined by HPLC. *Acta Agron. Hung.* 54: 133-140.

D'Arcy, W. G., and W. H. Eshbaugh. 1974. New World peppers (Capsicum-Solanaceae) north of Colombia: A résumé. *Baileya* 19: 93-105.

Dasgupta, P., and C. J. Fowler. 1997. Chillies: from antiquity to urology. Brit. *J. Urology* 80: 845-852.

Davis, C. B., et al. 2007. Determinaton of capsaicinoids in Habanero peppers by chemometric analysis of UV spectral data. *J. Agric. Food Chem.* 55L: 5925-5933.

De, A. K., ed. 2003. *Capsicum: The genus Capsicum.* New York: Taylor & Francis.

Deli, J., et al. 2001. Separation and identification of carotenoids from different coloured paprika (Capsicum annuum) by reversed-phase high-performance liquid chromatography. *Eur. Food Res. Technol.* 213: 301-305.

DeWitt, D., and J. Gerlach. 1990. Chile peppers: Growing fire in the garden. *Fine Gard.* 11: 54-57.

_____, and N. Gerlach. 1990. *The Whole Chile Pepper Book*. New York: Little, Brown and Co.

_____, and P. W. Bosland. 1993. *The Pepper Garden*. Berkeley, California: Ten Speed Press.

_____, and P. W. Bosland. 1996. *Peppers of the World: An Identification Guide*. Berkeley, California: Ten Speed Press.

Ellis, C. N., et al. 1993. A double-blind evaluation of topical capsaicin in pruritic psoriasis. *J. Amer. Acad. Dermatol.* 29: 438-442.

Eshbaugh, W. H. 1970. A biosystematic and evolutionary study of *Capsicum baccatum* (Solanaceae). *Brittonia* 22: 31-43.

_____. 1980. The taxonomy of the genus Capsicum (Solanaceae)–1980. *Phytologia* 47: 153-166.

_____. 1993. Peppers: History and exploitation of a serendipitous new crop discovery. *In New Crops*. Ed. J. Janick and J.E. Simon. New York: John Wiley & Sons. 132-139.

_____, et al. 1983. The origin and evolution of domesticated Capsicum species. *J. Ethnobiol.* 3: 49-54.

Estrada, B., et al. 1998. Effects of mineral fertilizer supplementation on fruit development and pungency in 'Padrón' peppers. *J. Hort. Sci. Biotechnol.* 73: 493-497.

Fang, J.-Y., et al. 1997. Percutaneous absorption and skin erythema: Quantification of capsaicin and its synthetic derivatives from gels incorporated with benzalkonium chloride by using non-invasive bioengineering methods. *Drug Dev. Res.* 40: 56-67.

Fujimoto, K., et al. 1980. Antioxidant activity and pungency of synthetic capsaicin homologues. *Yukagaku* 29: 419-422.

Fujiwake, H., et al. 1982. Capsaicinoid formation in the protoplast from the placenta of Capsicum fruits. *Agric. Biol. Chem.* 46: 2591-2592.

Fung, T., et al. 1983. The identification of capsaicinoids in tear-gas spray. *J. Forensic Sci.* 27: 812-821.

Galindo, H. S. G., et al. 1995. La capsaicina, el principio pungente del chile; su naturaleza, absorción, metabolismo y efectos farmacológicos. *Ciencia* 46: 84-102.

Gardner, C. S., and G. L. Queeley. 1999. Production guidelines for the Scotch Bonnet hot pepper. *Florida A&M Res. Ext. Bull.* Vol. 1, No. 1.

Glinsukopn, T., et al. 1980. Acute toxicity of capsaicin in several animal species. *Toxicon* 18: 215-220.

Gnayfeed, M. H., et al. 2001. Supercritical CO_2 and subcritical propane extraction of pungent paprika and quantification of carotenoids, tocophernols, and capsaicinoids. *J. Agric. Food Chem.* 49: 2761-2766.

Golcz, A., and P. Kujawski. 2004. Evaluation of the biological value of the fruit of several hot pepper (*Capsicum annuum* L.) cultivars. *Rocz. Akad. Roln. Pozn.* 38: 37-42.

Gómez, R., et al. 1998. Color differences in paprika pepper varieties (*Capsicum annuum* L) cultivated in greenhouse and in the open air. *J. Sci. Food Agric.* 77: 268-272.

Greenleaf, W. H. 1975. The Tabasco story. *HortScience* 10: 98.

Guadayol, J. M., et al. 1997. Extraction, separation, and identification of volatile organic compounds from paprika oleoresin (Spanish type). *J. Agric. Food Chem.* 45: 1868-1872.

Hanson, B., and P,. W. Bosland. 1999. *Chile Peppers: Hot Tips and Tasty Picks for Gardeners and Gourmets.* Brooklyn Bot. Gard.

Harness, J. 1982. Growing Hot Peppers. *Alcorn State Univ. Coop. Extens. Serv.* Publ. 851.

Haymon, L. W., and L. W. Aurand. 1971. Volatile constituents of Tabasco peppers. *J. Agric. Food Chem.* 19: 1131-1134.

Heiser, C. B., and B. Pickersgill. 1969. Names for the cultivated Capsicum species (Solanaceae). *Taxon* 18: 277-283.

_____, and B. Pickersgill. 1975. Names for the bird peppers (Capsicum–Solanaceae). *Baileya* 19: 151-156.

_____. 1976. Peppers. Capsicum (Solanaceae). *In Evolution of Crop Plants.* Ed. N. W. Simmonds. New York: Longman. 265-268.

Henderson, D. E., and S. K. Henderson. 1992. Thermal decomposition of capsaicin. 1. Interactions with oleic acid at high temperatures. *J. Agric. Food Chem.* 40: 2263-2268.

Howard, L. R. 2001. Antioxidant vitamin and phytochemical content of fresh and processed pepper fruit (*Capsicum annuum*). *In Handbook of Nutraceutical and Functional Foods.* Ed. R. E. C. Wildman. Boca Raton, Florida: CRC Press. 209-233.

_____, et al. 2000. Changes in phytochemical and antioxidaqnt activity of selected pepper cultivars (Capsicum species) as influenced by maurity. *J. Agric. Food Chem.* 48: 1713-1720.

Hudgins, S. 1993. Red dust: Powdered chiles and chili powders. *In Spicing up the Palate: Studies of Favourings—Ancient and Modern.* Ed. H. Walker. Totnes, England: Prospect Books. 107-120.

Iorizzi, M., et al. 2000. Chemical components of *Capsicum annuum* L. var. *acuminatum* and their activity on stored product insect pests. *In Flavor and Fragrance Chemistry.* Ed. V. Lanzotti and O. Taglialatela-Scafati. Boston: Kluwer Acad. Publ. 77-85.

IPGRI, AVRDC and CATIE. 1995. *Descriptors for Capsicum (Capsicum* spp.). Rome: Intern. Pl. Gen. Res. Inst.

Iwai. K., et al. 1979. Formation and accumulation of pungent principal of hot pepper fruits, capsaicin and its analogues, in *Capsicum annuum* var. *annuum* cv. Karayatsubusa at different growth states after flowering. *Agric. Biol. Chem.* 43: 2493-2498.

Jang, H.-W., et al. 2008. Antioxidant activity and characterization of volatile extracts of *Capsicum annuum* L. and *Allium* spp. *Flavour Fragrance J.* 23: 178-184.

Jarret, R., E. 2007. Morphologic variation for fruit variation for fruit characteristics in the USDA/ARS *Capsicum baccatum* L. germplasm collection. *HortScience* 42: 1303-1305.

_____, et al. 2007. Diversity of fruit quality characteristics in *Capsicum frutescens*. *HortScience* 42: 16-19.

Jaworski, C. A., and R. E. Webb. 1971. Pepper performance after transplant clipping. *HortScience* 6: 480-482.

Jensen-Jarolim, L. A., et al. 1998. Allergens in pepper and paprika. *Allergy* 53: 36-41.

Jun, H.-R., and Y.-S. Kim. 2002. Comparison of volatile compounds in red pepper (*Capsicum annuum* L.) powders from different origins. *Food Sci. Biotechnol.* 11: 293-302.

_____, et al. 2005. Comparison of volatile components in fresh and dried red peppers (*Capsicum annuum* L.). *Food Sci. Biotechnol.* 14: 392-398.

Jurentisch, J. 1981. Scharfstoffzusammensetzung in Früchten definierter Capsicum-Sippen-Konsequenzen für Qualitätsforderungen und taxonomische Aspekte. *Sci. Pharm.* 49: 321-328.

_____, et al. 1979. Einfache Bestimmung des Gesamt- und Einzelcapsaicinoidgehaltes in Capsicum-Früchten mittels HPLC. *Pl. Med.* 36: 54-60.

_____, et al. 1979. Nachweis und Identifizierung neuer Scharfstoffe in Capsicum-Früchten. *Pl. Med.* 36: 61-67.

_____, et al. 1979. Identifizierung kultivierter Capsicum-Sippen. Taxonomie, Anatomie und Scharfstoffzusammensetzung. *Pl. Med.* 35: 174-183.

_____, and R. Leinm‚ller. 1980. Quantifizierung von Nonylsäurevanillylamid und anderen Capsaicinoiden in Scharfstoffgemischen von Capsicum-Früchten und -Zubereitungen durch Gas-Flüssig-Chromatographie an Glaskapillarsäulen. *J. Chromatogr.* 189: 389-397.

Kang, J.-H., et al. 2007. Capsaicin, a spice component of hot peppers, modulates adipokine gene expression and protein release from obese-mouse adipose tissues and isolated adipocytes, and suppresses the inflammatory responses of adipose tissue macrophages. *FEBS Lett.* 581: 4389-4396.

Kang, J. Y., et al. 1995. Chili–protective factors against peptic ulcer? *Dig. Dis. Sci.* 40: 576-579.

Kawada, T., et al. 1991. Intake of sweeteners and pungent ingredients increases the thermogenin content in brown adipose tissue of rats. *J. Agric. Food Chem.* 39: 651-654.

Kirschbaum-Titze, P., et al. 2002. Pungency in paprika (*Capsicum annuum*). 1. Decrease of capsaicinoid content following cellular disruption. *J. Agric. Food Chem.* 50: 1260-1263.

_____, et al. 2002. Pungency in paprika (*Capsicum annuum*). 2. Heterogeneity of capsaicinoid content in individual fruits from one plant. *J. Agric. Food Chem.* 50: 1264-1266.

Kocsis, N., et al. 2002. GC-MS Investigation of the aroma compounds of Hungarian red paprika (*Capsicum annuum*) cultivars. *J. Food Comp. Anal.* 15: 195-203.

Kogure, K., et al. 2002. Mechanism of potent antiperoxidative effect of capsaicin. *Biochem. Biophys. Acta* 1573: 84-92.

Konisho, K., et al. 2005. Inter- and intra-specific variation of capsaicinoid concentration in chili pepper (*Capsicum* spp.). *Hort. Res. Japan* 4: 153-158.

Kurtz, O. 1972. *The Paprika Manual*. Englewood Cliffs, New Jersey: Amer. Spice Trade Assoc.

Lawless, H., et al. 1985. Effects of oral capsaicin on gustatory, olfactory, and irritant sensations and flavour identification in humans who regularly or rarely consume chili pepper. *Chem. Senses* 10: 579-589.

Lee, S.-A., et al. 2007. Capsaicin promotes the development of burst-forming units-erythroid (BFU-E) from mouse bone marrow cells. *Exp. Mol. Med.* 39: 278-283.

Locock, R. A. 1985. *Capsicum. Canad. Pharm.* J. 118: 516-519.

Long, A., C., and D. M. Medeiros. 2001. Evaluation of capsaicin's use in analgesic medicine. *J. Nutraceuticals Functional Med. Foods* 3: 39-46.

López-Carrillo, L., et al. 1994. Chili pepper consumption and gastric cancer in Mexico: A case-control study. *Amer. J. Epidemiology* 139: 264-271.

López-Carrillo, L., et al. 2003. Capsaicin consumption, Helicobacter pylori positivity and gastric cancer in Mexico. *Int. J. Cancer* 106: 277-282.

Lv, C.-s., et al. 2005. Light intensity affects pungency of hot pepper (*Capsicum annuum* L.) fruits. *J. Northeast Agric. Univ.* 12:33-36.

Maillard, M.-N., et al. 1997. Analysis of eleven capsaicinoids by reversed-phase high performance liquid chromatography. *Flavour Fragrance J.* 12: 409-413.

Maoka, T., et al. 2001. Cancer chemoprevention activity of carotenoids in the fruits of red paprika *Capsicum annuum* L. *Cancer Lett.* 172: 103-109.

_____, et al. 2001. Antioxidative activity of capsorubin and related compounds from paprika (*Capsicum annuum*). *J. Oleo Sci.* 50: 663-665.

_____, et al. 2004. Biological function and cancer prevention by paprika carotenoids. *Foods Food Ingred.* J. Jap. 209: 203-210.

Mateo, J., et al. 1997. Volatile compounds in Spanish paprika. *J. Food Comp. Anal.* 10: 225-232.

Matsufuji, H., et al. 1998. Antioxidant activity of capsanthin and the fatty acid esters in paprika (*Capsicum annuum*). *J. Agric. Food Chem.* 46: 3468-3472.

Mazida, M. M.,. et al. 2005. Analysis of volatile compounds of fresh chili (*Capsicum annuum*) during stages of maturity using solid phase microextraction (SPME). *J. Food Comp. Anal.* 18: 427-437.

Meek, A. J., and J. Gulledge. 1986. *Red-pepper Paradise.* New Orleans: Audubon Park Press.

Miller, M. 1991. *The Great Chile Book.* Berkeley, California: Ten Speed Press.

Minami, M., et al. 1998. Quantitative analysis of capsaicinoid in chili pepper (*Capsicum* sp.) by high performance liquid chromatography-operating condidtion, sampling and sample preparation-. *J. Fac. Agric. Shinshu Univ.* 34: 97-102.

Mínguez-Mosquera, M. I., et al. 1994. Influence of the industrial drying processes of pepper fruits (*Capsicum annuum* Cv. Bola) for paprika on the carotenoid content. *J. Agric. Food Chem.* 42: 1190-1193.

_____, and D. Hornero-Méndez. 1997. Changes in provitamin A during paprika processing. *J. Food Practice* 60: 853-857.

_____, and A. P. Gàlvez. 1998. Color quality in paprika oleoresins. *J. Agric. Food Chem.* 46: 5124-5127.

Molina-Torres, J., et al. 1999. Antimicrobial properties of alkamides present in flavour plants traditionally used in Mesoamerica: affinin and capsaicin. *J. Ethnopharmacol.* 64: 241-248.

Mósik, Gy., et al. 1997. *Capsaicin-sensitive Afferent Nerves in Gastic Mucosal Damage and Protection.* Budapest: Akad. Kiadó.

_____, et al. 2004. Capsaicin-sensitive afferent nerves and gastric mucosal protection in the human healthy subjects – A critical overview. In *Mediators in Gastrointestinal Protection and Repair.* Ed. K. Takeushi and Gy. Mósik. Kerala, India: Res. Signpost. 43-62.

_____, et al. 2005. Gastroprotection induced by capsaicin in healthy human subjects. *World J. Gastroenterol.* 11: 5180-5184.

_____, et al. 2005. Participation of vanilloid/capsaicin receptors, calcitonin-gene-related peptide and substance P in gastric protection of omeprazole and omeprazole-like compounds. *Inflammopharmacology* 13: 139-159.

Naj, A. 1992. *Peppers: A Story of Hot Pursuits.* New York: Alfred A. Knopf.

Noble, D. 1992. Cultivating peppers. *Green Scene* 21(1): 11-14.

Odoemena, C. S., K. E. Akpabio, and C. P. Nneji. 1998. Antibacterial activity of the essential oils from four selected varieties of *Capsicum annuum. Nig. J. Nat. Prod. Med.* 2: 49-50.

Pabst, M. A., et al. 1993. Ablation of capsaicin sensitive afferent nerves impairs defense but not rapid repair of rat gastric mucosa. *Gut* 34: 897-903.

Palevitch, D., and L. E. Craker. 1993. Nutritional and medical importance of red peppers. *Herb Spice Med. Pl. Dig.* 11(3): 1-4.

Park, H., and K-P. Park. 1993. Capsaicin induces acute spinal analgesia and changes in the spinal norepinephrine level. *Kor. J. Pharmacol.* 29: 3-41.

Park, K.-K., et al. 1998. Lack of tumor promoting activity of capsaicin, a principal pungent ingredient of red pepper, in mouse skin carcinogenesis. *Anticancer Res.* 18: 4201-4206.

Parrish, M. 1996. Liquid chromatographic method for determining capsacinioids in capsicums and their extractives: Collaborative study. *J. AOAC Intern.* 79: 738-745.

Pérez-Grajales, M., et al. 2004. Physiolgoical characterization of manzano hot pepper (*Capsicum pubescens* R & P) landraces. *J. Amer. Soc. Hort. Sci,.* 129: 88-92.

Perfumi, M., and M. Massi. 1996. Effect of capsaicin pretreatment in neonatial or adult rats on glucose load-induced hyperglycaemia. *Phytotherapy Res.* 10: S22-S24.

Perucka, I., and M. Materska. 2003. Antioxidant activity and content of capsaicinoids isolated from paprika fruits. *Pol. J. Food Nutr. Sci.* 12: 15-18.

Peusch, M., et al. 1997. Extraction of capsaicinoids from chillies (*Capsicum frutescens* L.) and paprika (*Capsicum annuum* L.) using supercritical fluids and organic solvents. *Z. Lebensm. Unters. Forsch.* A 204: 351-355.

Pino, J., et al. 2007. Characterization of total capsaicinoids, colour and volatile compounds of Habanero chilli pepper (*Capsicum chinense* Jack.) cultivars grown in Yucatan. *Food Chem.* 104: 1682-1686.

Porter, W. C., and W. W. Etzel. 1982. Effects of aluminum-painted and black polyethylene mulches on bell pepper, *Capsicum annuum* L. *HortScience* 17: 942-943.

Poyrazoğlu, E. S., et al. 2005. Determination of capsaicinoid profile of different chilli peppers grown in Turkey. *J. Sci. Food Agric.* 85: 1435-1438.

Proulx, E. A. 1985. Some like them hot. *Horticulture* 63(1): 46-54.

Purseglove, J. W., et al. 1981. *Spices* 2 vols. London: Longman.

Quinones-Seglie, C. R., et al. 1989. Capsaicinoids and pungency in various capsicums. *Lebensm.-Wiss. Technol.* 22: 196-198.

Reilly, C. A., et al. 2001. Quantitative analysis of capsaicinoids in fresh peppers, oleoresin capsicum and pepper spray products. *J. Forensic Sci.* 46: 502-509.

Rowland, B. J., et al. 1983. Capsaicin production in sweet bell and pungent jalapeno peppers. *J. Agric. Food Chem.* 31: 484-487.

Russo, V. M. 2003. Planting date and plant density affect yield of pungent and nonpungent jalapeño peppers. *HortScience* 38: 520-523.

Saga, K., and G. Sato. 2003. Varietal differences in phenolic, flavonoid and capsaicinoid contents in pepper fruits (*Capsicum annuum* L.). *J. Jap. Soc. Hort. Sci.* 72: 335-341.

Saimbhi, M. S., et al. 1977. Chemical constituents in mature green and red fruits of some varieties of chili (*Capsicum annuum* L.). *Qual. Pl.* 27: 171-175.

Saito, A., and M. Yamamoto. 1996. Acute oral toxicity of capsaicin in mice and rats. *J. Toxicol. Sci.* 21: 195-200.

Seller, H., et al. 1997. Activation of chemosensitive neurons in the ventrolateral medulla by capsaicin in rats. *Neurosci. Lett.* 226: 195-198.

Serra C., I., et al. 1996. Cáncer vesicular: estudio de casos y controles en Chile. *Rev. Chilena Cirugía* 48: 139-147.

Shannon, E. 1989. Chile Disease Control. *New Mexico State Univ. Coop. Extens. Serv. Guide* H-219.

Smith, P. G., and C. B. Heiser. 1951. Taxonomic and genetic studies on the cultivated peppers, *Capsicum annuum* L. and *C. frutescens* L. *Amer. J. Bot.* 38: 362-368.

_____, and C. B. Heiser. 1957. Taxonomy of *Capsicum sinense* Jacq. and the geographic distribution of the cultivated Capsicum species. Bull. *Torrey Bot. Club* 84: 413-420.

_____, and C. B. Heiser. 1957. Breeding behavior of cultivated pepper. *Proc. Amer. Soc. Hort. Sci.* 70: 286-290.

_____, et al. 1987. Horticultural classification of peppers grown in the United States. *HortScience* 22: 11-13.

Sundstrom, F. J., et al. 1987. Effect of seed treatment and planting method on Tabasco pepper. *J. Amer. Soc. Hort. Sci.* 112: 641-644.

Surh, Y.-J. 1997. Effects of capsaicin, a major pungent principle in hot red pepper, on chemically induced carcinogensis and mutagenesis. In Food Factors in Cancer Protection. Ed. H. Ohigashi, et al. *Tokyo: Springer-Verlag.* 257-261.

_____. 1998. Cancer chemoprevention by dietary phytochemicals: a mechanistic viewpoint. *Cancer J.* 11: 6-10.

_____, and S. S. Lee. 1995. Capsaicin, a double-edged sword: Toxicity, metabolism, and chemopreventive potential. *Life Sci.* 56: 1845-1855.

_____, and _____. 1996. Capsaicin in hot chili pepper: Carcinogen, co-carcinogen or anticarcinogen? *Food Chem. Toxic.* 34: 313-316.

_____, and K.-K. Park. 1997. Carcinogenic vs. anticarcinogenic properties of capsaicin in hot red peppers-An overview. *J. Korean Assoc. Cancer Prot.* 1: 55-61.

_____, et al. 1995. Chemoprotective effects of capsaicin and diallyl sulfide against mutagenesis or tumorigenesis by vinyl carbamate and N-nitrosodimethylamine. *Carcinogenesis* 16: 2467-2471.

_____, et al. 1998. Chermoprotective properties of some pungent ingredients present in red pepper and ginger. *Mutation Res.* 402: 259-267.

Suzuki, T., and K. Iwai. 1984. Constituents of red pepper species: Chemistry, biochemistry, pharmacology, and food science of the pungent principle of Capsicum species. *Alkaloids* 23: 227-299.

Swezey, L. B. 1998. Homegrown paprika beats the bottled spice. *Sunset* March: 74.

Tandan, R., et al. 1992. Topical capsaicin in painful diabetic neuropathy. *Diabetes Care* 15: 8-14.

Tanksley, S. D. 1984. High rates of cross-pollination in chile pepper. *HortScience* 19: 580-582.

Terpó, A. 1966. Kritische Revision der wildwachsenden Arten und der kultivierten Sorten der Gattung Capsicum L. *Feddes Repert.* 72: 155-191.

Todd, P. H., et al. 1977. Determination of pungency due to capsicum by gas-liquid chromatography. *J. Food Sci.* 42: 660-665, 680.

Van Rijswijk, J. B., and R. G. van Wijk. 2006. Capsaicin treatment of idiopathic rhinitis: the new panacea? *Curr. Allergy Asthma Rep.* 6: 132-137.

Vesper, H., and S. Nitz. 1997. Isolation and characterization of carotenoids in paprika (*Capsicum annuum* L.). *Adv. Food Sci.* 19: 124-130.

_____, and _____. 1997. Composition of extracts from paprika (*Capsicum annuum* L.) obtained by conventional and supercritical fluid extraction. *Adv. Food Sci.* 19: 172-177.

Viñas, P., et al. 1992. Liquid chromatographic determination of fat-soluble vitamins in paprika and paprika oleoresin. *Food Chem.* 45: 349-355.

Wall, M. M., et al. 2001. Variation in b-carotene and total carotenoid content in fruits of Capsicum. *HortScience* 36: 746-749.

Watanabe, T., et al. 1987. Capsaicin, a pungent principle of hot red pepper, evokes catecholamine secretion from the adrenal medulla of anesthetized rats. *Biochem. Biophys. Res. Commun.* 142: 259-264.

_____, et al. 1988. Effect of capsaicin pretreatment on capsicin-induced catecholamine secretion from the adrenal medulla in rats. *Proc. Soc. Exp. Biol.* 187: 370-374.

_____, et al. 1989. Effects of capsaicin pretreatment on 2-deoxy-D-glucose- and acetylcholine-induced catecholamine secretion from the adrenal medulla. *Agric. Biol. Chem.* 53: 3397-3309.

Wood, A. B. 1987. Determination of the pungent principles of chilies and ginger by reversed-phase high-performance liquid chromatography with use of a single standard substance. *Flavour Fragrance J.* 2: 1-12.

Woodbury, J. E. 1980. Determination of capsicum pungency by high-pressure liquid chromatography and spectrofluorometric detection. *J. Assoc. Off. Anal. Chem.* 63: 556-558.

Wu, C. M., and S.-E. Liou. 1986. Effect of tissue disruption on volatile constituents of bell peppers. *J. Agric. Food Chem.* 34: 770-772.

Yajima, M., et al. 2000. Isolation and structure of antimicrobial substances from paprika seeds. *Food Sci. Technol.* 6: 99-101.

Yao, J., et al. 1994. Supercritical carbon dioxide extraction of Scotch bonnet (*Capsicum annuum*) and quantification of capsaicin and dihydrocapsaicin. *J. Agric. Food Chem.* 42: 1303-1305.

Yeoh, K. G., et al. 1995. Chili protects against aspirin-induced gastroduodenal mucosal injury in humans. *Dig. Dis. Sci.* 40: 580-583.

Zewdie, Y., and P. W. Bosland. 2000. Pungency of chile (Capsicum annuum L.) fruit is affected by node position. *HortScience* 35: 1174.

_____, and _____. 2001. Capsaicinoid profiles are not good chemotaxonomic indicators for Capsicum species. *Biochem. Syst. Ecol.* 29: 161-169.

Zhang, Z., et al. 1997. Effects of orally administered capsaicin, the principal component of capsicum fruits, on the in vitro metabolism of the tobacco-specific nitrosamine NNK in hamster lung and liver microsomes. *Anticancer Res.* 17: 1093-1098.

Dr. Arthur O. Tucker (to his students at Delaware State University in Dover for almost 37 years) is a botanist specializing in the identification and chemistry of plants of flavor, fragrance, and medicine. In his capacity as Emeritus Professor and Co-Director of the Claude E. Phillips Herbarium, he has had the fortunate opportunity to work with all age groups, from young children to retirees, and a wide variety of ethnic groups to help them better appreciate herbs. As an advisor and writer for numerous scientific and popular gardening magazines, Art has helped untold numbers grow healthier herbs, bring in better harvests, and simply enjoy herbal flavors and fragrances more fully.

Herbed Chili Sauce

Marge Powell

SUMMER IS THE time for peppers, tomatoes, and fresh herbs. The miracle of canning lets us preserve those tastes long after the frosts have claimed the peppers and tomatoes. I love to use this chili sauce as a topping for meatloaf and my husband likes it on hotdogs (some of us prefer not to travel in that direction). But whenever we use it, it evokes the tastes of the summer past. The following recipe uses dried herbs, however fresh herbs can easily be substituted by doubling the amount indicated.

MAKES 5 TO 6 PINTS OR 10 HALF-PINTS

4 quarts (about 24 large) ripe, cored, and peeled tomatoes; Roma types are preferred but other tomatoes work well, too (See NOTE below)
3 cups onions, chopped
3 cups sweet red peppers, chopped (about 4 large)
2 1/2 teaspoons hot peppers, finely chopped
1 head of garlic, finely chopped (about 10 cloves)
1/2 cup white sugar
1/2 cup brown sugar
3 tablespoons sea salt
1 tablespoon each yellow mustard seed, celery seed, dried thyme, and dried dill weed
1 tablespoon dried rosemary, minced
3 tablespoons mixed pickling spices
2 1/2 cups apple cider vinegar
1/2 cup raw honey

NOTE: I like to prepare my tomatoes the night before I make the sauce by briefly dipping the tomatoes in boiling water for about 2 to 3 minutes, then coring them and slipping the skins off. I refrigerate them overnight and much of the vegetable "water" will drain off the tomatoes during this time. The vegetable "water" can be drunk or used for other cooking applications. This significantly cuts the cooking time for the sauce.

Place the tomatoes into a large non-reactive saucepan where the sauce will cook. Chop the tomatoes with a *mezzaluna* or *ulu* or a potato masher in the saucepan. Add the onions, sweet and hot peppers, garlic, sugars, salt, mustard seed, celery seed, thyme, dill weed, and rosemary. Cook over medium-high heat for 30 to 45 minutes, stirring often to prevent scorching. The mixture will thicken. Tie the pickling spices in a cheesecloth bag and add to the mixture; reduce heat to medium and cook another 30 to 45 minutes. Continue to stir frequently. Add the vinegar and cook slowly until the desired thickness is reached. Add the honey. Stir well.

Pour the hot chili sauce into hot, sterilized pint or half-pint canning jars; cap and process in a boiling water bath for 15 minutes. Let sit out on a counter for at least 24 hours to be sure jars have sealed and cooled completely before storing.

See bio on page 36

Red Pepper Paste
One of Life's Culinary Secrets

Stephen Lee

MARY VETRICE, MY paternal grandmother, was my culinary mentor from a very early age. She taught me the cooking basics and a world about herbs for flavoring, but most importantly, she made sure I learned that a good cook always cooks "smart."

She'd say never roast one chicken when you can just as easily roast two—you know you're going to be hungry tomorrow about this same time. I remember once I incurred a light scolding when she walked into the kitchen to discover that I was boiling a couple of eggs in a large saucepan. She explained that if you are going to bother to light the stove, it didn't take much more effort to go ahead and boil a full dozen eggs. They could then be used for so many different dishes in the next few days, and if nothing else, any left could be quickly pickled on the weekend.

She was the queen of expeditiousness in the kitchen. Anything you could do to lighten the load and move the existing cooking project forward was music to her ears. Understand, she was the second child of eight siblings and had ten children of her own. Feeding the troops was her life's work, and here she was feeding not only me but eight other folks in my father's house.

Grandmother was never a really big user of hot chiles, but she often made a tasty rendition of what she called San Antonio Chili-Stew. Not a real chili nor a real stew—but truly delicious—it was kind of a combination of the two. I think now on reflection it was a sneaky way for her to get more garden carrots, potatoes, and peas onto our plates.

My grandmother always had a pantry of culinary secrets. Many jars and miscellaneous containers were filled with herbal combinations, compounds, and concoctions. Each was specifically designed to simplify the cooking process for one or more of her many wonderful dishes. She told me she learned how to make the chili-stew from an old cowboy who was drifting through her western Kentucky hometown of Fancy Farm. He had stopped at their farm looking for work or a handout – whichever came first. She invited him to join the family and farmhands for lunch and he began regaling the group with stories of his life in Texas. She became really intrigued when he told of working on the cow trail and detailing the trials and tribulations of his on and off work as a chuckwagon cook - and with it the technique for making Red Pepper Paste.

> "Three little peppers and how they grew,
> so many peppers I smashed up two.
> Added some seasoning, a bit of oil new,
> a tasty condiment for the whole dang crew."

This red pepper paste is a real boon for any cook who is looking for substantial depth of western flavor obtained quickly. It reminds me a lot of the Spanish *sofrito*, a combination of onions, tomatoes, garlic, thyme, bay leaf, and salt that is cooked slowly in olive oil for a long period until the mixture becomes almost paste like, then jarred and squirreled away for quick use in the daily preparation of dishes like *paella* and *patatas bravas*.

Red Pepper Paste

Use the paste to enhance your favorite chili recipe or to flavor sauces, beans, vegetables, soups, and meat loaves or burgers. Keep refrigerated for several weeks or freeze in tablespoon-sized portions on waxed paper until solid and transfer into a zip-lock bag and store in the door of your freezer for up to a year.

MAKES ABOUT 1 1/4 CUPS

8 red serrano chile peppers, fresh (or pepper of your choice)*
1 cup boiling water
1 red bell pepper, seeded and chopped
2 large garlic cloves, peeled and minced
1 teaspoon smoked paprika
1 teaspoon cumin seed
1 teaspoon dried oregano
1 1/2 teaspoons Kosher salt
2 tablespoons apple cider vinegar
2 tablespoons corn oil
1 to 1 1/2 cups bread cubes, day old, crusts removed (I use sourdough)

Put the chile peppers into a heat-proof bowl and pour the boiling water over. Allow to sit for three minutes, pour into colander and cool under cold running water. Drain well. Remove stem, seed membrane, and seeds. Chop and put peppers into the work bowl of a food processor. Add the red bell pepper, garlic, smoked paprika, cumin seed, oregano, and Kosher salt. Process in pulses, scraping down the sides as necessary, to pulverize. Add the vinegar and corn oil and process to combine.

Add the bread a few cubes at a time; pulsing until the bread softens and blends into the puree forming a paste. Stop adding bread cubes when the paste is firm enough to your liking.

*If you need to use dried chiles instead of fresh simply soak them in the boiling water for about 20 minutes before draining and then proceed with the recipe.

Cook's Notes: Vary the heat of your paste depending on the likes of the folks you'll be feeding. If your group doesn't like much heat, substitute poblanos and a green bell pepper—you'll have a green pepper paste, but it will be delicious. If you regularly cook for hotheads, use habaneros peppers and a yellow bell pepper and watch the steam build.

Here is a list of the most commonly available peppers from mildest to hottest:

Bell, poblano, guajillo, 'Anaheim,' 'New mexico,' ancho, banana, pasilla, cascabel, jalapeño, chipotle, 'Red Finger,' 'Fresno,' serrano, cayenne, pequin, tabasco, macho, habanero, 'Ghost,' 'Carolina Reaper.'

You can mix and match a whole different bunch of peppers if your goal is to make a special formula paste that becomes a signature for you. I can't imagine using 'Ghost' or 'Carolina Reaper' peppers for this paste but I know there are adventurous folks out there.

I hope that I have tempted you to want to try to be a "smart" cook. Make your own batch of Red Pepper Paste and get cooking. Here is my Grandmother's recipe for San Antonio Chili-Stew, just as she gave it to me years ago. I've not changed a word; it tastes like home, and who really believes that you can't go home again, at least in your culinary dreams.

Mary Vetrice Lee's San Antonio Chili-Stew

MAKES 6 TO 8 SERVINGS

2 tablespoons flour, all-purpose
1 tablespoon paprika
2 teaspoons chili powder
2 teaspoons Kosher salt
2 1/2 pounds rump round beef, cut into 1/2-inch cubes
3 tablespoons lard (or vegetable oil)
2 large yellow onions, peeled and sliced thin top to bottom
1 large garlic clove, minced
2 teaspoons Red Chili Paste—more or less to your taste
28 ounce can tomatoes, diced
3 tablespoons chili powder
2 teaspoons ground cinnamon
1/2 teaspoon ground cloves
1 cup cold water
2 cups peeled potatoes, cut into 1/2-inch cubes
2 cups peeled carrots, cut into small cubes
1 cup green peas

Combine the flour, paprika, two teaspoons chili powder, and Kosher salt on a large serving plate. Put a large cast iron Dutch oven over medium-high heat; when hot add the lard (or oil) and allow to melt, swirling the pan to coat the bottom and sides.

Dredge the beef cubes with the flour mixture, and immediately put into the hot fat, turning to brown well. Add the onions, garlic, Red Pepper Paste, any remaining flour mixture and mix well. Reduce heat to medium low, then cook, stirring often, until soft. Add tomatoes, chili powder, cinnamon, cloves, and 1 cup of cold water. Stir to combine, cover, and cook on a low simmer for 2 hours, stirring occasionally. (Add additional water if the mixture becomes too dry.)

Add the potatoes and carrots and cook on simmer until the vegetables are done, about 30 minutes. Add the peas, stir well, and cook for 15 minutes more. Remove from heat and let sit for 15 minutes before serving. Taste and adjust seasonings to your satisfaction.

Known as the HerbMeister, Stephen Lee has enjoyed a diverse culinary career consistently interwoven with his love of herbs. He is the author of five books, including *About 8 Herbs* and *Go Withs*. He owned and operated *The Cookbook Cottage,* an internationally known source for rare and out-of-print cookbooks and Kentucky's only cooking school, for fifteen years.

Twice Chairman of the Cooking Schools and Teachers Committee of the International Association of Culinary Professionals, Stephen currently manages the Daily Lunch Program for the Homeless for the Archdiocese of Louisville, He is Superintendent of the Culinary Department of the Kentucky State Fair, a licensed and active Auctioneer, a Board Member of the IHA Foundation, and an honest-to-goodness Kentucky Colonel. Learn more at www.herbmeister.com.

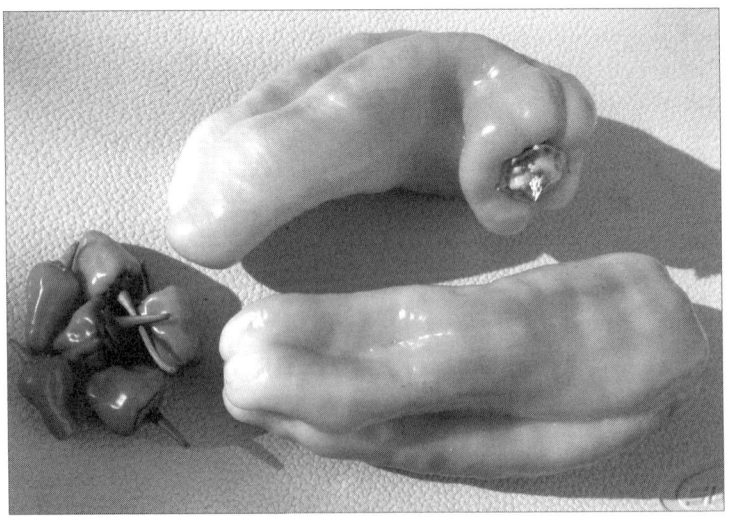

Small and Tall – Hinklehatz and Aconcagua, Karen O'Brien

Calling All Capsicums

Karen O'Brien

THERE ARE THREE items that I always have on hand in my larder, as I use them every day in my cooking, be it breakfast, lunch, dinner, or even a snack. Often, I use them together, in a particular recipe or to add to a meal. No matter what season, each of these find its way into my food everyday, sometimes raw, and othertimes cooked. My three essentials are garlic, onions, and peppers. The absence of any one of these sends me directly to the grocery store to replenish my supply. Time and again, I use these three indispensible ingredients to create a more complex dish, adding additional elements to elevate my cuisine.

In Cajun cooking, these three plus celery are known as the Holy Trinity, and form the basis of many regional dishes such as gumbo, jambalaya, red beans and rice, and more. In fact, the term Trinity is a general cooking term that refers to a combination of three ingredients gently sauteed to form a flavor base, which is indicative of a particular region or country. There are several noted bases:

Spain—garlic, onion, tomato—*Sofrito*

France—onion, carrot, celery —*Mirepoix*

Italy—carrots, onion, celery—*Soffrito*

China—garlic, ginger, hot pepper

German—carrots, celeriac, leek—*Suppengrün*

Puerto Rico—culantro, ajes dulces (small chiles)—*Recaito*

West Africa—chile peppers, onions, tomatoes

One great tip, for ease of preparation, is to chop these vegetables when you have extra time or when they are on sale in the peak growing season. As long as you will be cooking or sautéing them, the vegetables do not have to be blanched or pre-cooked. Simply slip them into freezer bags and try to get out as much air as possible. I usually squeeze as much air out as I can, close the bag almost all the way, and then stick a small straw into the end of the bag and suck out any more air that I can. Too much air will cause moisture to form, which in turn forms ice crystals. You can also use a vacuum sealer.

If I am making a marinade, I always use my trinity of garlic, onions, and pepeprs in some form. I might use chopped hot peppers, minced red onion, and minced garlic for lamb or beef kebabs. For an omelet or frittata, I may use garlic chives, red bell pepper, and a sweet onion. Soups or stews? - in goes my trinity. I've updated my mom's recipe for stuffed peppers, using a red bell pepper for stuffing instead of a green one. Add minced garlic and onion, sautéed, to cooked brown rice, throw in some cooked beans or lentils, add some homemade chili sauce (recipe below) and top with some grated cheese. Bake in a 350°F oven for 35 to 45 minutes. Delicious!

A NEW WORLD PLANT TRAVELS THE GLOBE

> *The greedy merchants, led by lucre, run*
> *To the parched Indies and the rising sun;*
> *From thence hot pepper and rich drugs they bear,*
> *Bartering for spices their Italian ware.*
>
> —John Dryden

Peppers are a New World plant, originating somewhere in South America. Christopher Columbus, searching for a route to the Spice Islands, stumbled on these plants accidently. He was seeking pepper, or *Piper nigrum*, and found the native people called Arawak using a plant they called *aga* or *aji* as a seasoning for their root vegetable *age*, or yam, as we know it today. This flavor was hot and pungent and reminded Columbus of pepper, and thus it was named. So began the plant's exodus to many other lands, as seeds and pods were distributed around the world. Five species had already been domesticated by the time of his arrival, and it's hard to believe that so many cultures have embraced it as their own.

Africa, Italy, India, and Mexico are a few of the countries with which peppers are associated. Many tropical locales use hot peppers, and with good reason. Hot peppers are considered "yin" and bring heat to surface capillaries, where it dissipates, resulting in a cooling sensation. It is said that in Mexico, because of a devoted consumption of fiery peppers, a man who unfortunately perishes in the desert will never be devoured by vultures, because the peppers cause their bodies to be too hot and spicy to eat! Colonial Puritans forbade the use of hot peppers, especially, as they believed it excited passions. There are even those who believe that peppers grow best if planted by redheads or those in an emotionally agitated state.

FAVORITES AND HOW TO USE THEM

I find hot peppers enjoyable to grow and use. My favorites are 'Fish,' a variegated pepper, 'Hinklehatz,' a German variety that grows extremely well and prolifically for me, and 'Bulgarian Carrot,' whose neon orange color adds a nice touch to salsas and gazpacho. As to sweet peppers, I love 'Aconcagua,' whose tall plants yield an abundant crop of 7 to 9 inch long, thin-walled peppers that ripen in my zone.

What to do with all the peppers you grow? There are lots of ways to preserve them. I love to pickle them, dry them in a dehydrator, use them in chili, spaghetti, or barbecue sauce. Or make a hot pepper vinegar, preserve them in sherry (you can use both the peppers and the sherry), and make Fire Cider. Hot peppers are especially useful to deter pests such as deer, bear, skunks, and squirrels. It is equally effective as a insecticide. Birds are not affected by the heat, so you can add some ground pepper to your bird seed to keep other critters from eating it. Or make a pepper spray by blending hot peppers and garlic in some water and a small amount of liquid soap. Strain, then put in a sprayer and apply to whatever plants need protection. Try growing peppers—you'll enjoy having your own and using the abundant fruits.

REFRENCES

Foster, Steven. *Herbal Renaissance*. Layton, VT: Gibbs Smith Publishing. 1993.

Grieve, Mrs. M. *A Modern Herbal Vol. 1*. New York: Harcourt Brace. 1931.

Griffin, Judy. *Mother Nature's Herbal*. St. Paul, MN: Llewellyn Publishing, 1997.

Kloss, Jethro. *Back to Eden*. NY: Benedict Lust Publishing, 2003.

Leyel, Mrs. C.F. *Herbal Delights*. Suffolk, England: Richard Clay Ltd., 1989.

Liebman, Malvina. *From Caravan to Casserole: Herbs and Spices in Legend, History, and Recipes*. Miami, FL: E.A. Seeman Publishing, 1977

Milodravich, Milo. *The Home Garden Book of Herbs and Spices*. NY: Doubleday & Co., 1952.

Sayre, James Kedzie. *Ancient Herbs and Modern Herbs*. San Carlos, CA: Bottlebrush press. 2001.

The City Cook.com/articles/2011-09-01-the-trinities. Accessed 8/30/15.

Grinding dried chiles. Susan Belsinger

Fish Pepper Dip

This dip is only slightly spicy and is equally good on crackers or with vegetables. You can use the peppers before they are ripe, when they are cream and green colored.

MAKES ABOUT 1 CUP

4 ounces cream cheese
4 ounces sour cream
3 to 4 'Fish' peppers (or other hot pepper), seeds and stem removed
2 scallions, white part only
1 tablespoon parsley

Place all ingredients in a food processor and blend. Let chill 3 to 4 hours before serving.

Fiery Vinaigrette

This can be used as a salad dressing or as a marinade for meats.

MAKES ABOUT 3/4 CUP

6 tablespoons hot pepper vinegar (directions below)
1/2 cup olive oil
2 cloves garlic, minced
2 tablespoons whole grain mustard
1/2 teaspoon paprika
1 teaspoon maple syrup

In a small bowl, whisk together vinegar and olive oil. Add garlic, mustard, paprika and maple syrup and continue to blend.

Hot Pepper Vinegar

This will be as spicy as you like, depending on the type of pepper you use.

MAKES 1 CUP

Assorted hot peppers (enough to fill an 8-ounce jar)
1 cup apple cider vinegar

Wash and dry the peppers. Pierce each one two or three times with a knife or ice pick. Place peppers into an 8-ounce canning jar, preferably wide mouth. Slowly pour the apple cider vinegar into the jar, pressing down gently on the peppers so the vinegar seeps into each pepper. Screw on the lid and set in a warm place for about three weeks. You can eat the peppers, as they will be "pickled" and use the vinegar in soups, stews, etc.

Herbed and Hot Chili Sauce

I make this when the garden is at its peak, with tomatoes ripe and bursting with flavor, and hot peppers available to add the necessary heat. Adapted from a recipe in Summer in a Jar, *by Andrea Chesman.*

MAKES ABOUT 5 QUARTS

12 pounds paste tomatoes, quartered (about 6 quarts)
1 cup apple cider vinegar
3 large, sweet onions, quartered
3 red sweet peppers, seeded and quartered
10 to 15 small hot peppers (you can add more if you like your sauce very spicy)
7 to 8 lovage stalks (can substitute 8 celery stalks)
6 garlic cloves
1/4 cup olive oil
4 tablespoons chipotle chile powder
4 tablespoons ground cumin
1 tablespoon whole mustard seed
1 tablespoon celery seed
1 tablespoon whole allspice

Combine tomatoes and vinegar in large non-reactive pan and cook until tomatoes become soft, around 15 to 20 minutes. Remove from heat.

Meanwhile, in a food processor, finely chop the onions, red peppers, hot peppers, lovage (or celery), and garlic. You can alternately chop the vegetables very finely by hand.

In a heavy, large, non-reactive saucepan, heat the oil. Add the chipotle powder and cumin and simmer until it foams, about 5 minutes (watch out – the fumes can knock you over!) Add the chopped vegetables and sauté until tender, 5 to 10 minutes. Remove from heat.

Puree the tomatoes with a stick blender, or in a blender. Add tomatoes to vegetables. Place the mustard seed, celery seed, and allspice in a muslin bag or tea ball and add to pan. Bring to a boil and simmer until sauce thickens, stirring occasionally. This could be three hours if your tomatoes are very juicy.

Pour into clean, hot quart jars, leaving 1/2-inch head space. Seal and process in a boiling water bath for 10 minutes. Cool undisturbed for 12 hours. Let jars sit for 6 weeks for flavors to develop.

Pepper sauce, Susan Belsinger

Lucille's Tomato Soup

My good herbal friend, Lucille Dressler, gave me this recipe years ago. I have added a few more herbs, as well as hot peppers, and I make this cold soup at least once in the season when the garden is bountiful.

SERVES 8 TO 10

5 to 6 cups ripe, cut up tomatoes (bite size — I used several different kinds, giving this soup great visual appeal)
1 red, orange, or yellow sweet pepper, finely chopped
2 or 3 hot peppers, finely chopped—optional
1/2 seedless cucumber, chopped
1/2 cup sweet onion, finely chopped
2 cans low sodium beef broth
1/4 cup red wine vinegar or any herbal vinegar
4 to 5 lovage stems and leaves, finely chopped
15+ garlic chive leaves, minced
20+ basil leaves, minced
8 salad burnet stems, leaves minced and stem discarded

Mix the tomatoes, sweet and hot peppers, cucumber, and onion in a large, non-reactive bowl. Add the broth, vinegar, and herbs, and mix well. Refrigerate overnight to blend flavors. Serve cold.

Lucille's Soup, Karen O'Brien

Chile Pistachio Butter

This butter is great on its own, or for vegetables, steaks, chicken, or fish.

MAKES ONE CUP

1/2 pound unsalted butter
3 minced garlic cloves
3 tablespoons fresh, chopped oregano (if you have 'Hot 'N' Spicy,' all the better!)
4 tablespoons ground chile powder
Pepper
4 tablespoons finely ground pistachio meats
1/2 cup chives, finely chopped

Bring butter to room temperature in medium bowl. Mix in garlic, oregano, chile powder, and pepper to taste. Shape into two logs. In a pie plate, mix together chives and pistachios. Roll each log in the chive mixture, coating well. Wrap in plastic wrap and chill until firm. This can be frozen.

Karen O'Brien's herbal business "The Green Woman's Garden" www.greenwomansgarden.com is located in the central Massachusetts town of Mendon. She has unusual herb plants, including medicinals and native herbs for sale, runs workshops on various herbal adventures, and occasionally participates at farmers markets and fairs. She is the Botany and Horticulture Chair of The Herb Society of America, currently serves as Co-Chairman of the New England Unit of H.S.A., is Secretary of the International Herb Association, and is Past President of the Greenleaf Garden Club of Milford. She is the editor and contributing author of several Herb of the Year™ books, including *Capsicum*, *Savory*, *Artemisia*, and *Elderberry*, produced by the IHA.

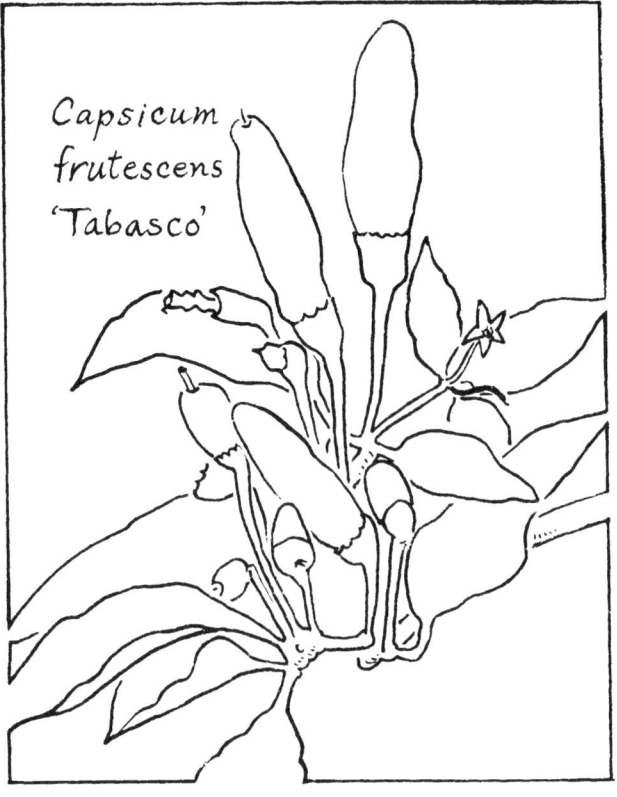

Capsicum frutescens, Pat Kenny

But Really, Why on Earth Do We Love Chiles Anyway?

Conrad Richter

A LOVE FOR herbs, a love for travel—two necessary prerequisites for any would-be herb explorer. New herbs are the lifeline of Richters Herbs, and getting out into the world, preferably the under-developed world, is one way we find new, interesting plants and seeds for our customers.

One year I found myself in Oaxaca City, in Mexico, where I treated myself to the local delights, like fried grasshoppers, on offer at the market near the *zocalo*. Not too bad, actually, except the legs get stuck between the teeth. I criss-crossed the market hunting for interesting items that might be fun to grow back in Canada, especially chiles— lots of different chiles, of different shapes, sizes, and colours. Like any self-respecting plant explorer, I saw gold in them chiles. I saw with my x-ray vision plantable seeds inside every pod, and I excitedly scooped up every available variety that the farmers offered. In my excitement it didn't occur to me to wonder what the vendors might think about the sight of a gringo stocking up on every type of chile, but they would have been quite right to think "This gringo is loco."

Back in my hotel room, I eagerly set up to remove the seeds from every chile bought, carefully keeping the varieties separate, and spreading the seeds out on labeled sheets of newspaper to dry. It was a tedious job in a hot room, and I kept reminding myself to never, ever wipe the sweat of my brows for fear of getting the hot burning oil of the chiles in my eyes. I remember priding myself for having had some training in Buddhist single-pointed mindfulness meditation, helping me, I thought, to resist the urge to wipe the sweat with my contaminated hands. Halfway through the seed extraction job, I felt the urge to pee. This was one urge that could not be resisted. I was annoyed because I was so excited about the seeds and wanted nothing to interfere with the job of getting them out of the pods. Reluctantly, I put the knife down and quickly slipped into the bathroom to urinate, and just as quickly I was back at the bed that was buried with newspapers covered in seeds— ready to resume work.

But something wasn't right. Something down 'there'. A warm tingle erupted into a violent blast of heat. The pain engulfed me, and gasping for air, I could only think of fire extinguishers and amputation. I made it to the shower but copious cold water had little effect. I figured I had two options: drag myself to the hospital, or wait until the pain subsided. Not relishing the humiliation of explaining what happened in broken Spanish, I opted for the latter. The seeds were worth it.

A few years earlier, while completing post-graduate studies in botany, I shared a house with several people. One of my housemates was a woman whose grown son became crippled after hitting his head on concrete in a running accident. After months of hospitalization, Vance moved into the house to be in the care of his mother. We could tell that the injury had had a profound effect on his personality. He had become more jovial, less restrained, and generally unsuspecting of the intentions of others, and his uplifting attitude toward life endeared us all to him.

One day we played a joke on Vance. We sprinkled some chili powder on his slices of a pizza that all of us were about to share. We waited for Vance to blurt out "Spicy!" but there was no reaction at all. Naturally the joke did not go over too well with his mother when she found out. A week later, Vance ordered a pizza for himself and decided to smother his pizza with chili powder. Not just a sprinkling but a thick layer slathered over the pizza with a knife. We were besides ourselves with alarm. Did he know what he was doing? We pleaded with him not to eat the pizza but he would not listen. In shock we watched him eat the entire pizza covered with perhaps a spice jar's worth of cayenne pepper. But this time the joke was on us—he had almost no reaction to the chili powder. We were in awe of what we had witnessed.

Thinking about the very different reactions to hot peppers, such as mine and Vance's, prompted me to learn more about hot peppers, why some of us handle them easily, and why the rest of us masochists endure the pain and eat them anyway. The story, as I discovered, has unexpected twists and turns, just like a good mystery.

Of the twenty or so species that belong to the pepper genus, *Capsicum*, five are domesticated. All the hot chiles that humans consume belong to one of these five species. The compounds responsible for the heat are a group of chemical constituents called capsaicinoids. The most important is capsaicin which accounts for more than two-thirds of all the heat activity in hot peppers. Capsaicin is mostly found in the pods, especially in the interior ribs to which the seeds are attached. It is a very interesting chemical: it acts like a key to turn on the pain system. It binds to ion channels in the membranes of neurons and when it does that, the channels open and let calcium into the neuron. The sudden influx of calcium is what triggers a constellation of events that lead to the sensation of pain.

Humans are not the only animals that are sensitive to capsaicin; many other mammals are too. Birds, significantly, are insensitive. In the wild, birds are the primary agents for the dispersal of pepper seeds; when they swallow a pod the seeds pass through the digestive system intact and germinate readily wherever the bird droppings fall. Rodents, on the other hand, are discouraged from eating hot peppers because they feel the pain. That is a darn good thing if you are a pepper plant because rodents have molars and they crush the seeds when they eat peppers, and are of no use for spreading seeds. This selective quid pro quo has important implications for us humans because we share 97.5% of our genome with mice, hence our common sensitivity to capsaicin. Effectively, we have been lumped in with the rodents as enemies of peppers.

But if capsaicin is important for seed dispersal, why are some peppers not hot at all? Even in the wild one can find peppers that are hot and others that are not. You might think that the hot ones are found in hot, dry areas while the mild ones are found in wet, cooler areas, but you'd be wrong. In Bolivia, the hot forms of the wild *Capsicum chacoense* are found in the cooler, wetter areas and the mild forms are found in the drier areas; a pattern that is repeated in Mexico and elsewhere where wild peppers grow. So what gives?

It turns out that, in the case of *Capsicum chacoense*, in cooler, wetter areas there is a bug that pokes holes in the pods in order to suck out the juice. The birds don't mind the holes in the pods and still do their job of scooping up the pods and dropping seeds here and there. But the holes are bad for the pepper plants because fungi enter and destroy the seeds, rendering the whole exercise of making seeds a waste of time. Having loads of capsaicin stored all around the seeds is pure genius because of capsaicin's other important property: it's a powerful antifungal agent that protects seeds from invading fungi. But bugs and fungi aren't a problem in hot, dry areas, so wild peppers there don't need to be as hot.

But then you may ask, why don't all peppers just produce loads of capsaicin just to be safe? The answer is that capsaicin is expensive insurance. It requires lots of nitrogen to manufacture, a key nutrient that is not in great abundance in soils where peppers grow. If capsaicin is not needed for the protection of the seeds then why bother wasting a valuable resource that could be used for other purposes? Plants that produce little or no capsaicin are in fact more drought resistant, which of course is of greater priority for pepper plants in dry areas.

Over the past few decades, capsaicin research has been, quite literally, hot. Thousands of research papers have been published, much of which is focused on pain research. Capsaicin is a valuable tool for understanding the pain signaling systems of the body. Remember those ion channels that I mentioned earlier? Those channels in the membranes of neurons also open up in response to excessive heat and to applied pressure such as pinpricks. So capsaicin can be used to mimic the effects of real pain caused by heat and by pressure. This first step of the pain signal, starting from the ion channels, is why we so easily conflate the type of pain we are experiencing. When we eat hot chiles we experience the pain as heat. Our brains interpret (or misinterpret) the signal as heat because the signal travels more or less along a common path. In pain research, capsaicin is used to turn on the ion channels like switches in order to study the pain mechanisms and to help in the search for new painkilling medicines.

But as anyone who has felt the wrath of hot peppers knows, there is a lot more to the pain of capsaicin than just the simple hijacking of the pain signaling system. We also sweat, often copiously, we get flushed, and our skin temperature rises. But surprisingly, for the first hour or so after ingesting chiles our bodies actually cool down. Hard to believe, but this was proven in experiments in which both the skin temperature and the temperature in the colon were measured simultaneously. In the first hour, the skin temperature jumps while the internal temperature drops. What happens is that the blood vessels dilate, allowing body heat to escape to the skin where it can dissipate more easily. The dilation effect brings blood closer to the skin surface, hence the flushed skin. And the rise in skin temperature initiates the flow of sweat. Both the flushed skin and the sweating cool the body, so after about an hour there is a net loss of body heat.

But soon after ingestion of capsaicin, a completely separate response mechanism kicks in, slowly increasing the rate of metabolism and creating new body heat. Over a period of twenty-four hours or so this new heat builds up slowly, bringing the body's temperature back to more or less where it was before ingestion. So, as always with anything involving herbs and the human body, nothing is simple.

Paradoxically, capsaicin not only causes pain but is also used as a painkiller. It is used in topical creams and patches for peripheral neuropathy, postherpetic neuralgia, osteoarthritis, and other chronic pain conditions. In both Canada and the United States, a number of prescription and over-the-counter products containing capsaicin are available in pharmacies. But how in the world does a pain-inducing product become a painkiller, you might ask. To answer this question, we need to understand the phenomenon of desensitization. As the use of a compound is repeated, its effect is diminished over time. In the case of capsaicin, there are two forms of desensitization. One is a short term desensitization that follows from the fact that the calcium signal can only be switched on so many times before it becomes unresponsive. If all the pain switches (i.e. the ion channels) are already thrown, adding more capsaicin, or applying more pressure, or turning up the heat more, won't cause more pain. This is graphically illustrated in a video that circulated on the Internet showing a man taking a bite of the world's hottest pepper, the 'Carolina Reaper,' 300-800 times hotter than a jalapeño pepper. The man falls to the floor, sweats profusely, and suffers terribly; yet he ultimately finishes eating the pepper. As Ed Currie, breeder of the 'Carolina Reaper,' claims in another video, the experience of taking a bite is "amazing," "incredible," and "pleasurable" once the peak heat passes. Presumably, all the pain switches that could be turned on are done so by the Reaper and there is not much more pain that can be experienced.

The second desensitization effect is a longer term one. This is the one that painkilling patches made with capsaicin rely on. When either a low dose of capsaicin is repeatedly applied or a high dose is applied once, a long-lasting insensitivity to pain results. This happens because repeated or strong stimulation with capsaicin causes the degeneration of sensory nerve fibres, and the painkilling effect lasts for months. People who grow up with hot peppers in their daily diet no doubt also become desensitized, probably in the same way that pain patches work— by destroying sensory nerves. But even where chiles are part of the daily diet, infants are not born with a tolerance to chiles. Mexican parents, for example, are known to give children packets of sugar spiked with chili powder to build up tolerance.

Genetic differences in the sensitivity to capsaicin have been reported but there is not a lot known yet. Korean scientists have studied an individual who was completely insensitive to capsaicin. This person had less than half a normal person's ion channels in his or her buccal mucosa, the lining of the cheeks and lips inside the mouth opposite the teeth. Because desensitization by capsaicin occurs in the nerve fibres further down the signaling pathway, and not on the ion channels at the start of the pathway, we know that this individual could not have lost all sensitivity by exposure to capsaicin. The scientists found several mutations in the DNA code for the ion channels and presumably these affected the receptor site for capsaicin, making it impossible for capsaicin to bind to the channels and turn them on. This is one of the few published reports showing genetic differences in the sensitivity to capsaicin.

There is also a report of genetic differences among female redheads that unsurprisingly elicited comment from a few wags. Compared to blond and dark-haired females, redheads were found to develop less sensitivity to pain after the application of a low dose capsaicin cream. Unlike high doses or repeated low doses, a single low dose makes people temporarily more, not less, sensitive to capsaicin, and this hypersensitivity effect was found to be less prominent in redheads. What exactly is the significance of this finding, I am not sure, but it does seem to suggest that genetic differences among human groups and races could be important and warrant further study.

What about Vance? Is he a genetic oddity, born with an insensitivity to capsaicin? Or did he acquire an insensitivity to it? Or was it something else? Actually, he was not as completely insensitive to the chili powder as I made him out to be. I fabricated a little there. He did get a little flushed and a little sweaty; but he did not experience pain. There was no involuntary pinched look or grimace as the effect of the capsaicin in the chili powder enveloped him. My guess is that his brain injury occurred in an area of the brain responsible for processing pain, such as the insular cortex. This area is also involved with the emotions, and we saw that his accident caused changes in his range of emotional expression. So, just maybe, Vance's ability to tolerate the effects of capsaicin and feel no pain reflected the possibility that his brain was now processing pain differently. But who knows?

So why *do* we eat this stuff? When did gastronomic pain become a good thing? An idea has emerged that humans—uniquely humans among mammals—seek out and enjoy hot peppers as a consequence of some trickery in the processing of pain in the brain. A mental sleight of hand dubbed "hedonic reversal" or "benign masochism" has been suggested to explain how we derive pleasure from the pain of chiles. Paul Rozin, professor of psychology at the University of Pennsylvania, has been studying the idea since the 1970s. He says that humans are able to dissociate the pain signal from the threat of danger, and can enjoy the thrill of danger without feeling the risk, in the same way that humans love the thrill of a roller coaster ride without worry of injury. Other mammals probably don't have the brain power to do this kind of mental calisthenics. For rats, any experience of pain means an immediate risk of danger, 100 per cent of the time, and nothing is going to change that. In an experiment, Rozin found that he was not able to condition rats to love chiles even when the rats were given the stark choice of food laced with chiles and food laced with a chemical that made them sick. Rats preferred the food that sickened them come hell or high water.

But despite a growing acceptance of Rozin's theory, it still does not quite rest well with me. I am not sure that "benign masochism" fully explains a love for chiles that goes back at least 9,500 years when the earliest use of chile peppers is known to have occurred. We know that chiles are a rich source of vitamins B and C, potassium and iron, so nutrition could have played a role. We know that chiles lower blood pressure and habitual use kills pain, so medicinal benefits could have played a role. And we know that capsaicin has antifungal properties that may have had a role in preserving food and may have helped decontaminate unhealthy food, or helped the body to resist the effects of eating unhealthy food. Rozin dismisses all these reasons for explaining our love for chiles.

In the comments section of an online *Scientific American* article on chiles, a devoted fan of the 'Bhut Jolokia' pepper, a pepper not quite as hot as the 'Carolina Reaper' but pretty darn close, summed up his take on Rozin's theory by suggesting a simpler, slimmed down alternative. He says eating very hot chiles everyday makes him feel good. "If I'm feeling lethargic before eating a very hot chile, I feel revitalized. It's a similar reward as when you lift weights (I do this too). Both make you feel good after enduring a little pain." It doesn't seem to me that this "revitalized" state is a mere figment derived from mental trickery, of relishing the relief of the cessation of pain, as Rozin would believe. To me, the Jolokia lover is referring to an actual physiological change in his metabolic state, one that overcomes lethargy. We know that there is an immediate inner cooling effect for about an hour after eating hot chiles, and maybe it is this simple change of state that has more to do with why he feels "revitalized" afterwards. Who knows?

But I am not loco enough to eat a 'Bhut Jolokia' to find out.

Conrad Richter has a Master of Science degree in botany from the University of Toronto. He has been involved with Richters since its inception in 1967 when he was still a child, helping in the greenhouses and in the fields after school and on weekends. His interest in herbs took flight when he helped his father prepare the first Richters herb catalogue in 1970. He has worked on every Richters catalogue since. His primary responsibility is research and development. Through his efforts many herbs new to gardeners in North America have been introduced for the first time. Conrad is responsible for the introduction of famous Richters varieties such as Orange Spice™ Thyme and Profusion® Chives. Conrad has been invited to speak at many conferences, and has appeared on television and radio, and frequently writes for gardening and herbal magazines.

Pepper seedlings. Karen O'Brien

Paprika plant. Pat Kenny

Some Like it Hot—Some Don't
Paprika, the Sweet Spice

Gert Coleman

PAPRIKA—THE GROUND FRUITS of the pepper *Capsicum annum*—is often a supporting player in cooking, offering color first, then flavor and "spiciness" without the heat and drama of its more spectacular *Capsicum* cousins, the cayennes and chiles that make mouths burn and foreheads sweat. But paprika can stand proudly on its own merits.

While I was growing up, every Sunday we had a roast. My parents seasoned beef, chicken, pork, lamb, and veal exactly the same way: with white salt, black pepper, and red paprika. Sometimes they'd add parsley, sometimes thyme, but for the most part the meat was speckled halfway through the cooking process with salt, pepper, and paprika. They didn't like foods too spicy or too hot. "Don't use too much!" they'd say when I played with flavors.

German-Hungarian on my father's side, Polish on my mother's side, I grew up loving paprika, thinking it was spicy and exotic. We always used the sweet paprika; I never even knew there were sharp, hot, and smoky varieties. In my adult life, the first time I substituted Hungarian Half-Sharp Paprika for the sweet one, I added the same amount called for in the recipe. Whew! Wasn't I surprised at how hot—and delicious—it tasted! My parents would never have liked it, but my husband—who's never met a hot seasoning he didn't like— loved it. Infused in a good olive oil, this particular paprika also makes a great finish for fish, meats, and roasted root vegetables.

Spices have long been used as flavoring, medicine, and currency; they have built empires, engendered massacres, scented the air, and preserved our foods. Confucius warned his followers in the days before refrigeration to avoid foods not seasoned properly or else pay the price in illness. The capsicums would have warmed his heart had he known them. While paprika may seem to the uninitiated to be a foreign, ancient spice, the capsicum family originated in subtropical Central and South America, emigrating to Spain with Christopher Columbus who mistakenly thought he had the black pepper plant (*Piper nigrum*), then spread rapidly across the Mediterranean region and globally as spice traders found its worth.

Paprika is always sold as a ground spice, its colors and flavors graded on color and sweetness/hotness scales. Though championed as Herb of the Year™, paprika, cayenne, and chile peppers are really spices. Connotatively, the word *spice* conjures up visions of Marco Polo in ancient, mystical ports; conversely, the capsicums only joined the global spice pantheon within the last few centuries. Though native to the Americas, an unexpected spice paradise, capsicums caught fire traveling through colonial empires and global trade routes to Europe, Africa, Asia, and eventually back to California, blending thoroughly into local cuisines.

Acclimating to Europe's temperate climate, *C. annum* varieties produced sweeter, less hot fruits, resulting in paprika, the ground red spice which today has become an integral part of Spanish, Portuguese, Croatian, Polish, Cajun, Creole, Mexican, Turkish, Moroccan, and especially Hungarian cuisines. Within a hundred years of Columbus, paprika or "red Turkish pepper" became a popular houseplant, garden ornamental, and scintillating seasoning.

Paprika peppers, originally hot in taste in its native habitat, evolved into a milder, sweeter spice with enough warmth and pungency that, by the nineteenth century, represented not only Hungarian cuisine but drove its economy as a national crop. In colorful ways this spice wove itself firmly into the cultural identity. Hungarian chicken and veal paprikash dishes depend heavily on paprika in sour cream sauces, while goulashes use paprika-dominated spice blends dictated by local tastes. Served on the table with salt, paprika is more popular than black pepper in many areas of Eastern Europe and, in fact, rose in popularity during World War II when black pepper was hard to find. Hungary, long considered to grow the finest paprika, is a major source of commonly used paprika, graded on eight levels from mild to pungent to hot, with colors varying from light to dark red, some with orange tones. Don't let those bright colors fool you; the strongest, hottest paprika (*erős*) is light brown.

One Hungarian legend suggests that a woman's capacity for consuming paprika reflects her capacity for romantic passion. An old Hungarian folk ritual to ensure the successful planting of paprika seeds in garden beds in early May, called *hempergőzés* (the roll in the bed), encourages the farmer and his wife to make love the same day to ensure good crops in all areas of procreation. Jancsi Paprika, the Hungarian folk hero with a capsicum pepper nose, embodies the national values of bravery, generosity, knowledge, humor, and ingenuity, and many Jancsi dolls are sold to tourists (*Whole Chile Pepper Book*).

Paprika adds color and flavor to spice blends, especially those for salt-free diets. Probably the most popular use of paprika is on deviled eggs, potato salad, and macaroni salad, but it's also a major flavor in many sausages, especially chorizo. Spanish paprika is typically sweeter than Hungarian varieties and excellent in fish, egg, and vegetable dishes. Pickled paprika peppers, known as pimentos, fill Spanish green olives as red accents. Spanish paprika (*pimentón*) comes in three versions: mild (*pimentón dulce*), moderately spicy (*pimentón agridulce*), and very spicy (*pimentón picante*). Some Spanish paprika, including *pimentón de la Vera*, derives its distinctive smoky flavor and aroma from being dried over oak fires. Herbal food writer Susan Belsinger highly recommends sprinkling this variety with a pinch of sea salt on popcorn, home fries, French fries, sweet potato fries, and corn on the cob.

Medicinally, paprika packs a wallop of easily soluble Vitamin C—1 tablespoon of paprika contains the same amount of Vitamin C as four lemons—along with Vitamins A, B1, and B2. Eating paprika can increase the appetite and stimulate sluggish circulation. Before it became their culinary star, Hungarians treated aches and pains with ground paprika in plasters and ointments, a remedy most associated today with cayenne. According to the Hungarian Paprika Museum website, "The crystalline capsaicin extracted from the paprika is used as a basis for medication for the treatment of arthritis as well as for creams and ointments to relieve minor aches and pains." Though it lacks cayenne's extraordinarily high capsaicin content, paprika's milder heat is currently combined with other herbs in massage creams and oils to encourage circulation in cellulite-reduction protocols.

Paprika stands out for its coloring outside of the culinary realm. Clothing manufacturers often market garments by using alluring, exotic spice words. *Paprika* often describes clothing in the red to orange range, colors I like to wear. Female cardinals, whose mates are often called "the red bird," sport paprika (or cayenne, depending on the light) beaks and wing feathers. Additionally, paprika was once added to canary food to enhance feather coloring. Paprika powder can be combined with henna to produce a reddish tint when coloring hair (*Wikipedia*).

Culinary experts have long decried America's wimpy use of paprika as merely colorful accents atop mayonnaise salads and deviled eggs. This flavorful spice has long been popular but arguably underused for its warm, pungent, and aromatic qualities, often overshadowed by cayenne. Hot peppers and chiles are really "in" these days but paprika is still an integral part of that spice family in both its own right and as a congenial supporting player. When hotter spices are unavailable, 2 teaspoons of paprika plus 1/2 teaspoon of cayenne can be substituted for one teaspoon each of ancho, mulato, or pasilla powders, according to spice expert Jennifer Mulherin. You can also reduce cayenne's heat by substituting paprika for part of the called-for amount. In fact, you can easily assess a recipe's hotness by looking at the ratio of cayenne to paprika and adjust accordingly.

Contributing to paprika's popularity is the fact that not everyone likes food blisteringly hot. I am one of those people, even though I have spent years judiciously (some might say timidly) adding cayenne, red pepper flakes, chili powder, and other warming spices to sauces, soups, stews, and other dishes, creating rather delicious effects.

While the mouth's tolerance for fiery foods may be genetic, cultural, or habitual, possibly even addictive, most folks are clear on their tolerance for hot, spicy food. My husband, his father, all of his brothers, and my son consume spicy foods with gusto, red-faced and sweating. On the other hand, as soon as my lips start to burn, I stop eating, unable to tolerate more than a few fiery spoonsful.

Paprika adds aromatic flavor, warmth, color, and pungency without overheating the palate. How dull my cooking would be without it!

BIBLIOGRAPHY

Belsinger, Susan. Phone interview. August 23, 2015.

Bown, Deni. *Herbal: The Essential Guide to Herbs for Living.* New York, NY: Barnes & Noble, 2001.

Bremness, Leslie. *The Complete Book of Herbs: A Practical Guide to Growing and Using Herbs.* New York: Viking Penguin, 1988.

Bunney, Sarah. *The Illustrated Encyclopedia of Herbs: Their Medicinal and Culinary Uses.* New York, NY: Viking Penguin, 1992.

Clairbourne, Craig. *Cooking with Herbs and Spices.* New York, NY: Bantam, 1978.

De la Tour, Shatoiya. *Earth Mother Herbal.* Gloucester, MA: Fair Winds Press, 2002.

DeWitt, Dave and Nancy Gerlach. *The Whole Chile Pepper Book.* Boston, MA: Little, Brown, and Co., 1990.

Duff, Gail. *A Book of Herbs and Spices: Recipes, Remedies, and Lore.* Topsfield, MA: Salem House Publ., 1987.

Hemphill, John and Rosemary. *The Book of Herbs and Spices.* New York, NY: Gallery Books, 1984.

Keville, Kathi. *American Country Living Series. Herbs: Techniques, Recipes, Uses, and More.* New York, NY: Crescent Books, 1991.

———- *Herbs: An Illustrated Encyclopedia.* New York, NY: Barnes & Noble, 1997.

Levtin, Estelle and Karen McMahon. *Plants and Society.* New York, NY: McGraw-Hill, 1996.

McHoy, Peter and Pamela Westland. *The Herb Bible.* New York, NY: Barnes & Noble, 1994.

Mulherin, Jennifer. *Spices & Natural Flavorings.* New York, NY: Macmillan, 1998.

Oster, Maggie. *Herb Mixtures and Spice Blends.* Massachusetts: Storey Books, 1986.

Paprika Museum. http://puszta.com/eng/hungary/cikk/paprika_tortenete_elterjedese. Accessed August 12, 2015.

Penzey's Spices. www.penzeys.com. Accessed August 18, 2015.

Reader's Digest Magic and Medicine of Plants. Pleasantville, NY: Reader's Digest Assoc., 1986.

Rodale's Illustrated Encyclopedia of Herbs. Emmaus, Pennsylvania: Rodale Press, 1987.

Root, Waverly. *Food: An Authoritative and Visual History and Dictionary of the Foods of the World.* New York, NY: Smithmark, 1996.

Sheen, Joanna. *The Country Book of Herbs and Spices.* London, GB: Anaya Publ., 1993.

Weiner, Michael. *Weiner's Herbal.* Mill Valley, CA: Quantum, 1990.

Wikipedia: http://en.wikipedia.org/wiki/paprika. Accessed July 15, 2015.

Lemon-Paprika-Garlic Chicken

This colorful dish can be served on its own or over noodles, with steamed spinach or broccoli as a side dish. If serving over noodles, increase the butter by a tablespoon and the lemon juice by a few squeezes. Do not overcook as overheating can cause paprika to darken and turn bitter.

SERVES 4

3 teaspoons paprika or 2 teaspoons half-sharp paprika for a pretty spicy version
Salt
Pepper
1/4 cup all-purpose flour
1 pound boneless chicken breast, sliced thinly into 2-inch strips
2 tablespoons butter
2 tablespoons extra virgin olive oil
3 to 4 cloves garlic, minced
Juice of one half lemon (or more, as needed)
3 teaspoons parsley, fresh or dried, as garnish

Mix paprika, flour, salt, and pepper in shallow bowl. Dredge the chicken strips in the paprika flour mixture till evenly coated. Sauté the strips in a combination of butter and oil until slightly browned without crowding in pan, about 4 minutes. Add more butter and oil, as needed. Then add garlic and sauté for 2 to 3 minutes. Add lemon, stir and cook until heated through, another few minutes. Check for flavor and add additional lemon and paprika, if desired. Sprinkle with parsley and serve.

Paprika Butter

Heat brings out the subtle, deeper flavor of paprika, so lavish this herb butter on warm dishes rather than as a cold spread on bread. Excellent on cooked carrots, cauliflower, corn on the cob, roasted veggies, mashed and fried potatoes, sweet potatoes, spaetzle, noodles, garlic bread, cornbread, and scrambled eggs. Increase cayenne in proportion to decreasing paprika for a more fiery effect. You can easily substitute savory, thyme, oregano, rosemary, or garlic for the parsley.

MAKES 1/2 CUP

8 ounces (1 stick) salted butter, at room temperature
2 teaspoons paprika
1 teaspoon dried parsley
1/2 teaspoon cayenne (optional)

In a small bowl combine the softened butter with the paprika, parsley, and cayenne and blend well. Store in the refrigerator for a week or so.

Paprika Pork Rub

Excellent for a barbeque with potato salad, sprinkled liberally with paprika, and coleslaw, or as an autumn harvest meal with mashed potatoes, also sprinkled with paprika, baked squash, and homemade applesauce. Amounts below are suggested. Increase or decrease the amounts according to personal preference.

SERVES 4 TO 6, DEPENDING ON APPETITES.

Spice Rub

2 teaspoons paprika
1 teaspoon ground coriander
1/2 teaspoon ground garlic
1/2 teaspoon cayenne
1/2 teaspoon ginger
1 teaspoon ground cumin
1/4 teaspoon turmeric
1/2 teaspoon chili powder
1/2 teaspoon dried rosemary, or one sprig, fresh rosemary, snipped finely
One pork tenderloin, 2 to 4 pounds
1 tablespoon extra virgin olive oil

In a bowl, combine the ingredients together for the spice rub, tossing well; set aside.

On a platter, spread the olive oil, and then roll the tenderloin in it to coat. This will help the spice rub to stick to the meat. Rub or spread the spice blend evenly on the meat, and allow to sit for 10 to 15 minutes (longer if you want a stronger flavor), then roast on the grill over medium heat about 25 minutes. Slice and serve.

Paprika Cabbage Wedges

This side dish goes well with pork, veal, and any kind of sausage.

SERVES 6 TO 8

1 small green cabbage, cut into 6 wedges
1 tablespoon sugar
2 tablespoons white wine vinegar
1 tablespoon butter or olive oil
2 teaspoons onion, diced
1/2 teaspoon celery seed
1/2 teaspoon salt (optional)
1/2 teaspoon sweet paprika or 1/4 half-sharp paprika

Heat about 1 inch water to boiling in large pot, and then add cabbage wedges. Cover and simmer until tender, about 15 to 20 minutes. Drain and remove to platter or large serving dish and keep warm.

Heat sugar, vinegar, butter, onion, celery seed, salt, and paprika to boiling. Stir for a few minutes, and then pour over cabbage wedges.

Paprika Cheese Crackers with Rosemary and Savory

I first made these crackers to take on a camping trip to spread with hummus. Now I make them as appetizers with a bit of tomato and goat cheese. You can use any kind of paprika but smoked paprika adds an extra special zest. Rosemary is my favorite herb here but savory makes an outstanding substitution.

Makes 2 to 3 dozen

8 tablespoons salted butter, softened
4 ounces Parmesan, finely grated
2 ounces sharp cheddar, grated
1 teaspoon dried rosemary, crumbled, or 1 teaspoon dried savory, crumbled
1 cup all-purpose flour
3 to 4 teaspoons paprika
1/2 teaspoon ground black pepper
Sea salt for sprinkling on top

Mix butter, Parmesan, cheddar, rosemary, flour, paprika, and black pepper with fork in large bowl until combined. Using hands, press mixture into a dough. Roll dough into a log about 2 inches in diameter and tightly wrap in wax paper. Chill 30 minutes or until just firm.

Preheat to 350°F. Lightly oil two baking pans with olive oil.

Remove paper from log and slice into 1/8-thick circles. Space evenly on pans. Sprinkle with sea salt and bake until a deep golden brown, about 15 minutes. Let crackers cool completely on pans. Store in an airtight tin.

Gert Coleman loves herbs, grows herbs, eats herbs, uses herbs, and reads avidly about them. As an herbal educator, she gives presentations on all aspects of herbs, and has 106 acres in Central New York where she and her husband are planting herbs, flowers, trees, and at-risk native plants. A recently retired Associate Professor of English at Middlesex County College in Edison, New Jersey, she lives across the bay in Staten Island, often walking the beaches with her husband and exuberant dog Thorne. As a member of the S. I. Herb Society, she helps maintain the Colonial Herb Garden at Conference House Park. Gert is Editor of the IHA newsletter and frequent contributor to the Herb of the Year™ book series, and often writes about the legends, lore, and poetry of herbs. As a naturalist, she developed and taught parent-tot nature programs at Staten Island parks and zoo, introducing children and parents to local plants, animals, and topography. In addition, Gert offers nature walks and workshops on nature writing in the parks and wild places of New York and beyond. You can contact her at gert.coleman@verizon.net

Fish pepper foliage, Karen O'Brien

Assortment of Hot Sauces. Jim Long

Hot Sauce or Salsa?

Jim Long

IT'S FUNNY, AND a bit baffling, that so many people confuse salsa and hot sauce. I'm even a bit irritated when I'm eating in a restaurant and ask the waitperson for hot sauce and they bring me a little dollop of salsa. To me it seems like being confused by the difference between pickle relish and catsup; while they are both condiments—they are entirely different.

Hot sauce is a near-liquid condiment made primarily from peppers, with other ingredients added for flavor. Hot sauce is meant to be added after the dish is served, to add heat and a zippy flavor, by the drop.

Salsa, on the other hand, is a chunky vegetable relish, often made from tomatoes, onions, and peppers (but not necessarily; I make salsa from any vegetable or fruit, from bananas to zucchini—See my book, *Sensational Salsas, from Apple to Zucchini*). Salsa is used for chip dipping, as a topping for sandwiches, hot dogs, and especially on tacos and enchiladas. Hot sauce is a seasoning; salsa is a dip.

HOW HOT IS HOT?

The nearer people live in relation to the equator, the hotter the food they eat. Capsaicin, the oil in peppers, causes the body to perspire, which is one of the natural methods the body has of keeping itself cool. In other words, what heats your mouth, cools your body! That's why you'll find food in Northern India to be milder than foods in Southern India, nearer the Equator. Alaskans traditionally don't eat hot peppers (sweating would not be a good thing in a cold climate), but if you visit Central America or Southern Mexico, you will find hot peppers to be a necessary, soothing, and pleasant part of daily life.

The amount of heat in peppers is measured by the Scoville Organoleptic Test, now simply called Scoville Heat Units, or SHU, and is named for a chemist, Professor Wilber Scoville, who developed the method for measuring heat levels of chile peppers in 1912. The heat factor is measured in multiples of 100 units, so a sweet bell pepper and a sweet banana pepper are rated at zero units, while a jalapeño is rated at between 2,500 and 8,000 SHUs.

COMPARISONS OF PEPPERS BY SHUS

SHU	Type Of Chiles
15 million	Pure Capsaician
2 million	U.S. Grade Pepper Spray
1,100,000 - 2,000,000	Trinidad Moruga Scorpion
1,000,000 - 1,100,000	Bhut Jolokia/Ghost Pepper
350,000 - 500,000	Red Savina Habanero
200,000 - 350,000	Habanero
50,000 - 100,000	Chiltepin
50,000 - 100,000	Thai
30,000 - 50,000	Cayenne
30,000 - 50,000	Tabasco
15,000 - 30,000	Arbol
5,000 - 20,000	Serrano
2,500 - 8,000	Jalapeño
2,500 - 5,000	Guajillo
1,000 - 2,000	Ancho
1,000 - 3,000	Pasilla
1,000 - 2,000	Poblano
800 - 1,400	New Mexico
500 - 1,500	Anaheim
100 - 500	Pimento
0	Sweet Bell

Hot sauce can be either cooked or raw, depending on the kind of sauce you want. It can also be refrigerated for several weeks, or canned for use later. Sauces can also be made from either fresh or dried peppers. For example, here's one of my favorite sauces made from dried peppers.

Drying peppers. Susan Belsinger

"Instant" Hot Sauce from Dried Peppers

This is a very simple, uncooked hot sauce that has a terrific smoky flavor. Like all hot sauces, the flavor improves after about a week. This can be refrigerated for several weeks, or it could be canned, as well, for longer storage.

MAKES 2 1/2 CUPS

2 to 3 ounces dry New Mexico chiles (about five to six whole chiles, stems removed, caps left on) See Note below
5 dry chile de arbol (also known as Mexican tree chile or bird's beak chile; you can substitute dried cayenne)
4 cloves garlic
1 tablespoon salt (I prefer canning or sea salt, but any salt will work)
1 cup apple cider vinegar
1 cup water
1 tablespoon sherry
1 tablespoon cocoa
2 teaspoons brown sugar

Rinse chiles and remove stems. Place chiles in a shallow bowl.

Bring enough water to a boil to completely cover the chiles and pour over the peppers. Set a plate on the chiles to hold them down in the hot water and set aside for 20 minutes, or until chiles are soft. Reserve the water from soaking.

Place chiles and garlic, salt, vinegar, water, and brown sugar in a blender in batches and puree until you have a smooth paste; add some of the water from soaking the chiles earlier to thin to a good consistency (discard any leftover water).

Add the cocoa and sherry at the last, blending briefly; add more salt if desired.

NOTE: *When removing the stems from peppers, leave on the little cap at the top of the pepper. It adds better flavor to your sauce and is traditional in many parts of the world.*

Garlic and Mixed Chile Hot Sauce

Makes about 6 cups

1/2 gallon glass container with lid
12 cloves garlic, peeled, crushed slightly
2 fresh habanero peppers, stems removed, cut in half
  (leave or remove seeds)
6 to 8 dried serrano or cayenne pepper pods,
  stems and most of the seeds removed
1 tablespoon canning or sea salt
5 to 6 cups distilled white vinegar

Place the garlic cloves in the bottom of the jar. Add the fresh habaneros, dried peppers, and salt.

Pour enough vinegar over the ingredients to completely cover. Cover jar with plastic wrap then loosely screw on a lid. Set aside for one week. Check to make sure ingredients are completely covered with vinegar, if not, add more vinegar.

Empty the entire ingredients into a blender in batches and blend until smooth. If the mixture is too thick, add more vinegar or water to make a pourable sauce. This can be kept refrigerated for several months.

Quick and Easy Hot Sauce

This is a tasty, versatile recipe, vary it with the ingredients you have on hand. Use it on scrambled eggs, grilled meats, or other dishes.

Makes 3 to 4 cups

4 cups coarsely chopped, fresh mixed peppers, such as jalapeño, cayenne, poblano, serrano, etc., stems removed, caps left on
2 1/2 cups distilled white vinegar
3 to 4 garlic cloves, peeled
2 teaspoons chili powder
1 tablespoon salt

Combine the ingredients in a blender and blend until nice and smooth. If the sauce is too thick, add a bit of water. Refrigerate for up to six weeks.

HOT, Jim Long

SRIRACHA HOT SAUCE

McIlhenny Co.'s Tabasco® Pepper Sauce was once the only hot sauce available. The McIlhenny family began making Tabasco® brand hot sauce in the 1860s on Avery Island in South Louisiana. Grown from a strain of *Capsicum frutescens* (the family maintains secrecy about the precise variety and guards the seeds vigorously), the peppers are packed in salt and aged in barrels for 3 years before being turned into the great American hot sauce we all grew up with. The flavor is simple, vinegary, and hot.

However in the past decades a myriad of hot sauces have come on the market. None has gained world-wide appeal as much as Sriracha, and this sauce has now overtaken the traditional Tabasco® as the number one hot sauce, not just in America, but around the world, as well.

Sriracha is named for the beach city of Si Racha in eastern Thailand where it originated. Originally it was served as a dipping sauce with seafood by street vendors along the seashore. Sriracha is made from red jalapeño peppers, with garlic, sugar, and vinegar, then fermented. The flavor includes a just-picked pepper fragrance with a fruity, garlicky, chile pepper taste, and a hint of sweetness with moderate heat.

You can easily make your own sriracha for use on crab cakes, black bean soup, Asian dishes, chicken, or just a simple omelet. Sriracha is delicious on noodles with a bit of chopped scallion, cilantro and sesame seeds, as well as any Asian dish, scrambled eggs, even plain hamburgers.

Homemade Sriracha-Style Sauce

According to authentic Thai recipes, you snip the stems of the peppers with scissors, leaving the green button at the top of the pepper to provide flavor of "the flower."

MAKES ABOUT 2 CUPS

1 pound fresh, red hot chiles, such as serrano, jalapeño, cayenne, or Thai chiles, stems removed and coarsely chopped
4 cloves garlic, peeled
2 tablespoons palm or brown sugar
1 1/2 teaspoons kosher salt
1/3 cup rice vinegar (or substitute white distilled vinegar, but rice vinegar is preferred)
1/4 cup water

Place the all the ingredients in a saucepan and bring to a boil. Lower the heat and simmer for five minutes. Remove from heat and allow to cool to room temperature.

Transfer to a blender or food processor and blend until smooth, adding a bit of water if needed.

Straining is a matter of personal preference: I processed mine until really smooth and left as is (the seeds practically disappear). I did strain some to test it, and I found the strained version to have a little more bite and heat, and the remaining pulp is a great chile paste. However, I preferred the non-strained version of the sriracha, which had a nice heat combined with a wonderful fruitiness (and so much easier than pushing the pulp through a sieve). Refrigerate for up to a month.

See bio on page 91

Paprika Promises

Pat Kenny

DEVILED EGGS
Kim Merryman

Smooth, white orbs, halved and emptied
Golden centers mashed
Mayo, pickle juice combined
Half orbs mounded high
Paprika adorned
Won't last long
Eat!

UNTIL RECENTLY, I had merely used paprika as an accent; an orange-red, slightly tasty decoration on deviled eggs, scalloped potatoes, and hummus. That's something I bet a lot of us could say, but paprika has dimensions much loftier than that. Come along with me on an adventure of appreciation.

PLANT FAMILY

Solanaceae, which includes not only economically important food plants such as potato, tomato, eggplant (or aubergines), green and red peppers, paprika, husk tomato, and tomatillo, but also showy garden ornamentals such as the petunia, angel's trumpet, datura, and the ornamental nightshades. Many of the food plants have medicinal uses as well as culinary uses; many of the others are inedible or toxic to animals but are used sparingly as medicine or pesticides.

DESCRIPTION

As you know by now, the New World *Capsicum* genus and its member species, not the Old World *Piper,* black pepper genus, is our Herb of the Year™ 2016. Some name reference guides say *Capsicum* comes from the Latin *capsa,* "box" or "case," yet the genus name is more likely from the Greek *kapto* "to bite" (*Encyclopedia of Herbs,* 2009), in reference to the pungent taste in the alimentary canal beginning on the tongue in the mouth and ending at the other end.

All species have stems that branch repeatedly, with pointed leaves that have long petioles. Their white-to-cream, green, or purple star-shaped flowers vary, having four to seven petal lobes, often five, that appear during July and August; fruit matures during the following months to October and the region's frost date, if grown in temperate climates. They create sweet and hot fruits in a variety of shapes, colors, tastes, degree of "heat" (burning sensation), and are more or less rich in Vitamins A and C, often depending on how ripe they are. The fruit of the chile pepper plant is really a berry. A berry is defined as a fleshy fruit that does not split open at seams or pores. When it becomes ripe, it is indehiscent; it is soft and fleshy throughout, before drying and shrinking. In the case of the capsicums, the fruit is a hollow box and it is usually 2-chambered. In the case of hot peppers the most pungency can be found where the flat seeds attach to the placenta. The seeds themselves only taste "hot" where and if they touch the placenta; wash them and little or no capsaicinoids can be detected.

There are five most listed species of capsicums: *Capsicum annuum, Capsicum baccatum, Capsicum chinense, Capsicum frutescens, Capsicum pubescens.* We are probably most familiar with the *Capsicum annuum* species, the native pepper that has been bred into the most cultivated varieties. Morphologically, this species has only one flower in each leaf axil. Every year new cultivars are introduced, thousands worldwide; at this writing, *Wikipedia* lists about 189 (last modified 8–16–2015). They are annuals in our climate (zones 4 through 8) or short-lived perennials unless grown through cold weather in bright hot houses. They are especially productive in warm, dry climates.

There are at least five groups of *C. annuum: Cerasiforme* (cherry), *Conioides* (cone), *Fasciculatum* (red cone), *Grossum* (pimiento, sweet bell), *Longum* (cayenne, chili). Paprika peppers are in the fifth group, the *Longum*, along with cayenne and jalapeño peppers. Since paprika peppers are round and globular one might think they would be grouped into the *Ceriforme* (cherry) or *Grossum* (pimiento, sweet bell) groups, but nooooo...obviously, I am not a taxonomist.

CAPSICUM HISTORY

Native to Central and South America, including Mexico and the Caribbean regions, the Capsicums were developed into a crop plant about 6000 B.C.E., some believe even earlier. Archaeological records reveal that early inhabitants of Mexico were using what I like to call "the Mother of All Capsicums", a pea-sized pepper, like the chiltepin or chiltecpin, *C. annuum* var. *aviculare*, (now *C. glabriusculum*), the wild "flea chilli" or "bird pepper", as far back as 7500 B.C.E.

In September 1493, Columbus set out on his second voyage with a Spanish physician, Dr. Diego Alvarez Chauca, who recorded in vivid detail the flora and fauna of the New World. He told of the *agi*, a red fruit that caused tongue blisters. The pods became "Ginnie cods" or "Indian Pepper" and, at first, were treated only as an ornamental, grown in pots, for the court of King Philip II of Spain. John Gerard (*The Herbal*, 1633) refers to writings of Dioscorides (first century), Actuarius (thirteenth century), and Clusius, a Belgian, also called "hunter of plants," Charles de l'Ecluse (1526–1609), who called the plant *piperitis*, having a taste similar to *Piper*, different from that of *Zingiber* or *Panax*. Sea-faring Greeks called the peppers they got from Italy *peperi* or *piperi*.

Although his search for exotic Asian spices was often considered to be a failure, Columbus found peppers and allspice, both of which Europeans called *pimiento*, hoping the latter was oversized black pepper. For that reason confusion continues as many recipes calling for pimento or pimiento may be referring to allspice, sweet red capsicum pepper, or even black pepper, *pimienta* in Spanish.

Jean Andrews, author of *Peppers: The Domesticated Capsicums*, has written a scholarly history of how the Capsicums made their way around the world. We know that monasteries were often the centers of gardening and medicine, and so it follows that Spanish priests and botanists who accompanied explorers, traders, and conquistadors would be interested in collecting and spreading seeds of plants as well as dispersing religious and cultural stories. Western monks and botanists probably received peppers from the Iberian Peninsula as a result of these explorations.

From Portugal, Spain, Morocco, back and forth to Brazil and East Africa, Capsicum peppers spread all over the world. Early sailors and traders of Spain, Portugal, England, and France, as well as local traders who made exchanges with them, continued the pepper progression to colonies in East Africa, India, Indonesia, and the rest of what was called the Orient. The arrival of Capsicum peppers in Central Europe is thought to coincide with the invasion by the Ottoman Turks in the sixteenth century. Suleiman the Magnificent conquered Mediterranean areas, one-by-one, then occupied Hungary between 1538 and 1548. Some sources say that the Turks acquired the cultivated New World peppers from Portuguese colonies in Persia and India and then took them with other spices and New World foods through Hungary to the Balkan Peninsula. Hungary was plagued by invasions and migrations but these were people who loved gardening and cooking so the cultivation of the spice encouraged times when the country could rebuild and flourish.

Art Tucker tells a story about a young Hungarian girl forced into becoming a member of a harem of the pasha of Buda. Confined to the palace and looking out the window, she watched how the gardeners grew the peppers. After armed Hungarians retook the palace, she ran back to her village with the peppers and taught the villagers how to grow them. The Hungarians called the spice *paparka*, from the Bulgarian *piperka*, which came from the Latin *piper*. It became a condiment added to cauldrons over the open fires of the herdsmen of the country, fishermen of the Danube, and then the peasantry whose diet depended upon pigs, poultry, and "fattened oxen".

Zoltan Halasz, (*Hungarian Paprika Through the Ages*, 1963), calls all New World peppers *paprika*, reminding us that peppers from the Americas were all "hot"; the cultivation of the mild paprika came about much later and with much deliberation. Napoleon's campaigns have been said to start the career of the well-known Szeged paprika. Realizing that Napoleon seemed to be taking over the European continent,

Britain enacted a naval blockade of the French coasts. The British ruled the seas but France's greater population and agriculture had nurtured an intercontinental trade among other European economies. Because of the continental blockade by both adversaries, people had to find substitutes for products they had previously been able to get through trading: cane sugar was replaced with beet sugar and paprika began to be used in place of black pepper. By that time the progeny of paprika farmers had improved growing and processing techniques and were ready and willing to share their spice, heretofore thought of as only holding "a unique and privileged position in the realm of spices"(Halasz).

TASTE AND SCENT

The famed bright red-orange powder called paprika, pronounced PAP–rika in Hungary, is made from fleshy, thick-walled peppers; in fact, any *Capsicum annuum* that is thick, red, and relatively mild can be used. In my opinion, there can be mighty hot paprikas. According to DeWitt and Bosland, U.S. California Sweet is lowest on Scoville Heat Unit Scale at 0; Hungarian hot paprika falls between 100–500 SHUs. Tastes and aromas are described as sour to sweet, bland to hot, fruity, spicy to pungent. To taste your paprika more easily, let it soak in some vegetable oil for a while. The aroma is hard for me to describe without saying, "Hmm, smells like paprika!" I leave that to those of you with better and more discriminating noses.

Paprika's ability to color and flavor foods is obvious, but I ran across an additional use of adding it to henna for an even brighter head of red hair. Along with marigold petals, feeding chickens a small quantity of mild Hungarian paprika in their daily meal deepens the yellow color of egg yoke. The color is mostly due to xanthophyll carotenoid zeaxanthin (*Project Gutenberg Self-publishing Press*, 2015).

PAPRIKA'S HISTORICAL BACKGROUND

Each country to which Capsicums were introduced bred and adapted the species to its own climate and soil type. Even though hot peppers were present in Central Europe since the beginning of the Ottoman

Conquest, then traveled to colonies throughout Africa and Asia, the paprika pepper, as we know it, did not become popular and cultivated in Hungary until the late nineteenth century. The most important regions for growing paprika peppers are between three rivers, the Tisza, the Maros, and the Danube, and two towns, Szeged and Kalocsa, the latter to the west on the Danube. "The Hungarian Plain," Zoltan Halasz says, had many microclimates and it took years of research to breed a fruit with the characteristic bright red color and spicy aroma and flavor. He relates that there were as many local varieties as there were towns in the region. Selection for the best variety to choose for improvement as to large size, early fruition, drought, and disease-resistance took much experimentation.

The length of the growing season was about five months on the Plain, April to September. The soil was good, sandy, and well-drained, but the climate was temperate (yearly average was 2000 hours of sun), not dry and tropical. At the turn of the eighteenth to nineteenth century, the "paprika-people" had developed practices in reaction to the hazards of weather, frost and heat, and avian pests. Superstitious traditions and beliefs were created to appeal to the supernatural powers for protection. Three customs emerged:

1. Vine-shoots were gathered and set afire in the yards; holy water was sprinkled on the smoldering vine-shoots which were then thought to be infused with magic power to keep away witches. The burnt vine-shoots were then buried in the corners of the field of paprika to keep evil away from the young plants; this was called "kindling of fire."

2. Drills that were used to insert seedlings were never to be stuck into the soil when not being used; the drill was to be laid with care aside the planted bed.

3. Most important, and still proper to observe even today, family members were cautioned to forget all anger or differences with neighbors at the time of planting, encouraging all "to help each other in this most urgent work" (Halacz).

At the beginning of the twentieth century, many countries began seeking a non-pungent variety of paprika as well. Master processors, the Palffy Brothers of Szeged, noticed that they could decrease the pungency of the powder by washing the seeds. However, that was too much work, so they attempted, and finally grew, a non-pungent pepper. Unfortunately, after a few generations, the original pungency reappeared. It was found that some women had planted what they were calling "eating paprika" alongside their "seasoning-paprika" beds; cross-pollination had occurred. Ferenc Horvath, a Kalocsa research worker at the Agricultural and Chemical Paprika Research Station, selected 300 non-pungent "mother plants" and divided them between the two towns. During generation after generation, the non-pungent paprika plants were saved and propagated. The liberation of Hungary in 1945 after World War II provided a much wider range for research, which was encouraged by a network of institutes and experimental farms. Two new hybrid varieties were developed and cultivated on Szeged and Kalocsa lands.

Because of all this work over the years, there now exists a wide range of paprika powders, from the faintly pungent kind to a variety known as "rose," paler in color and definitely hot-tasting; there is also a variety named "brown" for the brown-red color, extremely pungent, only used in small quantities. Dried, powdered paprika can be of one variety or a mixture of sweet and hot varieties.

CULTIVATION

Today, the growing of paprika peppers is the same as for any member of *Solanaceae;* germinate from seed started early, over a heat mat to maintain constant temperatures, and under fluorescent lights (using both warm and cool tubes) for seven to ten weeks. Move strongest plants to full sun in well-draining, composted garden soil after all danger of frost is past and when the soil temperature warms (month of May in the mid-Atlantic region). Space seedlings two to three feet apart in moderately fertile soil having a pH range of between 5.5 to 6.8.

HARVESTING

Traditionally, September 8th, the Feast of the Holy Virgin's Nativity, heralds the beginning of the paprika harvest. The ripest peppers are chosen first, then the rest are picked subsequently as they ripen. Initially, everything in Hungary was done by hand: picking the harvest "with good cheer and perseverance," letting the peppers rest for three to four weeks to allow color and flavor to intensify, and threading eight to ten foot garlands of pods for hanging and drying on white-washed walls. The drying process was completed in earthen ovens until they rattled; the dried peppers were bagged, stomped upon underfoot, sifted, then ground in huge mortars with pestles. Each family had its own method of processing.

You can grow and prepare your own paprika pepper for a fresher, more flavorful product. Harvest the peppers when they are completely red with no tinge of green or chocolate color. In 1992, Ohio grower Meyer Hoffer described drying instructions that include the use of silica gel in a plastic bag (*The Avant Gardener* newsletter, Vol. 24, N0. 10, p. 76, July 1992).

CULINARY USES

Mild or sweet types are seeded and dried, with both placenta and seeds removed before grinding. Hot paprika is prepared with sweet peppers whose flesh contains less heat; some seeds and placentas may be added. Most are blends that fall between mild, sweet, and hot. The European Traveler website*(europeantraveler.net/archives/taste-of-europe/paprika.php)* lists eight types which range from "*Kulonleges* (Special), The brightest red paprika of all, with good aroma and very mild, sweet flavor; *Edesnemes* (Noble Sweet), Bright red in color but with only a mildly spicy flavor. Most of the paprika exported to the rest of the world is this type; to *Eros* (Hot), The hottest variety, pale rust-red to light brownish-yellow in color."

Most cooks agree that the finest paprika is grown and ground in a region of southern Hungary called Szeged. Depending upon the amount of pungency (*capsaicin*), members of the genus *Capsicum* are said to have bacteria-deterrent and antioxidant qualities that can extend the keeping periods of fats, meats, and casseroles (*The Joy of Cooking*).

Besides being used as a garnish or decoration, paprika has traditional use in *gulyasleves* ("herdsman soup" with meat, vegetables, paprika, other spices), chicken paprikas, paprikash potatoes, and Hungarian goulash. Paprika is also used in making soups, stews, sauces, and pastes. When cooking with paprika, always dissolve the spice in hot oil or fat to release its flavor and aroma, then quickly add the vegetables, meat, or a liquid to lower the temperature and keep the spice from burning. This is good advice to practice with almost any spice or herb.

MEDICINAL USES

When in the West Indies on Columbus' voyage, Dr. Chauca witnessed native rituals using drinks containing the "God of Fire" for mystical purposes, as well as a relish-type seasoning at meals. Zoltan Halasz tells of a Jamaican beverage made of "a certain cucumber-variety," lemon juice, onion, Madeira wine, and a lot of paprika (or *Capsicum* varieties) which is still prescribed for malarial fevers today. Franciscan monks who functioned as gardeners and physicians in Hungary used the red pods to treat malaria-stricken people living along the river marshes. The people of the Balkan Peninsula have used it as a preventive against fevers since the beginning of the eighteenth century.

No one knows what it was about paprika that instilled trust in food and drink seasoned with it. "But one thing is certain:" Halasz says, "even in the beginning of the twentieth century, the favourite medicine of the Hungarian peasant of the Plain was brandy with paprika." It was used for stomach-ache or an unexpected fever. Among the working people, traditional remedies employed paprika powder for night-blindness, as a digestion stimulant, a disinfectant for small wounds, and in plasters for boils. During the rest of the twentieth century, many scientific studies on animals and humans took place. In 1931, curious about the physiological effects of noble-sweet paprika, two Szeged doctors worked with rabbits, dogs, and frogs on questions about effects on nutrition, digestion, blood pressure, and heart activity. It was found that noble-sweet paprika enhanced digestion, whereas highly pungent paprika irritated stomach lining, therefore interrupting secretion of gastric juices. Capsaicin extracted from paprika caused blood pressure to rise only if it was injected directly into the circulatory system; if ingested by mouth, the slight quantity in noble-sweet paprika had no effect.

The red color in paprika indicates the presence of carotenoids. Hungarian biochemist, Professor Laszlo Cholnoky (1899-1967), demonstrated that paprika has much more vitamin A than carrots. Sylvie Tremblay (*Livestrong.com* December 18, 2013) says that "one tablespoon of paprika contains 3,349 international units of vitamin A, more than 100% of the daily intake requirement for men and women, set by the Institute of Medicine." Albert Szent-Gyorgyi (1893-1986), Hungarian physiologist, was the first to discover one of our most essential vitamins, vitamin C, first in adrenal gland tissue (*hexuronic acid* in 1930); then in later experiments, used paprika as a source for the vitamin C. Lesley Bremness claims in her book *Herbs* (1994) that paprika helps prevent seasickness.

STORAGE

Meyer Hoffer suggests storing dried peppers in an airtight mason jar with a small amount of silica gel. Do not be tempted to grind it all at once, because within two to four weeks the flavor will deteriorate to that of tasteless red food coloring (just like the store-bought paprika). As do many herbs, paprika loses color and flavor with age, so it is best to purchase freshly milled and carefully-packaged paprika, or grind your own from dried pods. Perhaps the best dry, dark place away from heat and sunlight might be your kitchen cabinet for the whole and/ or powdered paprika, which, Taste-of-Europe writer Sharon Hudgins suggests using within a year from purchase. According to McCormick Spice Company, "Spices should not be stored in the freezer. Freezing does not extend the shelf life of regularly used dried spices and herbs. If stored in the freezer, and repeatedly removed for use, condensation will form in the bottles and accelerate loss of flavor and aroma."

PLANTS

Francesco DeBaggio, Stephen Facciola, and Art Tucker (1998), list the following open-pollinated varieties:

'Alma Paprika' has a small, round or somewhat flattened fruit, thicker-fleshed, smooth white skin turning red when ripe, pungent, often processed into pickles; it is the most widely-grown hot pepper in Hungary, where ground dried paprika is considered to be the national spice and nicknamed "Red Gold."

'NuMex R. Naky' and 'NuMex Conquistador' are two "mild" hot peppers grown for making paprika powder; others recommended are 'Hungarian' and 'Paprika Supreme' (Tucker, 2009). DeWitt and Bosland (2009), say, "New Mexican pods are the basis for the green chile, the red chile, and much of the paprika production in the world".

'Papri Mild II' which matures in 78 days, deep green ripening to bright dark red, high in flavor but mild in pungency (hotness), can be dried in sun or dehydrator and powdered for kitchen use, selected for quick-drying and dark color at maturity (Facciola 1998).

'Paprika' (culinary paprika, paprika mild) 85 days, upright plant; short, flattened, 4-lobed fruit, thin- walled, very mild & flavorful, excellent for drying and powdering, especially popular in Hungarian cooking. (Facciola, 1998). In the latest *Joy of Cooking* (2006), the chapter "Know Your Ingredients" speaks of *Capsicum tetragona* which could be another name for this cultivar. Spain has a similar pepper called *pimiento* with pointed heart-shaped fruit used to make *pimenton*, a ground spice similar to paprika; in fresh form it's most familiar as stuffing for Spanish olives.

The following are listed by Wikipedia under *Capsicum annuum* cultivars that produce Hungarian paprikas (8-31-15):

'Alma Paprika'– 10,000 SHU (Scoville Heat Units); so far, ours this year, labeled "hot", was sweet; perhaps it did not get enough hot sun.

'Leutschauer Paprika'– no further info.

'Paradicsom Aluka'– no further info.

'Ram Horn Fireboy'– 35, 000 SHU

A SEED SOURCE

PepperGal@bellsouth.net offers at least five paprika-type seeds by the following names: Feher Ozon Paprika Sweet Pepper Seed, Conquistador Sweet Pepper Seed, Szegedi Giant Sweet Pepper Seed, Krimzon Lee Hybrid Hot Pepper Seed, and Alma Paprika Hot Pepper Seed.

The following is a famous quote by the novelist Zsigmond Moricz :

"Under the eaves, over the fences, on the trees and on the dove-cots – garlands of paprika, everywhere. So exotic is this decoration that for its sake tourists will want to come from Calcutta, London and other places, because this is a wondrous specialty. Beautiful! Inconceivably beautiful is the village courtyard at such times…" *Hungarian Paprika through the Ages*

Just saying the word PAPrika! makes me feel happy.

REFERENCES:

Andrews, Jean. 1995. *Peppers: The Domesticated Capsicums.* Univ. Texas Press Austin.

Andrews, Jean. 1999. *The Pepper Trail-History and Recipes from Around the World.* Univ. of North Texas, Denton TX.

Bremness, Lesley. 1994. *Herbs.* New York, NY, DK Publishing Inc., 237.

DeBaggio, Francesco. 2015. *DeBaggio Herbs catalog*, Chantilly, Virginia, 35-38.

DeVore, Sally and Thelma White. 1978. *The Appetites of Man - An Introduction to Better Nutrition from Nine Healthier Societies.* Anchor Books, Garden City, 31, 37, 55.

DeWitt, Dave and Paul W. Bosland. 2009. *The Complete Chile Pepper Book – A Gardener's Guide to Choosing, Growing, Preserving and Cooking.* Timber Press, Portland/London, 53, 163.

DeWitt, Dave and Nancy Gerlach. 1990. *The Whole Chile Pepper Book.* Little Brown, Boston, 173-177.

Elpel, Thomas J. 2013. *Botany In A Day.* Hops Press, Pony MT, 146-148.

Facciola, Stephen. 1998. *Cornucopia II.* Kampong Publications, Vista CA, 476, 479, 480.

Foster, Stephen. 1993. *Herbal Renaissance*. Gibbs-Smith Publishers, Salt Lake City, 62-64.

Halasz, Zoltan. 1963. *Hungarian Paprika through the Ages*. Corvina Press, Budapest.

Heiser, Charles B, Jr. 1980. *Peppers of the Americas*. A folder U.S. National Arboretum distributed.

Heywood, V.H., ed. 1993. *Flowering Plants of the World*. Oxford Univ. Press, New York, 228-229.

Kaufman, Sheilah. 2002. *Sephardic Israeli Cuisine: A Mediterranean Mosaic*. Hippocrene Books, Inc., New York.

Ortiz, Elisabeth Lambert. 1994, *The Encyclopedia of Herbs, Spices, and Flavorings*. Dorling Kindersley, London, 72.

Rombauer, Irma S., Marion Rombauer Becker and Ethan Becker. 2006. *The Joy of Cooking*. Scribner, New York, 553, 1006-7.

Rosengarten, Jr. Frederic. 1969. *The Book of Spices*. Livingston Press, Wynnewood PA, 59, 130-131,134-137.

Tucker, Arthur and Thomas De Baggio. 2009. *The Encyclopedia of Herbs–A Comprehensive Reference to Herbs of Flavor and Fragrance*. Timber Press, Portland OR, 187-204.

van Wyk, Ben-Erik. 2006. *Food Plants of the World*. Timber Press, Portland OR, 116.

Viard, Michael. 1995. *Fruits and Vegetables of the World*. Longmeadows Press, Ann Arbor, 42-45.

Heimburger's European Traveler. www.europeantraveler.net/archives/taste-of-europe/paprika.php

www.budapest-tourist-guide.com/hungarian-paprika.html

Hungarian World Encyclopedia. www.library.obu.edu/Hungarian World Encyclopedia

Deviled eggs with paprika Susan Belsinger

Pat Kenny—Medical illustrator retired from NIH, volunteer herb publicist giving photo-illustrated herb talks and demos neighborhood-to-nation, member of IHA since it was IHGMA, Herb Society of America since 1979, and supporter of the nation's largest public herb garden, the National Herb Garden, where every year there is a Chile Pepper Celebration early in October.

Paprika Choices, Pat Kenny

Cayenne—A Fiery Friend in our Herbal Apothecary

Carol Little R.H.

CAYENNE (*CAPSICUM ANNUUM*) is a well-loved and much-used member of my herbal apothecary. This fiery fruit has a long tradition in the herbal world and a very long list of healing attributes.

It offers a stimulating jolt to formulas with a definite warming effect and so is used in a small quantity.

Let me begin with some of the highlights of cayenne as an herbal medicine. Please see the glossary on page 241 for help with any unfamiliar terms.

HIGHLIGHTS OF CAYENNE FRUIT IN HERBAL MEDICINE:

- Analgesic
- Antibacterial
- Anti-emetic (also emetic in large doses)
- Anti-inflammatory
- Antioxidant
- Antispasmodic
- Anti-thrombotic
- Blood pressure 'regulator'
- Cardiac tonic
- Carminative
- Circulatory stimulant
- Decongestant
- Diaphoretic (warming)
- Digestive stimulant
- Hypolipidemic
- Lymphatic
- Rubefacient
- Stomachic
- Styptic

All of the attributes above are achieved with cayenne tincture, although cayenne powder has its place in the apothecary as well. As well as a tincture, cayenne powder makes a super addition to your first aid kit. I keep some cayenne powder handy in a small container as a wonderful styptic to stop bleeding.

Cayenne tincture, as a circulatory stimulant, adds clout to a formula. It can boost the ability of a formula to reach all areas of the body quickly. It's a super choice when the formula is quite full with other important herbs as only a small amount is needed to be effective. Herbalists use it as a potent stimulant for poor circulation for those with cold hands and feet, as well as any other imbalances due to a lack of circulation. It is believed to boost metabolism, so can be helpful in detoxifying tonics where it is thought to help rebuild tissues and facilitate weight loss.

Cayenne can be very helpful in cases where blood clots are a concern, in the case of heart attack or stroke, for example. It is revered for ability to reduce plaque formation in arteries and is often used in formulas to normalize blood pressure. Additionally, cayenne tincture can be used as a cardiac tincture to lower or raise blood pressure and has been known to decrease blood fats and lower cholesterol.

Cayenne helps to improve digestive function. It is is the most potent of digestive stimulants, notably helpful for small intestine disorders and various stomach conditions. Cayenne combines well with bitters and carminatives to heal everything from digestive upset to ulcers. It can also be used to help to stimulate appetite after an illness. Eating disorders can be helped with good nourishing tonic formulas and cayenne tincture can provide the extra oomph to get that formula into every corner of the body and to every cell. As a lymphatic, cayenne helps to support the entire lymph system and can be a welcome addition to immune boosting formulas. The respiratory system welcomes cayenne for help with inflammatory lung conditions, tightness in the chest, and even a loose cough. It can elevate a decongestant formula with its own decongesting movement-oriented abilities. Cayenne can be an excellent help in rheumatic conditions, both internally and externally. In the case of aches, pains, bruises, and strains, it can assist topically when incorporated into healing salves or liniments. Cayenne in a salve is a well-respected rubefacient remedy and easy to make.

Honey with a Kick

Every autumn, I visit my local beekeeper at our farmers' market and make a series of herb-infused honeys in preparation for winter. Infusing hot peppers into honey makes a tasty, rather spicy condiment that can be used in lots of ways. Add a healing heat to your warm tea, sauce, marinade, or vinaigrette. I love to take a spoonful of this hot honey with chopped garlic cloves, at the first sign of any viral visitor.

This recipe is more of a 'guideline'. You can make a small jar or a very large one! It's up to you.

Choose the number of peppers you want to use.

Find a glass jar with a good lid that is appropriate to the size needed. Put the peppers in the jar.

Cover the peppers with raw honey.

Use a chopstick or wooden utensil to poke the peppers a bit as this ensures that any air bubbles are able to rise to the surface.

Add more honey if needed to cover the peppers.

Put the lid on the jar and allow to blend for a few weeks.

ENJOY!!

Cayenne Hot Salve

Cayenne is well known for reducing many types of pain, especially nerve and nervous system pain. It has the ability to block Substance P, which is a neurotransmitter that relays information and results in pain. It can assist with many types of pain issues, from arthritis and back pain to bruises, shingles, and even diabetic neuropathy. I've also used it successfully treating migraine headaches. We use it predominantly for closed cuts as it may very likely be irritating to unhealed wounds. Use externally only and within 4–6 months for best results. Remember that this is a healing salve, and may take a week or two to achieve results. Salves are easy to make. I make salves from many different infused olive oils. In this case, the olive oil is infused with fiery cayenne powder.

Please note: If cayenne comes in contact with your eyes, it will burn! I have a very vivid memory of an encounter with jalapeño peppers and my eyes. . . never to be repeated! Take care to wash hands thoroughly and I'd suggest the use of gloves at all times, both when making and even when applying salve.

If you are using this salve to relieve painful hands or feet, apply in the evening and leave gloves on hands or cotton socks on your feet all night.

MAKES ABOUT 4 OUNCES

1/2-cup good quality olive oil
15 grams cayenne powder (or about 2 teaspoons)
1/2 ounce of beeswax

First, infuse the olive oil with the cayenne powder.

You can use a double boiler, or use a glass or stainless steel bowl over a pot of simmering water. A crock pot is another idea, and creates a good infusion. If you are organized, you can do this ahead of time.

Pour the olive oil into the bowl or top of the double boiler and add the cayenne powder.

Heat gently until quite warm and then turn off. Cover.
Allow to steep with the heat off for 15-20 minutes.

Turn the heat on again, on low and watch the oil.

When it is quite warm, again turn off the heat. Cover.

Repeat this process for a couple of hours.

Now you know why I have suggested the crockpot idea. If it has a low setting it works like a charm. Infuse the oil this way for 12-24 hours if you like. Take care not to burn it.

Strain the infused oil through a piece of cheesecloth into a small pot. Discard the cheesecloth.

Add the beeswax to another small pot and heat gently.

When the beeswax is liquefied, add the infused oil.

Keep stirring. The slightly cooler oil may cause lumps to form. At the moment when the entire mixture is in liquid form, it's ready for pouring. Carefully pour the mixture into small jars or tins, reserving a tiny amount of the mixture if you can.

Salve makers' trick: Allow the salve to set. It will often solidify with a small depression in the top. Add the still warm reserved beeswax-cayenne oil very slowly to form a very tiny top layer after a few hours, to avoid this small puddle, which often cracks and takes away from the smooth finish.

Label the jars. This is very important as this hot salve should be used with care!

Cayenne Tincture

There are many ways to make this potent powerhouse medicine. Some folks fill a blender with fresh or dried cayenne peppers and fill it with vodka, then blend and transfer to a glass canning jar with a tight-fitting lid.

Alternatively, don a pair of kitchen gloves and chop the peppers, removing the stem pieces. Place the chopped peppers, including seeds, into a glass canning jar and cover with 40 (or 50) proof alcohol. Add a tight-fitting lid and give a gentle shake. Top up the jar with more alcohol after a day or so if necessary, so that the peppers are covered.

In both cases, label the jar with the contents and date. Allow to steep for a month, shaking often to mix thoroughly. Strain into amber glass jar for storage and label.

There is so much more to write. Experiment with cayenne medicine. This fiery friend is worth getting to know!

Rosemary Gladstar http://www.sagemountain.com
I love to share Rosemary's online course:
    http://bit.ly/sagemountainonline
Michael Vertolli offers local classes and online traditional herbalism
    http://www.livingearthschool.ca

STUDIO BOTANICA
GLOSSARY OF HERBAL ACTIONS

Analgesic: relieves pain

Anesthetic: produces insensibility to pain

Anodyne: relieves pain

Antibacterial: kills or prevents growth of bacteria

Antidote: counteracts effect of poison

Anti-fungal: inhibits growth or multiplication of, or destroys fungi

Anti-inflammatory: reduces inflammation

Antimicrobial: helps destroy or resist pathogenic micro-organisms

Anti-rheumatic: eases inflammation and pain in joints and muscles

Antiseptic: a topical antimicrobial

Antispasmodic: relieves cramps, prevents or relaxes muscle spasms

Anti-thrombotic: reduces the formation of blood clots

Aperient: gentle laxative

Aromatic: pleasant odour, stimulates digestive system function

Astringent: contractions and firms tissue, reduces secretions & discharges

Cardiac Tonic: beneficial supportive action on heart and circulatory system

Carminative: helps to encourage better digestion

Circulatory Stimulant: improves blood flow throughout the body

Decongestant: reduces thick fluid build-up in nose, throat, sinus or chest

Demulcent: soothing to mucus membranes

Diaphoretic: induces perspiration, helps body to sweat

Emollient: softening, soothing

Expectorant: promotes mucus discharge from respiratory passages

Hemostatic: arrests blood flow

Hypolipidemic: reduce the lipid level (triglyceride and cholesterol) in the blood

Lymphatic: assists detoxifying by effect on lymph tissue. Supports immune system

Mucilage: contains gelatinous or gummy constituents

Nervine: calms nerves and supports nervous system

Nutritive: nourishes and sustains life

Parturient: hastens labour in childbirth

Relaxant: relieves tension, relaxes

Rubefacient: increases superficial circulation, producing irritation

Stimulant: excites or increases vital action

Styptic: stops bleeding

Stomachic: strengthens and stimulates the stomach

Sudorific: produces perspiration

Tonic: increases functional tone of the system

Trophorestorative: healing and restorative action on specific organ or tissue

Vulnerary: stimulates healing of wounds

http://www.studiobotanica.com

Green Farmacy
Medicinal Spices - Pepper

Dr. James A. Duke

Bell Pepper, Capsicum, Cayenne, Hot Chile, Paprika, Red Pepper, Aji (Cuba); Piman (Haiti); Bruhi, Lanka (Sanskrit)

SOLANACEAE

CAPSICUM

Widely distributed and growing wild after cultivation (FAG; JTR). The hotter ones are often *C. frutescens*, the sweeter ones *C. annuum*, but the intermediates are often confused taxonomically. For example, JFM treats only the hot pepper as *Capsicum annuum* var. *minimum* (synonym, or often recorded as, *C. frutescens, C. baccatum*, or *Capsicum frutescens* var. *baccatum* Irish). We treat it as *C. frutescens* in our *Handbook of Spices* (HOS). Teuscher subsumes his *Capsicum* information under paprika. I'm subsuming all my *Capsicum annuum/frutescens* info in this cluttered writeup. "All chiles have healing properties...If there's no heat, there's no capsaicin. If there's no capsaicin, it's not a chile. Most studies show that capsaicin cream brings relief to nearly 75 percent of people who use it. It even works for extreme pain."

COMMON NAMES (CAPSICUM)

Aakale Morich (Ban.; RAH); Ahi (Ese Eja; Sp.; AVP; MD2); Ahmur (Arab.; NAD); Ají (Sp. AVP; LOR; MDD); Ají Agujeta (Cuba; AVP); Ají Bobito (D.R.; AHL); Ají Boniato (Dom.; AVP); Ají Bravo (Sp.; Sal.; AVP); Aji Caballero (Sp.; P.R.; AVP; JFM); Aji Caribe (Dr.; Ven.; AVP;

Capsicum Combo. Pat Kenny

TRA); Aji Chinchana (Sp.; SOU); Aji Chirel (Col.; Ven.; AVP); Aji Chivata (Sp.; JFM); Ajicito montesino (Dr.; AHL); Ají Comun (Cuba; JTR); Aji Dulce (Sp.; Dr.; Ven.; AHL; AVP); Aji de Gallina (Dr.; AHL); Ají de Plaza (Cuba; JTR); Aji Guaguao (Sp.; Cuba; AVP; JTR); Aji Largo (Sp.; Peru; AVP); Aji Limon (Sa.; RAR); Ajillo (Pan.; AVP); Ají mono (Sp.; SOU); Ají Montaña (Sa.; RAR); Ají Montecino (Dom.; AVP); Ají Moron (Dr.; AHL); Ají Morron (Sp.; Dom.; AVP); Ají Pajarito (Sp.; Col.; AVP; JFM; JTR); Ají Picante (Sp.; Pr.; AVP; JFM); Ají Picantel (Sp.; Cuba; AVP); Ají Quinillo (Sp.; SOU); Ají del Salon (Dr.; Peru; AHL; JAD); Ají Titi (Dr.; AHL); Angmak (Ulwa; ULW); Anmak (Ulwa; ULW); Ardeiu (Romania; KAB); Arnaucho (Peru; AVP); Ati (Garifuna; C.A.; IED); Barkono (Africa; Hausa; AVP; KAB); Beissbeere (Ger.; EFS; TAN; TEU); Bell Pepper (Eng.; FAC; VOD); Bilber (Turkey; EB54:155); Bird Chilli (Eng.; HOS); Bird Pepper (Eng.; AVP; JFM; JTR); Birdseye Chili (Eng.; WIK); Birosi (Rai; NPM; Bisho (Ese Eja; MD2); Brasilianischer Pfeffer (Ger.; TEU); Bruhi (Sanskrit; EFS; NAD); Caja (Kuna; Pan.; IED); Capsique (Fr.; BOU); Cayenne (Eng.; FAC); Cayenne Pepper (Eng.; AVP; VOD); Chabai (Mal.; KAB; NAD); Chabai Sabrong (Malaya; EFS); Chakeai (Malaya;

Pictured at left: Capsicum Combo . From the ground up:
1. The roots of the "Long codded Ginnie Pepper" copied in ink from The Herbal or General History of Plants by John Gerard, The Complete 1633 Edition as Revised and Enlarged by Thomas Johnson, Book 2, Chapter 71, p. 364, 1633 (Dover Publications unabridged reproduction, 1965).
2. Capsicum annuum/Cayenne, inspired by the drawing by DD Dowden, p. 63, Herbal Renaissance by Steven Foster, Gibbs Smith, 1993.
3. Typical Capsicum flowers, National Herb Garden, from pk photographs.
4. Two views Capsicum baccatum var. pendulum/Bishop's Hat , Christmas Bell, or Peppadew; "wings" have sweet pepper taste, central placenta and seeds are hot, from pk photographs.
5. Capsicum annuum/Sweet Green Pepper, from County MG Demo Garden, pk photograph.
6. Capsicum chinense/'Aji Dulce', Hot Pepper, County MG Demo Garden, pk photograph.
7. Capsicum frutescens/Tabasco, National Herb Garden, from pk photo.
8. Capsicum pubescens 'Manzano'/purple flower and apple-shaped fruit converted to ink from photos, p. 19, The Complete Chile Pepper Book by Dave DeWitt and Paul W. Bosland, Timber Press, 2009; foliage said to be pubescent, having noticeable hairiness on the leaves.

KAP); Chalie (Mal.; WO2); Charapilla (Sp.; SOU); Chile Bravo (Sp.; JFM); Chile Chiltepen (Mex.; AVP); Chile Juipin (Mex.; AVP); Chile Largo (Sal.; AVP); Chile de Monte (Sp.; JFM); Chile de Velleno (Sp.; Sal.; AVP); Chile de Zope (Sp. Sal.; AVP; JFM); Chilillo (Sp.; JFM); Chili Padi (Thai; WIK); Chili Pepper (Eng.; FAC; TEU; VOD); Chilla (Berber; BOU); Chilli Pepper (Eng.; HOS); Chilpepe (Sal.; AVP); Chilpete (Cr. AVP); Chiltepe (Sp.; JFM); Chiltepen (Mex.; AVP); Chinche uchu (Sa.; SOU); Chirel (Col.; Ven.; AVP; JLH); Chivato (Col.; AVP); Chojnya huaica (Aymara; SOU); Choxnya wayk'a (Aymara; DLZ); Chyoots (Amuesha; SOU); Conguito (Col.; AVP); Corail des Jardins (Fr.; AVP; BOU); Corallo (It.; KAB); Du (Sunwar; NPM); Felfel ahmar (Arab.; BOU); Felfel haar (Arab.; BOU); Felfel helw (Arab.; BOU); Felfel rumi (Arab.; BOU); Felfel torshi (Arab.; BOU); Felfila (Arab.; BOU); Fibl e Abmar (Arab.; KAP); Filfile Ahmer (Arab.; EFS; KAB; NAD; WOI); Filfile Ahmar (Iran; NAD); Franchiao (China; KAP); Fulfilisurkh (Iran; KAB); Gachmaich (Bengal; KAB); Gach Mirichi (Hindi; NAD; WOI); Galakonda (Tel.; NAD); Garho Mirch (Sin.; NAD); Gasmiris (Sin.; NAD); Gemeiner Paprika (Ger.; TEU); Gewürzpaprika (Ger.; TEU); Gnnayoke (Burma; KAB); Goat Pepper (Eng.; JFM); Golakonda (Tel.; KAB); Green Pepper (Eng.; TEU); Guindilla (Sp.; EFS); Hot Pepper (Eng. HOS; TEU; VOD); Hov txob nplej (Hmong; EB57:365); Huaica (Aymara; SOU); Hugn (Huachipaeri; MD2); Ifelfel (Berber; BOU); Ik (Maya; AVP); Iki (Cocama; SOU); Indianischer Pfeffer (Ger.; TEU); Indischer Pfeffer (Ger.; TEU); Jahfiilla (Ocaina; SOU); Jeeray (Sikkim; SKJ); Jhal (Ben.; Hindi; NAD); Jima (Aguaruna; SOU); Kacha Morich (Ban.; RAH); Kambuzi Pepper (Eng.; WIK); Kapur (Kuna; Pan.; IED); Katuvira (Sanskrit; KAB; KAP; NAD); Kelekeke (Sudan.; AVP); Khorsani (Gurung; NPM); Khursani (Danuwar, Magar, Majhi, Nepal; NPM; SUW); Khursani (Nepal; SUW); Khurshaney (Sikkim; SKJ); Khursya (Chepang; NPM); KidachiTogorashi (Japan; TAN); Kirmizii Biber (Turkey; EFS); Komlu (Piro; Yine' MD2); Krasniy Peretz (Russia; KAB); Kua txob (Hmong; EB57:365); La Chiao (China; EFS); Lada Mutia (Malaya; EFS); Lalmarch (Urdu; KAB); Lal Mirch (Hindi; ADP; SKJ); Lalmircha (Hindi; KAB); Lalmirchi (Hindi; KAP); Lalmirichi (Ben.; NAD); Lalmoricho (Oriya; WO2); Lanka (Ben.; Sanskrit; ADP); Lanka Maric (Ben.; KAP); Lanka Marich (Ben.; NAD); Lankamirch (Ben.; SKJ); Lara (Pi.; KAB); Lavungi Mirchi (Mah.; NAD); Locoto (Sa.; SOU); Lombok (Dwi.; KAB); Lombokpeper

(Dutch; EFS); Malabari (India; EFS); Malabhata (Nepal; KAP); Malagueta (Sa.; SOU; WIK); Malawian Pepper (Eng.; WIK); Malta (Newari; NPM); Marcha (Guj.; Tamang; NAD; NPM); Marchawangun (Kashmir; WO2); Marchi (Limbu; NPM); Marchu (Guj.; NAD); Marich (Ben.; Sanskrit; ADP); Maricha (Bihar; SKJ); Marichiphalam (Sanskrit; NAD); Mattisa (Punjab; NAD); Mattisa Wangru (Kumaon; NAD); Menashinakayi (Kan; KAB; NAD; WOI); Mensina Kai (Kan; WOI); Meris (Sinh.; KAP); Mexikanischer Paprika (Ger.; TEU); Milagay (Tam.; ADP; WOI); Mirapa (Tel.; ADP); Mira Pakaya (Tel.; SKJ; WOI); Mirch (Bhojpuri; Guj.;Hindi; KAB; NPM; SKJ); Mircha (Tharu; NPM); Mirchai (Mooshar; NPM); Mirchi (India; Mar.; EFS; WO2); Mirch Surkh (Iran; Yunani; KAP); Mirch Wangum (Kashmir; NAD); Mirsang (Kon.; NAD); Mirsinga (Mah.; NAD); Mishqui uchu (Quechua; DLZ; SOU); Molagay (Tam.; NAD); Morich (Ban.; RAH); Moricha (Ban.; Santal; RAH); Mulaku (Mal.; ADP; WOI); Mullagay (Tamil; KAB); Municion uchu (Bol.; DLZ); Muragay (Tam.; SKJ); Nayop (Burma; NAD); Nayusi (Burma; KAP); Nupu Uchu (Sa.; SOU); Ot (Vn.; EB42:413); Paprica (Romania; KAB); Paprika (Eng.; Fr.; Hungary; FAC; KAB; TEU); Pasitis (Tagalog; KAB); Pepe de Guinea (It.; EFS); Peper (Sur.; AVP); Peperone (It.; AVP; EFS); Petit Piment (Fr.; TRA); Pichirina (Sa.; SOU); Piemento (Ger.; TEU); Pilipili (Fr.; Swahili; KAB; TRA); Piman (Creole; Haiti; TRA; VOD); Piman Bouk (Creole; Haiti; VOD); Piman Zwazo (Creole; Haiti; VOD); Piment (Fr.; Haiti; AVP; BOU); Pimenta (Sp. AVP); Piment anuele (Fr.; AVP; KAP; TEU;); Pimentao (Por.; AVP); Pimentão comprido (Por.; AVP); Pimentão cumari (Por.; AVP); Pimentão de Caiene (Por.; EFS); Pimentão de Cheiro (Por.; EFS); Pimentão maca (Por.; AVP); Piment Bouc (Haiti; AVP); Piment Cabresse (Guad.; AVP); Piment Capsique (Fr.; EFS); Piment Caraibe (Fwi.; JTR); Piment Cultivee (Fr.; BOU); Piment de Cayenne (Fr.; TRA); Piment Chien (Haiti; AHL); Piment de Cayenne (Gabon; JLH); Piment des jardines (Fr.; BOU); Piment Doux (Haiti; AHL); Piment Enrage (Fr.; AVP; JTR); Piment des jardins (Fr.; AVP); Pimineto Maleguete (Sa.; SOU); Piment Oiseau (Fr.; AVP); Pimento (Eng.; FAC); Piment Plomb (Guad.; AVP); Piment Zouezeau (Haiti; AHL); Piment Zouezo (Haiti; AHL); Pimiento (Eng.; AVP); Pimiento Aji (Sp.; AVP); Pimiento de la India (Sp.; EFS); Pimienton (Sa.; SOU); Piperus (Moldavia; KAB); Piri Piri (Eng.; WIK); Pod Pepper (Eng.; AVP); Poivre de Cayenne (Fr.; TEU); Poivre de Guinee (Fr.; BOU; EFS); Poivriere de Cayenne (Fr.; AVP); Poivrier long (Fr.;

BOU); Poivre d'Espagne (Fr.; AVP; TEU); Poivre d'Indie (Fr.; BOU); Poivre long (Fr.; Gaud. AVP); Poivron (Fr.; AVP; BOU; TAN); Pucuna Uchu (Bol.; DLZ); Puca Uuchu (Quechua; DLZ); Pucunucho (Peru; DAV); Puk Morich (Ban.; RAH); Pway Kayèn (Creole; Haiti; VOD); Q'ellu Uchu (Quechua; DLZ); Q'ellu wayk'a (Aymara; DLZ); Q'omer uchu (Quechua; DLZ); Quiticot (Visayan; KAB); Quiya Cumari (Brazil; KAB); Red Chili (Eng.; HOS); Red Pepper (Eng.; AVP; JTR; TEU; VOD); Rocoto (Col.; IED); Roter Pfeffer (Ger.; TEU); Saghakar (Lepcha; NPM); Sakaipilo (Madagascar; JLH); Schotenpfeffer (Ger.; TEU); ili Biberi (Turkey; EFS); Siling Labuyo (Thai; WIK); Soodimirapakaaya (Tel.; WO2); Spaanse Peper (Dutch; EFS); Spanish Pepper (Eng.; KAP); Spansicher Pfeffer (Ger.; AVP; TEU); Spansk Peber (Den.; EFS); Spansk Peppar (Sweden; EFS); Spansk Pepper (Norway; KAB); Spur Pepper (Eng.; HOS); Tabasco Pepper (Eng.; HOS; TEU; VOD; WIK); Thai Pepper (Eng.; WIK); Thilly Pepper (Eng.; AVP); Tiffile (Iran; EFS); Ti-Piment (Guad.; AVP); Togarashi (Japan; KAP; TAN); Touanka (Africa.; AVP); Tsikame (Matsigenka; MD2); Tsi-tra-ka (Tibet; NPM); Türkischer Pfeffer (Ger.; TEU); Uchu (Arg.; Quechua; AVP; DLZ); Upperparanki (Mal.; NAD); 'Ugn (Amarakaeri; MD2); Usimulagay (Tam.; WO2); Wasa (Calaway ; DLZ); Wayk'a (Aymara; DLZ); Wila Wayk'a (Aymara; DLZ); Wild Pepper (Eng.; JFM; JTR); Yuchi (Amahuaca; Shipibo/Conibo; MD2). Teuscher says the terms paprika, Spanish pepper, and chili are very often used interchangeably in the literature (TEU) as well as bell pepper, capsicum, cayenne, chile, hot, paprika, and red pepper.

ACTIVITIES (CAPSICUM)

Acaricide (1; X24496493); ACE-Inhibitor (1; HOS); Adrenergic (1; HOS; LIB; SPI; XX3375268; X19390166); AGE-Inhibitor X25868614; Allergenic (1; TEU; X25944018); Alpha-amylase-Inhibitor (1; X21663471; X21792679; X25750185); Alpha-glucosidase-Inhibitor (1; X21663471; X25868614); ALT-Inhibitor (1; X24723459 Analgesic (f12; APA; BHA; HOS; TEU; ULW; VOD; WAM; X17202897; X24235936; X24661126; X25536022); Anaphylactic (1; HOS); Androgenic? (1; HOS); Anesthetic (1; BHA; HOS; TAD); Anorectic (1; BHA); Antacid (1; BHA; X25675368); Antemetic (1; X 24472460); Antiacetylcholinesterase (1; X18361755); Antiacne (1; HOS);

AntiAGE (1; X23570003); Antiaggregant (1; BH2; HOS; PH2; SKY); Antiaging (1; HOS); Antiallergic (1; HOS; X21875363); Antiamylase (1; X18361755); Antiangiogenic (1; AGG); Antiarrhythmic (1; BHA; HOS); Antiarthritic (f1; MCK; X24661126); Antiasthmatic (1; HOS; X21875363); Antiatherogenic (1; HOS); Antiatherosclerotic (1; HOS); Antibacillary (1; LIB; X17365137); Antibronchitic (1; HOS); Anticancer (f1; HOS; TAD; X21898818; X23747734; X24341783); Anticancer, breast (1; X24341783); Anticancer, colon (1; AGG); Anticancer, liver (1; AGG MCK); Anticancer, lung (1; AGG; MCK; NR54:S71; X23747734); Anticancer, prostate (1; AGG); Anticancer, skin (1; AGG); Anticancer, stomach (1; AGG; MCK); AntiCandida (1; X23896704); Anticarcinogenic (1; AGG; X23747734); Anticarcinomic (1; HOS); Anticephalalgic (1; X23627937); Anticholangiocarcinoma synergic with 5-fluorouracil (1; X 25933112); Anticolonospasmic (1; HOS); Anticoronary (1; HOS); Anticystytic X24341783; Antidermatotic (1; HOS); Antidiabetic (1; DIA; X18361755; X18668490; X21663471; X25868614); Antidote (f; IED); Antiedemic (1; HOS; X23794063; X24235936); Antiendometriotic (1; AGG); AntiEscherichia (1; X23896704); Antiflu (1; HOS); Antiglucosidase (1; X18361755); Antiheadache (1; X23627937); Antihemorrhagic (1; HOS); Antihemorrhoidal (1; HOS); Antiherpetic (1; X23456596); Antihistaminic (1; HOS); Antiichthyotic (1; HOS); Antiinflammatory (f1; APA; BHA; HOS; TAD; TEU; WAM; WO2; X24235936); Antiischemic (f1; HOS; TAD); Antileukemic (1; AGG); Antileukoplakic (1; HOS); Antilithic (1; X25675368; X26147513); Antilowbackache (2; X25536022); Antilupus (1; HOS); Antimaculitic (1; HOS); Antimastotic (1; HOS); Anti-MDR (1; AGG; X16158935; X25047005); Antimelanomic (1; AGG); Antimetastatic (1; AGG; X24341783); Antimigraine (1; X23865915); Antimutagenic (1; TEU); Antimyalgic (1; X23627937); Antineuralgic (1; HOS); Antineuroblastomic (1; X17365137); Antinitrosaminic (1; HOS; JNU); Antinociceptive (f1; APA; 60P); Antinyctalopic (1; HOS); Antiobesity (2; X19489540; X22835261; X24246368; X24630935); Antiodontalgic (1; HOS); Antiosteoarthritic (1; X23728701); Antioxidant (1; AGG; HOS; SKY; TAD; WAM; X21898818); Antiozenic (1; HOS); Antiperoxidant (1; AGG); Antipharyngitic (1; HOS); Antiphotophobic (1; HOS); Antipityriasic (1; HOS); Antiplatelet (1; MCK); Antiporphyric (1; HOS); Antiproliferant (1; AGG; HOS); Antiprostaglandin (1; HOS; X145302140); AntiPseudomonas (1; X23896704); Antipsoriatic (1;

HOS; X20707875; X22389862); Antiradicular (1; HOS; X25868614); Antiseptic (f1; 60P; HDN; HOS; PNC; X21858615; X21882663); Antispasmodic (f1; HOS; PED); Antistreptococcic (1; X21858615); Antistress (1; HOS); Antitachycardic (1; BHA; HOS); Antithrombic (1; BHA; HOS); Antitumor (1; HOS; TEU; X173121750; X19489540); Antitussive (1; HOS); Antiulcer (f1; APA; BGB; HOS; PED; TEU; X25675368); Antiviral (1; WO2; X23456596); Antixerophthalmic (1; HOS); Antiyeast (1; X17572465; X18608885; X22120089; X23896704); Aphrodisiac (f; BOU; HOS; LIB; PHR); Apoptotic (1; AGG; X19489540) Arteriodilator (1; HOS); Astringent (f1; PED); ATPase-Inhibitor (1; HOS); Bacillus (1; LIB; X17365137); Bactericide (1; HOS; PED; PH2; TEU; TRA; X21858615); Bradycardic (1; WO2); Bronchoconstrictor (1; HOS; TAD); Bronchodilator (f1; APA); Calcium-Channel-Blocker (1; BHA; HOS; TAD); Candidicide (1; X17572465; X22120089; X23896704); Carcinogenic (f1; AGG; HOS; TAD; TEU); Cardioprotective (1; BHA; HOS); Cardiotonic (f1; HOS; NAD; TEU; FT61:266); Carminative (f1; 60P; BGB; PED; RAH); Caspase-3-Activator (1; AGG; Catabolic (f1; HAD; TEU; 60P); Catecholaminigenic (1; HOS); Chemopreventive (1; AGG; X16158935; X25675368); Choleretic (f1; TRA); Circulatory Stimulant (f1; KAB; PED; TEU); CNS-Stimulant (f; LIB); Corticosteronigenic (1; WO2); Counterirritant (f12; APA; HOS; PED); COX-1-Inhibitor (1; X20184029); COX-2-Inhibitor (1; HOS; X145302140; X20184029); Curare (f1; HDN); Cyclooxygenase-Inhibitor (1; HOS); Cytotoxic (1; X17365137; X16158935); Dart Poison (f; WBB); Decongestant (f1; APA; DAD; HOS; RIN; TRA); Detoxicant (f; BOW); Diaphoretic (f1; BGB; HOS; PED); Digestive (f1; AHL; APA; HOS; TEU); Diuretic (f; BOU; HOS; JFM); Energizer (12: JAD MJB); Endocrine-Active (1; HOS); Epinephrenergic (1; XX3375268); Erythemic (1; BHA); Expectorant (f1; HDN; HOS); Febrifuge (f1; HOS; TAD); Fibrinolytic (f1; BHA; LIB; MAB; PH2); Fungicide (1; HOS; X22120089; X24817604); Gastrogogue (f1; APA); Gastroprotective (f12; BHA; TEU; XX7895549; X23627937; X25675368); HIF-1alpha-Inhibitor (1; X22389862): HDL-Genic (1; BHA); Hemolytic (f1; BGB); Hemostat (f; 60P); Hepatotoxic (1; LIB; X17365137); Herbistatic (1; X22835261; X23471827; X24723459); Hyperemic (2; KOM); Hypocholesterolemic (1; APA; BHA; HOS; LE2; X23471827; X25675368; X26147513); Hypoglycemic (1; DAD; DIA; HOS; X18361755; X21792679); Hypokeratotic (1; HOS); Hypotensive (1; HOS); Hypotriglyceridemic

(1; APA; X22835261; X23471827; X24723459); IL1B-Inhibitor (1; AGG); IL6-Inhibitor AGG; IL8-Inhibitor AGG; Immunomodulator (1; X173121750; X17306834); Immunostimulant (1; HOS); Insecticide (1; UPW; WBB); Insulinogenic (1; DIA); Interferonogenic (1; HOS); Irritant (1; APA; HOS); Insulinotropic (1; X18668490); Interferon-Synergist (1; HOS); Ixodicide (1; X24496493); Lacrymatory (1; MCK); Lactase-Promoter (1; HOS); Laxative (1; HOS); LDL-Lytic (1; BHA; X23471827; X24723459); Lipase-Promoter (1; JE50:167); Lipolytic (f; TAD); 5-Lipoxygenase-Inhibitor (1; HOS; MCK); Maltase-Promoter (1; HOS; JE50:167); Mitogenic (1; X17082928); Mucogenic (1; BHA; HOS; X25675368); Mucoirritant (1; HOS); Mutagenic (1; HOS); Myorelaxant (1; HOS); Neurotonic (f1; AHL; BHA); Neurotoxic (1; HOS; KOM; TEU); NF-kappaB-Inhibitor (1; AGG; X15659827;X21663483); NO-Inhibitor (1; AGG); iNOS-Inhibitor (1; AGG); Orexigenic (f1; APA; BOU; HOS; PR14:401); Peristaltic (1; X23730892); Phagocytotic (1; HOS); Phytoalexin (1; HOS); PPAR-Activator (1; X17152989); PPAR-Gamma-Activator (1; X15383218); Prooxidant (1; HOS); Propecic (f1; PR14:401); Proteinase Inhibitor X24559910; Quinone-Reductase-Inducer (1; HOS); Radioprotective (1; HOS; WO2; X10775394); Repellent (1; HOS); Respirasensitizer (1; HOS); Retinoprotective (1; HOS); Rubefacient (f12; APA; BOU; FAG; HOS; NPM; PED; TRA); Satiating (2; X24630935); Secretagogue (1; HOS); Sedative (1; HOS); Sialogogue (f1; APA; HOS; TEU; WBB); Spasmolytic (f1; PED); Splenotoxic (1; LIB; X17365137); Stimulant (f1; AHL; BGB; BOU; IED; NPM; PED); Stomachic (f; BOU; FAG; IED; NAD; NPM; WBB); Sucrase-Promoter (1; HOS; JE50:167); Synergist (1; PED); Tachyphylactic (1; HOS); Thermogenic (f1; HOS; LIB; SAB; XX3375268; X19390166; X19489540; X25675368); Thymoprotective (1; HOS); TNF-alpha-Inhibitor (1; AGG; X21663483); Tonic (f1; APA; PNC; RAH; WAM); Ulcerogenic (f1; WO2); Urease-Inhibitor (1; X16158935); Uterocontractant (f1; TRA); Vasodilator (1; HOS; TEU; X20459996); Vasoconstrictor (f; TRA); VEGF-Inhibitor (1; AGG); Vermifuge (f; UPW); Vulnerary (f1; WO2; X24341783).

INDICATIONS (CAPSICUM)

Acne (1; HOS); Adenoma (1; X11604990); Aging (1; HOS); Ague (f; IED); Alcoholism (f1; HH2; HOS; NAD; PHR; PH2; WO2); Allergy (1; HOS; X21875363); Alopecia (f; PR14:401); Ameba (f; HDN); Angina (f; FAG; HOS; LIB; MAB); Anorexia (f1; APA; HOS; PHR; WBB; WO2); Anorexia nervosa (f; PH2); Anxiety (f; VOD); Apocrine Chromhidrosis XX1656616; Arteriosclerosis (1; PHR; PH2); Arrhythmia (f1; FNF; HOS); Arthrosis (Pain) (f12; AGG; APA; HOS; PHR; PH2; TRA); Asthma (f1; HOS; JFM; JNU; X21875363); Atherosclerosis (1; HOS); Atony (f; ADP) Bacillus (1; HOS; X10548758 X17365137); Backache (f12; AGG; APA; HOS; WBB; X17202897; X14581111); Bacteria (1; HOS; X17002415; X10548758); Bleeding (f1; DAD; HOS); Boil (f; HOS; IED; JFM; UPW); Bronchosis (f1; APA; HOS); Bubonic Plague (f; UPW); Burn (f; HOS; LIB); Burning Mouth Syndrome (1; PR14:401); Bursitis (f1; HOS; SKY); Cancer (f1; JLH; X16158935; X23747734;); Cancer, brain (1; BHA); Cancer, breast (f1; HOS; JLH); Cancer, cervix (1; HOS); Cancer colon (1; AGG; HOS; X17177533; X11604990); Cancer, esophagus (1; AGG; BHA); Cancer, liver (1; AGG; BHA; MCK); Cancer, lung (1;AGG; MCK; NR54:S71; X10668493; X23747734); Cancer, mouth (f1; JLH; X16158935); Cancer, nose (f; HOS; JLH); Cancer, prostate (1; AGG; BHA; X21992488); Cancer, skin (f; AGG; HOS; JLH); Cancer, stomach (1; AGG; BHA; MCK); Candida (1; X17572465; X18608885; X22120089; X23896704); Carcinoma (1; X16158935); Cardiopathy (f1; BHA; HOS; PHR; PH2; UPW; X17177533); Caries (f; HDN); Cataract (1; DAD; HOS); Cephalalgia (1; X23627937); Chest Cold (f; JFM; UPW); Chickenpox (f1; APA; HOS); Chilblains (f1; BGB; HOS;PNC; WO2); Childbirth (f1; HOS; 60P); Chills (f; APA; HOS); Cholera (f; ADP; HOS; IED; PH2; JAF49:31010); Chromhidrosis (1; HOS; LIB); Ciguatera (f; AHL); Circulosis (1; HOS); Clostridium (1; HOS; MCK); Cluster Headache (1; APA; BHA; HOS); Cold (f1; APA; HOS; JFM; RIN); Colic (f1; APA; HOS; JFM; PNC); Coma (f; HDN); Congestion (f1; DAD; HOS; JFM); Conjunctivosis (f; HDN); Consumption (f; UPW); Convulsion (f; HDN; MD2); Costosis (f; HDN); Cough (f'1; HOS; JFM; PH2); Cramp (f12; HOS; KOM; PH2); Cystosis (f1; LIB; PR14:401; X24341783); Dandruff (f; WO2); Delirium (f; HOS; KAB; LIB; NAD); Dermatomycosis (1; X18608885); Dermatosis (f1; HOS; RAH; ULW; X1078907; X18608885;

X24211679); Detrusor Hyperreflexia (1; PR14:401); Diabetes (f1; AGG; APA; DIA; HOS; RAH; X1737545; X18361755; X21792679; X25868614); Diabetic Neuropathy (1; HOS; SKY); Diarrhea (f; HOS; PHR; PH2); Dipsomania (f1; HH2; NAD; PHR; PH2; WO2); Diptheria (f; HOS; LIB; NAD); Dropsy (f; IED; HOS); Dyspepsia (f1; APA; BGB; BHA; HOS; IED; NPM; PH2; VOD; WO2); Dyspnea (f; DAV; HOS; WO2); Dysuria (f; HDN); Earache (f; ADP; HOS; IED); Eczema (f; RAH); Edema (f1; HOS; PH2; X23794063); Embolism (1; BHA; X17177533); Endometriosis (1; AGG); Enterosis (f; HOS; PH2; TEU); Epithelioma (f; HOS; JLH); Escherichia (1; HOS; X17365137; X10548758; X23896704); Exanthema (f; UPW); Fever (f1; HOS; IED; PHR; TAD; VOD); Flu (f; DAV; HOS; MD2); Frostbite (f; BGB; HOS; PHR; PH2; SPI); Fungus (1; HOS; X10548758); Gangrene (f; HOS; LIB); Gas (f1; APA; DAV; HOS; NAD); Gastrosis (f1; BHA; HOS; JFM; PH2; TEU; TRA; WO2; X17002415); German Measles (f; HDN); Giddiness (f; HOS; IED); Gonorrhea (f; WO2); Gout (f; IED; HOS; KAB; NAD; PH2); Hayfever (1; HOS; RIN); Headache (f1; APA; BHA; HOS; WAM; X23627937); Headcold (f1; HOS; RIN); Helicobacter (1; X17002415; X16158935); Hemorrhoid (f1; ADP; BOU; FAG; HOS; IED; JFM; WBB); Hepatosis (f1; BHA; HOS; WBB; WO2); Herpes Zoster (1; DAV; HOS; SKY; VOD); High Blood Pressure (f1; HOS; VOD); High Cholesterol (1; APA; BHA; HOS; LE2; TRA); High Triglycerides (1; APA; HOS); Hoarseness (f; ADP; HOS; KAB; PHR); Hydrocele (f; HDN); Ichythyosis (1; HOS); Impotence (f; BOU; HOS; LIB; PHR); Incontinence (1; HOS; MCK); Induration (f; HOS; JLH); Infection (f1; HDN; HOS; IED; PH2; ULW); Inflammation (f1; AGG; HOS; TRA; WO2); Inorgasmia (f; HOS; PHR); Insomnia (1; HOS); Ischemia (1; HOS; TAD); Itch (f12; ABS; HOS; MCK); Jaundice (f; HDN; WO2); Kernel (f; JLH); Labor (f1; 60P); Laryngitis (f; HOS; PNC); Leukemia (1; AGG; BHA); Leukoplakia (1; HOS); Lichen Planus (1; X17294586); Lumbago (f1; APA; HOS; NAD; PHR; PH2; PNC); Lupus (1; HOS); Maculosis (1; HOS); Madness (f; HDN); Malaria (f; HOS; IED; KAB; NAD; PHR; PH2); Mastosis (f; HOS; JLH); Melanoma (1; AGG); Migraine (f1; FNF; NMH; VOD; X23865915); Multiple Myeloma (1; AGG); Myalgia (f1 APA; KOM, PNC; X23627937); Mycosis (12; HOS; X17572465; X10548758); Myosis (f12; HOS; PHR; PH2); Nausea (f; AGG; MD2; VOD); Nephrosis (f; HOS; LIB); Nervousness (f; VOD); Neuralgia (f1; AGG; APA; HOS; SKY; VOD; WO2; XX9647450);

Neuropathy (1; AGG; BHA; HOS; TAD; X17177533; X1737545); Notalgia Paresthetica (1; PR14:401); Numbness (1; BHA); Nyctalopia (1; HOS); Obesity (f1; HOS; HAD); Oliguria (1; HOS); Ophthalmia (f; VOD); Osteoarthrosis (f1; HOS; LIB; TAD); Otosis (f; HOS; PH2); Ozena (1; HOS); Pain (f12; AGG; APA; BGB; BHA; HOS; PH2; VOD; WBB; X17202897; X1737545); Paralysis (f; WO2); Pharyngosis (f1; DAD; HOS; PH2; WOI); Photophobia (1; HOS); Pityriasis (1; HOS); Plague (f; HOS; WBB); Pneumonia (f; HOS; LIB); Poor Circulation (1; WAM); Porphyria (1; HOS); Postherpetic Neuralgia (1; BHA); Proctosis (f; HOS; LIB); Prurigo (f12; ABS; HOS; X1078907); Pseudomonas (1; X23896704); Psoriasis (f1; APA; HOS; SKY; X20707875); Pulmonosis (f; IED; HOS; ULW; 60P); Rabies (f; HDN); Respirosis (f; IED; HOS; RAH; ULW); Retinosis (1; HOS); Rheumatism (f12; AGG; APA; HOS; PHR; PH2; TRA); Rhinosis (f; HDN; HOS; JLH; PR14:401); Ringworm(f; MD2); Saccharomyces (1; X22120089; X23896704); Salmonella (1; WO2); Scabies (f; MD2); Scarlatina (f; ADP); Scarlet Fever (f; HOS; PH2); Sciatica (f1; HOS; PH2); Seasickness (f; HH2; HOS; PH2); Shingles (f1; APA; BHA; HOS; VOD; XX1656616); Snakebite (f; IED; HOS; 60P); Sore (f; HOS; LIB); Sore Throat (f1; ADP; AGG; HOS; JFM; KAB; PHR; PH2); Spasm (1; HOS); Sprains (f1; ADP; APA); Steatosis (1; BHA); Strains (f1; APA); Stomachache (f; HOS; JFM; JAF49:3101); Stomatosis (f; HOS; LIB); Streptococcus (1; X21858615) Stress (1; HOS); Stroke (1; HOS; PHR; PH2); Streptococcus (1; HOS; LIB; MCK); Surfeit (f; JFM); Swelling (f1; DAD; HOS; WBB; X23794063); Tachycardia (1; HOS); Tendinitis (f1; HOS); Tennis Elbow (1; HOS; JAD); Tension (f12; HOS; PH2); Thrombosis (1; HOS; X17177533); Thumb-Sucking (1; APA; BGB; HOS); Thyropathy (f; HOS; PED); Tonsilosis (f; ADP; AGG; HDN; HOS; LIB); Toothache (f1; DAV; HOS; 60P); Trigeminal Neuralgia (f1; X10333823; X20402746; X20490990); Tuberculosis (f; UPW);Tumor (f; NAD); Typhoid (f; IED; HOS); Typhus (f; HOS; KAB; JAF49:3101); Ulcer (f12; BGB; BHA; HOS; LIB; MCK; X17002415; X16158935; X7895549); UTI (f; HOS; PH2); Varicose Veins (1; HOS; JAD; WBB; WO2); VD (f; WO2); Vertigo (f; VOD); Virus (1; HOS; WO2); Vomiting (f; AGG); Vulvar Vestibulitis (1; XX1656616);Whitlow (f; VOD); Worm (f; UPW); Wound (f1; HOS; JFM; VOD; WO2); Xerophthalmia (1; HOS); Xerostoma (1; HOS); Yaws (f; UPW); Yeast (1; HOS; X22120089; X17572465; X16784815; X10548758); Yellowfever (f;

HOS; KAB; PH2; JAF49:3101); Germany's Commission E did not approve the oral administration of cayenne for medicinal purposes.

INDICATIONS SUMMARY

Arthrosis (Pain) (f12); Backache (f12); Cramp (f12); Itch (f12); Myalgia (f12); Myosis (f12); Pain (f12); Prurigo (f12); Rheumatism (f12); Tension (f12); Ulcer (f12).

DOSAGES

Fruits widely eaten, raw, cooked, dried, or preserved; leaves steamed as potherb or added to stews and soups, e.g., Andean *locro* with Koreans use dry pepper leaves, thin threads of red pepper and a hot-pepper flavored soybean paste (kochugang); Thais add the green leaves to green their green curry paste (gkaeng kiow wahn) (FAC; TAN; EB54:155). 1/4-1/2 tsp. spice/cup water/after meals (APA); 1/4-1/2 dropper tincture (APA); 30-120 mg fruit, 3 x/day (CAN); 0.3-1.0 ml fruit tincture (CAN; SKY); 0.6-2.0 mg oleoresin (CAN); topical maximum strength 2.5% (CAN); 2-3 450 mg capsules 3x/day (NH); 1 StX 450 mg capsule 3x/day (NH); 1/2 cup fresh fruit (PED); 100-300 mg dry fruit (PED); 200 mg dry fruit:1 ml alcohol/1 ml water (PED); 1-3 g cayenne (PIL); 30-120 mg powdered cayenne (PNC); 0.3-1 ml fruit tincture (PNC); 0.05-0.15 strong fruit tincture (PNC); 0.6-2 mg capsicum oleoresin (PNC). Topical StX should contain, methinks 0.0225-0.075% capsaicin, but I see reports of 0.25-0.75% capsaicin (SF); 0.5-1 tsp. dry fruit/cup water (SF). Some people work with stronger ointments than mine (0.025-0.075% capsaicin); Steve Foster gives levels 10 times higher, and CAN 100 times higher (for capsaicinoids). I consider these higher level rather too strong, if not dangerous).

- Asian Indians take fruit decoction with opium and fried asafetida for cholera (ADP)
- Asian Indians suggest plaster of amber, black pepper, capsicum, and garlic for lumbago (NAD)
- Asian Indians suggest *Capsicum* tea with cinnamon and sugar for calming delirium tremens and the cravings of dipsomanics. West

Indians use *Capsicum* to relieve the sinking "at the epigastrium felt by drunkards" (NAD)
- Bahamans and Curacaons apply crushed leaves with or without castor oil to boils (JFM)
- Bengali use as antiscorbutic, carminative, insectifuge, and tonic; for dermatitis, diabetes, dyspepsia, eczema, and respirosis (RAH)
- Caribs use fruit juice (not hot pepper I hope) as eyedrops in ophthalmia (VOD)
- Costa Rican BriBri take root decoction for colic and gastrosis after overeating (JFM)
- Cubans and Guadelupans eat fruit dietarily for hemorrhoids (FAG JFM)
- Dominican Caribs pound leaves in shark oil to poultice onto sores and wounds (VOD)
- Dominicans give chili pepper leaf infusion with basil and *Tabebuia* for pediatric anxiety (BOD)
- Dominicans take bell pepper leaf decoction for high blood pressure (VOD)
- Gabonese apply the plant to cancers of the nose (JLH)
- Guianans take the fruit with cinchona for malaria (KAB)
- Haitians apply greased leaves to forehead for migraine and vertigo (VOD)
- Haitians dress leaves onto whitlows and wounds as cicatrizant and vulnerary (VOD)
- Haitians rub fruit tincture onto rheumatism (VOD)
- Haitians use ripe fruit infusion for dyspepsia, fever, nausea and nervousness (VOD)
- Madagascans eat fruits for DT's (KAB); apply powdered fruits (*C. minimum*) to epitheliomas (JLH)
- Seeds tamped in cavities for toothache
- Sheila Humphrey, RN, suggests inhaling a few grains of cayenne for migraine (NMF)
- Trinidadians take leaf decoction for asthma, chest colds and cough (JFM)

DOWNSIDES

Class 2d. Contraindicated on broken skin or near eyes (AHPA, 1997). Commission E reports contraindications of damaged skin, hypersensitivity and adverse effects of irritant properties; rarely allergic reactions. Not to be used for more than two days, with 14-day lapse before reapplying (this is not often followed in this country) (AEHD). The Herbal PDR suggests the same. Newall, Anderson, and Phillipson (1996) report capsaicinoids to be irritant, "The toxicity of the capsaicinoids has reportedly not been ascribed to any one specific action but may be due to their causing respiratory failure, bradycardia, and hypotension."

Excessive consumption may cause gastroenterosis, hepatic, renal damage (CAN), or ulcers (SKY). Chronic administration of capsicum extract (0.5 ug capsaicin/kg body weight; that would be 50 ug (micrograms) for this 100-kilo rat) to hamsters has been reported toxic (CAN). The oral LD50 in rats is 190 mg/kg) (CAN). The oral LD50 97-294 orl mus in mice is such that led TAD to calculate that for me, a 220 lb (100 kg) rat, I'd need to ingest some 135 to 415 ounce of hot pepper. No way (TAD). Capsicum may interfere with blood pressure medicines and MAOIs (CAN). Antigens have been associated with anaphylaxis and rhinononjunctivitis (PH2).

Not for children under two years (WAM). Paprika and/or *Capsicum* may speed other medications (reading that, I went and tried a mixture of grapefruit juice with black pepper and tabasco; three well known potentiators of medications). Interesting. Spicy but good. Sure beats taking my less spicy herb (or synthetics for those more unfortunate than I). Digestive properties of capsaicin may be attributed to an enhancement of digestive enzyme activities or to indirect effects on vascular endothelia, smooth muscles and mast cells, resulting in increase of vascular permeability and of mucosal blood flow. Hot spices can promote antigen transfer through epithelia and thereby augment sensitization or allergic reactions. Unfortunately it may also speed up hepatic metabolism of many drugs effectively rendering them weaker. Many of my correspondents find the capsaicin cure worse than their aching ailment. Fleming *et al.* (1998) have some heavy duty toxicity information regarding toxic dosages possibly leading to life-threatening hypothermia by affecting the thermoreceptors. Prolonged consumption of high doses can cause chronic gastrosis, kidney and liver damage, and neurotoxicity (PHR). Prolonged exposure may deaden the sensitivity to any pain (PED). "Prolonged exposure to mucosa will make the mucosa insensitive to industrial pollution" (PED). (I don't know whether that's supposed to be a plus or a minus. (JAD). Chile, like garlic, can aggravate vasodilation in TKI therapy for myeloid leukemia (X20459996).

EXTRACTS (CAPSICUM)

One recent Korean study published in the *Journal of Food Science*, Hot peppers exhibit vasculotropic and vasoconstrictory activities. Capsaicin decongestant and rubefacient activities (TRA). *Capsicum* fruit extract is four times as toxic to mice as pure capsaicin. Apparently the capsaicin derivatives or other components have a synergistic effect (HDN). As a corollary, I confess or chide that such synergies would also prevail, on average, in medicinal activities as well. *Capsicum* extracts of both species and other spp inhibit various pathogens, including *Bacillus cereus, Bacillus subtilis, Clostridium sporogenes, C. tetani,* and *Streptococcus pyrogenes*, while individual capsicuninoids were not (MCK). (=) Capsidiol was more efficacious (MIC = 200 ug/ml) than metronidazole (MIC = 250ug/ml) at arresting growth of *Helicobacter in vitro* (X17002415). Capsaicin has hypoglycemic and insulinogenic activities in dogs (DIA). Japanese scientists have found and quantified some Capsiconinoids, a group of nonpungent capsaicinoid analogues. Capsiconinoids have agonist activity for transient receptor potential vanilloid type 1 (TRPV1), which is reported to be a receptor for capsaicin. Their study describes and quantifies capsiconinoid content in fruits of 35 *Capsicum* cultivars: 18 cultivars of *C. annuum*, seven of *C. baccatum*, five of *C. chinense*, four of *C. frutescens*, and one of *C. pubescens*. Ten cultivars contained capsiconinoids. Capsiconinoid Baccatum (CCB) (*C. baccatum* var. *praetermissum*) showed the highest capsiconinoid content (3314 μg/g DW) and Charapita (*C. chinense*) had the second highest content. Capsiconinoid content in CCB fruits increased until 30 days after flowering and then decreased rapidly until 40 days after flowering (X19489540).

AGGREGATED *C. ANNUUM*   ACETIC-ACID FR TEU FR
    WITH *C. FRUTESCENS*   X17766077
    (For disaggregated see Taxon   ACETOIN FR TEU
    Capsicum database.)   ACETONE FR JAF48:2454
ACETALDEHYDE FR JAF48:2454   ACETYLCHOLINE 15NM/G PC
                                                PAN

ACETYLCHOLINE 105NM/G SD PAN
ACETYLFURAN FR AAS170:141
ACYLATED-STERYL-GLUCOSIDE FR JAF49:622
AESCULETIN SP HH2
ALANINE 350-4,774 (6,691) FR USA
ALUMINUM 1-44 FR AAS HHB USG
P-AMINO-BENZALDEHYDE 6 RT WO2
AMMONIA(NH3) 382 FR PAN
BETA-AMYRIN SD PAN
ANTHERAXANTHIN 0.5-165 JAF44:711 FR HHB JBH X15186108 X21535519
APIGENIN 272 FR JAF49:3106
APIGENIN-7-O-APIOSYLGLUCOSIDE FR HH2
APIGENIN-6-C-BETA-D-GLUCOPYRANOSIDE-8-C-ALPHA-L-ARABINOPYRANOSIDE FR X15740069
APIGENIN-GLUCOPYRANOSIDE-ARABINOPYRANOSIDE FR X17091773
APIGENIN-C-GLUCOSIDE FR X21514607
APIGENIN-O-GLUCOSIDE FR X21514607
APIIN FR HHB PH2 TEU
APIOSE PL HH2
APO-12'-CAPSORUBINAL FR JAF49:1601
APO-8'-CAPSORUBINAL FR JAF49:1601
BETA-APO-8'-CAROTENAL FR PAN
APO-8'-ZEAXANTHINAL FR JAF49:1601
APO-10'-ZEAXANTHINAL FR JAF49:1601
APO-12'-ZEAXANTHINAL FR JAF49:1601
APO-15-ZEAXANTHINAL FR JAF49:1601
APO-11-ZEAXANTHINAL FR JAF49:1601
APO-14'-ZEAXANTHINAL FR JAF49:1601
APO-13-ZEAXANTHINONE FR JAF49:1601
APO-9-ZEAXANTHINONE FR JAF49:1601
ARACHIDIC-ACID FR CCO
ARGININE 410-5,592 (-7,835) FR USA
ARSENIC 0.00355-0.015 FR USG
ASH 5,000-122,000 FR AAS CRC USA USG
ASCORBIC-ACID 230-20,982 (-21,580) FR CRC USA WO2 X21514607 X21535734
L-ASPARIGINASE FR PAN
ASPARAGINE FR HHB
ASPARTIC-ACID 1,200-16,500 (-23,335) FR USA
AUROCHROME FR HHB
AUROXANTHIN-1 0-0.5 FR JAF44:711
AUROXANTHIN-2 0-0.5 FR JAF44:711
BARIUM 2-8 FR USG
BEHENIC-ACID FR CCO
BENZALDEHYDE FR X10563930

2-BENZALDEHYDE FR ACS170:138
BETAINE 0.8-12 FR JN133(9):2918
BETAINE FR CCO
BISHOMOCAPSAICIN FR WO2
BORON 1-18 FR USG (-74) BOB PAN
BROMINE 0.1-111 FR AAS
1,3-BUTANDIOL FR TEU
2,3-BUTANDIOL FR TEU AAS170:141
2-BUTANONE FR AAS170:141
BUTYRIC-ACID RE PAN
CADMIUM 0.005-0.33 FR AAS USG
CAFFEIC-ACID 11-32 FR PAN WO2
1-O-CAFFEOYL-BETA-D-GLUCOSE FR PAN
CALCIUM 36-2,100 (-3,900) FR CRC USA USG WO2
CAMPESTEROL 20-530 FR CCO GAS
CAMPESTERYL GLUCOSIDE FR JAF49:622
CAMPESTERYL (6'-O-LINOLEOYL) GLUCOSIDE FR JAF49:622
CAMPESTERYL (6'-O-PALMITOYL) GLUCOSIDE FR JAF49:622
CAMPESTERYL (6'-O-STEAROYL) GLUCOSIDE FR JAF49:622
CAMPHENE FR AAS170:142
CAMPHOR FR AAS170:141
CAPROIC-ACID RE PAN
CAPRYLIC-ACID-VANILLYLAMIDE FR HH2 TEU
CAPSAICIN 0-6,640 (-60,000) FR HHB PH2 TEU X17147411 X21514607
CAPSAICIN-BETA-D-GLUCOPYRANOSIDE FR X16881699
CAPSAICINOIDS 0.7- 800 FR X20184029; X21514607 X23471827
CAPSAICINOIDS (ACID AMIDES) 0-7,000 (-53,600) FR HHB PH2 TEU X17147411 X20184029
CAPSANTHIN 0-4,810 FR TEU WOI JAF44:711 JAF49:1517 X15186108 X21535519 X 21535734
CIS-CAPSANTHIN 0-630 FR JAF44:711 X15186108
9-CIS-CAPSANTHIN 0.5-140 FR JAF44:711
13-CIS-CAPSANTHIN 0-205 FR JAF44:711
CIS-9'-CAPSANTHIN FR PAN
CIS-13-CAPSANTHIN FR PAN
CIS-13'-CAPSANTHIN FR PAN
CAPSANTHIN-3,6-EPOXIDE 0-165 FR JAF44:711
CAPSANTHIN-5,6-EPOXIDE 0-185 FR JAF44:711 WO2 X15186108 X21535519
CAPSANTHONE 0-45 FR TEU JAF44:711
CAPSANTHONE-3,6-EPOXIDE FR JAF49:3965
CAPSIAMIDE 20-200 FR CCO PH2 TEU
CAPSIANOSIDE-1 FR X17002415
CAPSIANOSIDE-2 FR X17002415
CAPSIANOSIDE-3 FR X17002415
CAPSIANOSIDE-4 FR X17002415

CAPSIANOSIDE-A 33-250 FR PAN
CAPSIANOSIDE-B 2-18 FR PAN
CAPSIANOSIDE-C 35-103 FR PAN
 X17666836
CAPSIANOSIDE-D 21-38 FR PAN
 X17666836
CAPSIANOSIDE-E 15 FR PAN
 X17666836
CAPSIANOSIDE-F 5 FR PAN
 X17666836
CAPSIANOSIDE-I 18 FR PAN
CAPSIANOSIDE-II 43-138 FR 125
 FR JAF50:4310;
CAPSIANOSIDE-III 15-105 FR PAN
 X17666836
CAPSIANOSIDE-IV 9 FR PAN
CAPSIANOSIDE-V 2 FR PAN
CAPSIANOSIDE-VIII FR
 X17015971
CAPSIANOSIDE-IX FR X17015971
CAPSIANOSIDE-X FR X17015971
CAPSIANOSIDE-XIII FR
 X17015971
CAPSIANOSIDE-XV FR X17015971
CAPSIANOSIDE-XVI FR
 X17015971
CAPSIANSIDE-A 300 FR JBH PAN
CAPSIATES 98-1,000 FR
 JAF50:7396 X21514607
E-CAPSIATE FR X19415923
CAPSICIDINE SD PH2
CAPSICONINOIDS <300-3,314 FR
 X19489540
CAPSICOSIDE-A 585 FR
 JAF50:4310;
CAPSICOSIDE-A SD TEU
CAPSICOSIDE-A-1 530 RT HDN
 PAN
CAPSICOSIDE-B SD TEU

CAPSICOSIDE-B-1 620 RT HDN
 PAN
CAPSICOSIDE-C SD TEU
CAPSICOSIDE-C-1 600 RT HDN
 PAN
CAPSICOSIDE-C-2 RT HDN
CAPSICOSIDE-C-3 RT HDN
CAPSICOSIDE-D SD TEU
CAPSICOSIDE-D-1 RT HDN
CAPSICOSIDE E 195 FR
 JAF50:4310;
CAPSICOSIDE-E-1 RT HDN
CAPSICOSIDE F 120 FR
 JAF50:4310;
CAPSICOSIDE-G 295 FR
 JAF50:4310;
CAPSICOSINE FR HDN
CAPSICUOSIDE-A FR X24066587
CAPSIDIOL 29 FR PAN
CAPSIDOL PL JSG
CAPSINOIDS FR X19415923
CAPSOCHROME FR WO2
(8S)-CAPSOCHROME FR WO3
CAPSOLUTEIN FR HHB
CAPSORUBIN 0-800 FR TEU
 JAF44:711 JAF49:1517 WO2
 X15186108
CARBOHYDRATES 53,100-849,000
 FR CRC USA
DELTA-3-CARENE FR AAS170:142
CARNAUBIC-ACID SD HHB
ALPHA-CAROTENE 0-210 FR
 JAF44:711 JAF48:1713 PH2
BETA-CAROTENE 0-1,440 FR TEU
 JAF44:711 JAF49:1517 CRC
 USA 1/
CIS-BETA-CAROTENE 1-60 FR
 JAF44:711 CRC USA 1/

BETA-CAROTENE-EPOXIDE FR HHB
NEO-BETA-CAROTENE ZETA-CAROTENE FR PAN
CAROTENOIDS 115-12,000 FR TEU JAF44:711 JAF48:3857 X17822289 X21948863
CARPOXANTHIN FR TEU
CARVONE FR AAS170:141
CARYOPHYLLENE FR AAS170:142
CAY-1 PL X18608885
CHLORINE 150-1050 FR WO2
CHLOROGENIC-ACID FR PAN
CHLOROPHYLL 0-195 FR JAF44:711 X21535734
CHLOROPHYLL 2,115-21,500 LF X21535734
CHOLINE 297 PC PAN
CHOLINE 360 SD PAN
CHOLINE 35-360 FR JN133:1302
CHROMIUM 0-0.546 FR USG
CHRYSOERIOL-7-O-(2-APIOSYL-6-ACETYL)-GLUCOSIDE FR X15186108
CINNAMIC-ACID TC PAN
CITRIC-ACID FR HHB WO2
CITROSTADIENOL SD PAN
CITROXANTHIN FR HHB
CITRULLIN FR HHB
COBALT 0.001-0.1 (-151 PED) FR AAS USG
ALPHA-COPAENE FR AAS170:142
COPPER 0.5-105 FR AAS CRC USA USG WO2
P-COUMARIC-ACID 79-540 FR PAN WO2
N-TRANS-P-COUMAROYL-OCTOPAMINE 1 RT WO2
N-TRANS-P-COUMAROYL-TYRAMINE 2 RT WO2
P-CRESOL FR TEU
BETA-CRYPTOXANTHIN 0.7-150 FR JBH X15186108
CRYPTOCAPSIN 0.2-75 FR JAF44:711 HHB
CRYPTOXANTHIN 40-960 FR HHB TEU WO2
ALPHA-CRYPTOXANTHIN 1-25 FR JAF44:711
BETA-CRYPTOXANTHIN 0.03-510 FR JAF44:711
CIS-CRYPTOXANTHIN 0-65 FR JAF44:711
CUCURBITACHROME 0-400 FR JAF44:711
CUCURBITAXANTHIN-A 0-910 FR TEU JAF44:711 JAF49:1517 X15186108
CUCURBITAXANTHIN-B 0-110 FR TEU JAF44:711
CYCLOARTANOL SD PAN
CYCLOARTENOL SD PAN
CYCLOEUCALENOL SD PAN
CYCLOHEXANONE FR AAS170:141
CYCLOPENTANOL FR AAS170:141
CYCLOVIOLAXANTHIN 0-70 FR TEU WO3 JAF44:711
P-CYMENE FR AAS170:142
CYSTINE 160-2,182 (-3,100) FR USA
DECA-TRANS-2,5-DIENAL FR WO2
DECANOIC-ACID-VANILLYL-AMIDE 1-68 FR USA

DECYLIC-ACID-VANILLYLAMIDE FR TEU
DEHYDROASCORBIC-ACID 20,000 FR PAN
DELPHINIDIN-3-TRANS-COU-MAROYLRUTINOSIDE-5-GLUCOSIDE FR X16989312 X18222931
9,9'-DIAPO-10,9'-RETRO-CAROTENE-9,9'-DIONE FR JAF49:1601
(5'R)-3,4-DIDEHYDRO-BETA,KAPPA-CAROTEN-6'-ONE FR X14738402
DIGALACTOSYLDIACYLGLYCEROL FR JAF49:622
DIHYDROCAPSAICIN 0-3725 (-5,760) FR HHB PH2 TEU X17147411
DIHYDROCAPSAICIN-BETA-D-GLUCOPYRANOSIDE FR X16881699
CIS-9,10-DIHYDRO-CAPSENONE 1 TC PAN
DIHYDROCAPSIATE 60-600 FR JAF50:7396
6',7'-DIHYDRO-5',5'''-DICAPSAICIN FR JNP66:1094
5,6-DIHYDROXY-5,6-DIHYDRO-ZEAXANTHIN FR PAN
DIKETOGLUCONIC-ACID FR WO2
DIMETHOXYPHENOL FR TEU
4-ALPHA-24- DIMETHYL-CHOLESTA-7,24-DIEN-3-BETA-OL SD PAN
2,3-DIMETHYL-5-ETHYLPYRAZINE FR AAS170:142
2,3-DIMETHYLPYRAZINE FR AAS170:142
DIN-N-PROPYL-AMINE 0.3 FR PAN
DITERPENE-GLYCOSIDES FR X17015971
DITHIOLS FR X18163560
DITHIOLANES FR X18163560
EO 500-26,000 FR HHB TEU WO2
3,6-EPOXIDE-5-HYDROXY-5,6-DIHYDRO-ZEAXANTHIN FR CAP
3,6-EPOXYCAPSANTHIN FR WO3
5,6-EPOXYCAPSANTHIN FR WO3
ERIOCITRIN FR TEU
ERIODICTIN FR HHB
ETHYL-ACETATE FR TEU
ETHYL-DODECANOATE FR AAS170:142
1-ETHYLINDOLE FR X17766077
24-(R)-ETHYL-LOPHENOL SD PAN
ETHYL-3-METHYLBUTYRATE FR AAS170:142
ETHYL-OCTANOATE FR AAS170:142
ETHYL-TETRADECANOATE FR AAS170:142 EUGENOL FR AAS170:142
FAT 100,000-300,000 SD HHB TEU
FAT 1,000-277,000 FR CRC USA WO2
TRANS-P-FERULYL ALCOHOL-4-O-[6-(2-METHYL-3-HYDROXYPROPIONYL] 1-O-FERRULOYL-BETA-D-GLUCOSE FR PAN
FERULOYL-GLUCOPYRANOSIDE FR X17091773

TRANS-P-FERULOYL-BETA-D-GLUCOPYRANOSIDE FR X15740069
N-TRANS-FERULOYL-OCTOPAMINE 1-2 RT WO2
N-CIS-FERULOYL-TYRAMINE 2 RT WO2
N-TRANS-FERULOYL-TYRAMINE 12 RT WO2
FIBER 12,000-351,000 FR CRC USA WO2
FLAVONOIDS 1665 FR JAF49:3106 TEU
FLUORINE 0.03-1 FR AAS WO2
FOLACIN 0-3 (-65) FR USA WO2
FOLIAXANTHIN FR HHB
FRUCTOSE 50,000-90,000 FR TEU
FRUCTOSE SD WO2
FRUCTOSYLSUCROSE SD WO2
FUCOSTEROL SD WO2
FUNKIOSIDE RT PAN
2-FURANMETHANOL FR X17766077
GALACTOSAMINE FR PAN
GALACTOSE FR HHB
GERANYLACETONE FR AAS170:141
GERANYL-GERANIOL FR WO2
GITOGENIN PL HDN
GITONIN RT WO2
GLUCOCEREBROSIDE FR JAF49:622 L
GLUCOSAMINE FR PAN
GLUCOSE 10,000-30,000 FR HHB TEU
GLUCOPYRANOSIDE FR X15740069 4-ALPHA-D-GLUCOPYRANOSYLPLANTEOSE SD WO2
GLUTAMIC-ACID 1,120-15,277 (-21,540) FR USA
GLUTAMINASE FR PAN
GLUTATHIONE LF X21965607
GLUTATHIONE RT X21965607
GLUTATHIONE ST X21965607
GLYCERIC-ACID FR WO2
GLYCEROPHOSPHOCHOLINE ND FR JN133:1302
GLYCINE 310-4,228 (-6,035) FR USA
GRAMISTEROL SD PAN
GROSSAMIDE 3 RT WO2
HENEICOSANE FR CCO
HEPTADECANE FR CCO
HEPTANOIC-ACID FR AAS170:141
2-HEPTANETHIOL FR X14733513 X18163560
2-HEPTANONE FR AAS170:141
(3 E)-3-HEPTEN-2-ONE FR X18163560
HESPERIDIN FR HHB TEU
HESPERIDINE-GLUCURONIDE FR X17091773
HEXADECANE FR CCO
HEXANAL FR CCO
HEXA-CIS-3-ENOL FR WO2
HEXAN-1-AL FR PAN
N-HEXANAL FR AAS170:141
HEXANOIC-ACID FR AAS170:141
1-HEXANOL FR AAS170:141
2-HEXANOL FR AAS170:141
3-HEXANOL FR AAS170:141
CIS-3-HEXEN-1-OL FR AAS170:141
TRANS-2-HEXEN-1-OL FR AAS170:141
2-HEXANONE FR AAS170:141
HISTIDINE 170-2,319 (-3,345) FR USA

HOMOCAPSAICIN 2-90 FR CRC HHB
HOMOCAPSAICIN-I FR TEU
HOMOCAPSAICIN-II FR TEU
HOMODIHYDROCAPSAICIN 2-90 FR CRC HHB
HOMODIHYDROCAPSAICIN-I FR TEU
HOMODIHYDROCAPSAICIN-II FR TEU
HYDROXYBENZOIC-ACID FR HDN
HYDROXYBENZOIC-ACID-4-BETA-D-GLUCOSIDE FR WO3
3-HYDROXY-2-BUTANONE FR TEU
OMEGA- HYDROXYCAPSAICIN FR JNP66:1094
5-HYDROXY-CAPSANTHIN-5,6-EPOXIDE FR HHB
HYDROXY-ALPHA-CAROTENE FR HHB
3-HYDROXY-ALPHA-CAROTENE FR HHB
(3R,5'R)-3-HYDROXY-BETA,KAPPA-CAROTEN-6'-ONE FR X14738402
OMEGA- HYDROXYCAPSAICIN FR JNP66:1094
5-HYDROXY-CAPSANTHIN-5,6-EPOXIDE FR HHB
HYDROXY-ALPHA-CAROTENE FR HHB
3-HYDROXY-ALPHA-CAROTENE FR HHB
HYDROXYCINNAMIC-ACID FR HDN
6-HYDROXY-4,6-DIMETHYL-3-HEPTENE-2-ONE FR WO2
22-HYDROXYFURASTANOL-BIDESMOSIDE SD TEU
(2S,4R)-4-HYDROXY-1-METHYL-2-PYRROLIDINE-CARBOXYLIC-ACID LF X17284863
HYDROXYPYRIDINE FR X17766077
IODINE 0.54 FR WO2
BETA-IONONE FR JAF48:2454
IRON 4-286 FR CRC USA WO2
2-ISOBUTYL-3-METHOXYPYRAZINE FR WO2
3-ISOBUTYL-2-METHOXYPYRAZINE FR ACS170:138
ISOBUTYRIC-ACID RE PAN
28-ISOCITRADIENOL,31
ISOFUCOSTEROL SD WO2
ISOHEXANOIC-ACID RE PAN
ISOHEXYL-ISOCAPROATE FR AYL
ISOLEUCINE 270-3,683 (-5,300) FR USA
ISOPHORONE FR WO2
3-ISOPROPYL-2-METHOXYPYRAZINE FR ACS170:138
ISOTHUJONE FR AAS170:141
ISOVALERIC-ACID RE PAN
KAEMPFEROL? PL PAN
KARPOXANTHIN 0.5-150 FR JAF44:711 WO3
LANOSTENOL PL JSG
LANOSTEROL SD PAN
LANOST-8-EN-3-BETA-OL SD WO2
LATOXANTHIN 1-25 FR JAF44:711
LAURIC-ACID RE PAN

3,3'-LAUROYLMYRISTOYL-CAP-
SANTHIN FR TEU
LEAD 0.004-2 FR AAS USG
LEUCINE 440-6,002 (-8,565) FR
USA
LIMONENE FR AAS170:142 WO2
LINALOOL FR AAS170:141 WO2
LINOLEIC-ACID 1,040-29,871 FR
USA
ALPHA-LINOLENIC-ACID
50-3,001 FR USA
LITHIUM 0.284-0.4 FR USG
LOPHENOL SD PAN
LUPEOL SD PAN
LUTEIN 0-95 FR JAF44:711
JAF48:1713 JNU X15186108
X21535519
LUTEIN LF 100 -1,115 LF
X21535734
CIS-LUTEIN 1-10 FR X15186108
LUTEOLIN 13-31 (-1035) FR
JAF49:3106
LUTEOLIN-7-O-BETA-APIOGLU-
COSIDE LF WO2
LUTEOLIN-7-O-[2-(BETA-D-
APIOFURANOSYL)-BETA-
D-GLUCOPYRANOSIDE] FR
X15740069
LUTEOLIN-7-O-[2-(BETA-D-
APIOFURANOSYL)-4-(BETA-
D-GLUCOPYRANOSYL)-
6-MALONYL]-BETA-D-GLU-
COPYRANOSIDE. X15740069
LUTEOLIN-7-O-(2-APIOSYL)-
GLUCOSIDE FR X15186108
LUTEOLIN-7-O-(2-APIOSYL-
6-ACETYL)-GLUCOSIDE FR
X15186108
LUTEOLIN-7-O-(2-APIOSYL-
6-DIACETYL)-GLUCOSIDE
FR X15186108
LUTEOLIN-7-O-(2-APIOSYL-
6-MAONYL)-GLUCOSIDE FR
X15186108
LUTEOLIN-ARABINOPYRANO-
SIDE-DIGLUCOPYRANO-
SIDE FR X17091773
LUTEOLIN-7-O-BETA-DIGLUCO-
SIDE LF WO2
LUTEOLIN-GLUCOPYRANO-
SIDE-ARABINOPYRANOSIDE
FR X17091773
LUTEOLIN-C-GLUCOSIDE FR
X21514607
LUTEOLIN-O-GLUCOSIDE FR
X21514607
LUTEOLIN-7-O-GLUCOSIDE PL
PH2 TEU WO2
LUTEOLIN-7-O-BETA-D-GLUCO-
SIDE LF HH2 WO2
LUTEOLIN-6-C-BETA-D-GLUCO-
PYRANOSIDE-8-C-ALPHA-L-
ARABINOPYRANOSIDE FR
X15740069
LUTEOLIN-GLUCURONIDE. FR
X17091773
LUTEOLIN-7-MONOGLUCOSIDE
FR
LUTEOXANTHIN-1 2-40 FR
JAF44:711
LUTEOXANTHIN-2 7-110 FR
JAF44:711
LYSINE 380-5,183(-7,260) FR USA
MAGNESIUM 118-2,340 (-3,000)
FR PED USA USG
MALIC-ACID FR WO2
MALONIC-ACID LF FR WOI

4-ALPHA-MALTOPYRANOSYL-
PLANTEOSE SD WO2
MANGANESE 0.7-39 (-175) FR
AAS USA USG WO2
MARGARIC-ACID FR CCO
MELATONIN FR 31 to 93ng/g
X24629979
MERCAPTO-KETONES FR
X18163560
MERCAPTO-ALCOHOLS FR
X18163560
MERCURY 0.00071-0.001 FR USG
METHANOL FR JAF48:2454
METHIONINE 100-1,364 (-1,955)
FR USA
2-METHOXY-3-ISOBUTYL-
PYRAZINE FR PH2 WO2
X18163560
P-METHYL-ACETOPHENONE FR
AAS170:141
N-METHYL-ANILINE 13.1 FR PAN
2-METHYL-BUTANAL FR TEU
AAS170:141
3-METHYL-BUTANAL FR TEU
AAS170:141
2-METHYL-BUTAN-1-OL FR
AAS170:141
2-METHYL-BUTAN-2-OL FR
AAS170:141
2-METHYL-BUTYRIC-ACID FR
AAS170:141
3-METHYL-BUTYRIC-ACID FR
AAS170:141
22-O-METHYLCAPSICOSIDE-A
835 FR JAF50:4310;
22-O-METHYL-CAPSICOSIDE-D
245 FR JAF50:4310;
22-O-METHYLCAPSICOSIDE-G
365 FR JAF50:4310;

4-ALPHA-METHYL-5-ALPHA-
CHOLEST-8(14)-EN-3-BETA-
OL SD WO2
24-METHYLENE-CYCLOARTA-
NOL SD PAN
METHYL-DECANOATE FR
AAS170:142
METHYL-DODECANOATE FR
AAS170:142
24-METHYLENELA-
NOST-8-EN-3BETA-OL SD
WO2
2-METHYL-5-ETHYLPYRAZINE
FR AAS170:142
4ALPHA-METHYL-24-ETHYL-
CHOLESTA-7,24-DIENOL SD
WO2
5-METHYL-2-FURFURAL FR
AAS170:141
4-METHYL-HEPTADECANE FR
PAN
METHYL-HEPTANOATE FR
AAS170:142
6-METHYL-5-HEPTEN-2-ONE FR
JAF48:2454 X10888567
4-METHYL-HEXADECANE FR
PAN
METHYL-HEXADECANOATE FR
AAS170:142
4-METHYLINDOLE FR X17766077
4-METHYL-LANOST-9(11)-EN-3-
BETA-OL SD PAN
24-METHYL-LOPHENOL SD PAN
METHYL-8-METHYL-6-NON-
ANOATE FR AAS170:142
METHYL-NONANOATE FR
AAS170:142
8-METHYL-NONANOATE FR
AAS170:142

8-METHYL-NONANOIC-ACID FR AAS170:142
8-METHYL- TRANS-6-NONE-NOIC-ACID FR X18489121
24-METHYL-31-NORLANOST-9(11)-EN-OL SD WO2
28-METHYL- TRANS-6-NONE-NOIC ACID FR X18489121
24-METHYL-31-NORLANOST-9(11)-EN-OL SD WO2
METHYL-OCTADECANOATE FR AAS170:142
METHYL-OCTANOATE FR AAS170:142
7-METHYL-OCTANOIC-ACID FR AAS170:142
4-METHYLPENTADECANE FR CCO
METHYL-PENTANOATE FR AAS170:142
4-METHYL-PENTANOIC-ACID FR AAS170:141
4-METHYL-PENTAN-1-OL FR AAS170:141
2-METHYL-PENTAN-2-OL FR AAS170:141
3-METHYL-PENTAN-3-OL FR AAS170:141
4-METHYL-3-PENTEN-2-ONE FR AAS170:141
3-METHYL-1-PENTYL-3-METHYL-BUTYRATE FR AYL
4-METHYL-1-PENTYL-2-METHYL-BUTYRATE FR AYL
METHYL-PHENYLACETATE FR AAS170:142
METHYL-BETA-PHENYLPROPIO-NATE FR AAS170:142
2-METHYLPROPANAL FR JAF48:2454
2-METHYL-PROPIONIC-ACID FR AAS170:141
METHYL-SALICYLATE FR WO2
4-METHYLTETRADECANE FR CCO
N-(13-METHYLTETRADECYL)-ACETAMIDE PL PH2
METHYLTHIO-THIOLS FR X18163560
4-METHYLTRIDECANE FR CCO
MEVALONIC-ACID 0.5 FR PAN
N-(13-METHYLTETRADECYL) ACETAMIDE 300-400 FR CCO PAN
MOLYBDENUM 0-15 FR AAS USG
MONOGALACTOSYLDIACYLG-LYCEROL FR JAF49:622
MUTATOXANTHIN-1 0-40 FR JAF44:711
MUTATOXANTHIN-2 0.5-295 FR JAF44:711
MYRCENE FR AAS170:142
MYRICETIN <1-172 (-235) FR JAF49:3106
MYRISTIC-ACID 10-136 FR USA
NEOCHROME FR WO2
NEOXANTHIN 0-18 FR JAF44:711 WO2 X15186108
NIACIN 4-172 FR CRC USA
NICKEL 0.05-5.5 FR AAS USG
NIGROXANTHIN FR TEU
NITROGEN 1,900-23,330 FR AAS
N-NITROSO-DIMETHYLAMINE FR PAN

P-NITROSOGLUTATHIONE LF X21965607
P-NITROSOGLUTATHIONE RT X21965607
P-NITROSOGLUTATHIONE ST X21965607
N-NITROSO-PYRROLIDINE FR PAN
NONADECANE FR CCO
NONA-TRANS,CIS-2-6-DIENAL FR WO2
NONANOIC-ACID FR AAS170:142
NONANOIC-ACID-VANILLYL-AMIDE 2-45 FR WO2 2/
1-NONEN-4-ONE FR JAF48:2454
NONYL-ACID-VANILLYLAMIDE FR HH2
TRANS-BETA-OCIMENE FR WO2
2, 4-NONADIENAL FR X10563930
NONA-TRANS,TRANS,2,5-DIEN-4-ONE FR WO2
NONANOIC-ACID-VANILLYL-AMIDE 2-45 FR CRC 2/
1-NONEN-4-ONE FR X18163560
(2 E)-2-NONEN-4-ONE FR X18163560
(2 E,5 E)-2,5-NONADIEN-4-ONE FR X18163560
NON-1-ENE-4-ONE FR WO2
NONIVAMIDE FR TEU
NON-TRANS-2-EN-4-ONE FR WO2
NORCAPSAICINE FR PAN
31-NORCYCLOARTANOL SD PAN
NORDIHYDROCAPSAICIN 8-1,530 FR HHB HDN TEU
31-NOR-LANOST-9(11)-ENOL SD WO2
31-NOR-LANOST-8-EN-3-BETA-OL SD PAN
31-NOR-LANOST-9(11)-EN-3-BETA-OL SD PAN
OBTUSIFOLIOL SD PAN
TRANS-BETA-OCIMENE FR WO2
OCTANE FR AAS170:142
OCTANOIC-ACID FR AAS170:142
2-OCTENOIC-ACID FR AAS170:142
OCTOPAMINE 234 LF JBH UPW
OLEIC-ACID 110-3,582 FR USA
OLEIC-ACID SD HHB
OLEORESINS 150,500-174,600 FR WO2
OXALIC-ACID 257-1,171 FR WBB WO2
OXALATE 562 FR WO2
PALMITIC-ACID 150-6,820 FR USA
PALMITIC-ACID SD HHB
PALMITOLEIC-ACID 0-409 FR USA
PANTOTHENIC-ACID 0-5 FR USA
PECTIN-METHYLESTERASE FR X15373415
PENTADECANE FR CCO
PENTADECANOIC-ACID FR CCO
PENTANOIC-ACID FR AAS170:141
1-PENTANOL FR AAS170:141
N-PENTYLAMINE 3 FR PAN
2-PENTYLFURAN FR AAS170:142 WO2
2-PENTYLPYRIDINE FR AAS170:142
PETUNIDIN-DICLYCOSIDES FR WO2
ALPHA-PHELLANDRENE FR AAS170:142

BETA-PHENETHYLACETATE FR AAS170:142
PHENOL FR TEU
PHENYLACETALDEHYDE FR JAF48:2454
PHENYLALANINE 260-3,546(-5,055) FR USA
PHOSPHATIDYL-GLYCEROL FR PAN
PHOSPHODIESTERASE TC PAN
PHOSPHOCHOLINE 12-120 FR JN133:1302
PHOSPHATIDYLCHOLINE 7-75 FR JN133:1302
PHOSPHORUS 186-3,885(-6,690) FR AAS USA USG WO2
PHYLLOQUINONE 0.020-0.060 FR JN126:1183S
PHYTOENE FR WO2
PHYTOFLUENE FR WO2
PHYTOL FR WO2
PHYTOSTEROLS 90-1,750 FR GAS
ALPHA-PINENE FR AAS170:142
BETA-PINENE FR AAS170:142
PIPERIDINE 5.2 FR PAN
PLANTEBIOSE SD WO2
PLANTEOSE SD WO2
POLYPHENOLS FR X21898818
PORPHOBILINOGEN-OXYGENASE LF PAN
POTASSIUM 1,862-35,000 FR CRC USA USG WO2
PROLINE 370-5,047 (-7,095) FR CRC USA
N-PROPYLAMINE 2.3 FR PAN
PROTEIN 8,000-184,000 FR CRC TEU USA WO2
PROTO-DEGALACTO-TIGONINE SD TEU
PULEGONE FR CCO
PYRROLIDINE 1.4 FR PAN
QUERCETIN 60-450 FR JAF49:3106
QUERCETIN-C-GLUCOSIDE FR X21514607
QUERCETIN-O-GLUCOSIDE FR X21514607
QUERCETIN-RHAMNOPYRANOSIDE FR X17091773
QUERCETIN-RHAMNOPYRANOSIDE-GLUCOPYRANOSIDE FR X17091773
QUERCETIN 3-O-ALPHA-L-RHAMNOPYRANOSIDE-7-O-BETA-D-GLUCOPYRANOSIDE FR X15740069
QUERCETIN 3-O-ALPHA-L-RHAMNOPYRANOSIDE FR X15740069
QUERCETIN 3-O-RHAMNOSIDE FR X15186108
QUERCETIN 3-O-RHAMNOSIDE-7-0-GLUCOSIDE FR X15186108
QUINIC-ACID FR WO2
RIBOFLAVIN 0-27 FR CRC USA WO2
RUBIDIUM 0.38-10 FR AAS
SABINENE FR AAS170:142
SALICYLATES 6-2,030 FR X16608205 JAD85:9501
SALICYLIC-ACID 30-110 FR X16608205
SAPONINS SD PH2 TEU CAY-1 PL X18608885
SCOPOLETIN FR CRC

SCOPOLETIN SP HH2
3-(SEC-BUTYL)-2-
 METHOXYPYRAZINE FR
 ACS170:138
SELENIUM 0.00142-0.002 FR USG
SERINE 340-4,638(-6,525) FR USA
SESQUITERPENOIDS PL
 X15568784
SHIKIMIC-ACID FR WO2
SILICON 1-33 FR AAS
SILVER 0.071-0.1 FR USG
TRANS-P-SINAPOYL-BETA-D-
 GLUCOPYRANOSIDE FR
 X15740069
BETA-SITOSTEROL 60-1,190 FR
 GAS PAS
BETA-SITOSTERYL GLUCOSIDE
 FR JAF49:622
BETA-SITOSTERYL
 (6'-O-LINOLENOYL)
 GLUCOSIDE FR JAF49:622
BETA-SITOSTERYL
 (6'-O-LINOLEOYL)
 GLUCOSIDE FR JAF49:622
BETA-SITOSTERYL
 (6'-O-PALMITOYL)
 GLUCOSIDE FR JAF49:622
BETA-SITOSTERYL
 (6'-O-STEAROYL)
 GLUCOSIDE. FR JAF49:622
SKATOLE-PYRROLO-
 OXYGENASE LF PAN
SODIUM 25-735 FR CRC USA WO2
SOLANIDINE FR HHB WO2
SOLANINE FR HHB WO2
SOLANINE 500 LF PAN
SOLASODINE FR CRC

SPHINGOMYELIN ND FR
 JN133:1302
STEARIC-ACID 30-2,180 FR USA
STEARIC-ACID SD HHB
STERYL GLUCOSIDE FR
 JAF49:622
STIGMASTEROL 10-180 FR CCO
 GAS
STRONTIUM 2-12 FR USG
SUCCINIC-ACID FR WO2
SUCROSE 4,000-20,000 FR TEU
SULFOQUINOVOSYL-DIACYL-
 GLYCEROL FR PAN
SULFUR 190-2,440 FR AAS USG
 WO2
GAMMA-TERPINENE FR
 AAS170:142
TERPINEN-4-OL FR AAS170:141
ALPHA-TERPINEOL FR
 AAS170:141
TERPINOLENE FR AAS170:142
TETRADECANE FR CCO
TETRAMETHYLPYRAZINE FR
 AAS170:142
THIAMIN 1-15 FR USA WO2
THIOPHENE-THIOLS FR
 X18163560
THREONINE 310-4,228(-6,035)
 FR USA
ALPHA-THUJENE FR AAS170:142
THUJONE FR AAS170:141
TIMOSAPONIN-I2 180 FR
 JAF50:4310;
TIN 5 FR PED
TITANIUM 0.355-16 FR USG
TOCOPHEROL 24 FR WOI
ALPHA-TOCOPHEROL 12-291 FR
 TOT WO2 JAF49:3101

BETA-TOCOPHEROL 1.4-7 FR X17263473
DELTA-TOCOPHEROL 0.2-1 FR X17263473
GAMMA-TOCOPHEROL 2.5-12.5 (-7,750) FR X17263473 X21535734
GAMMA-TOCOPHEROL 70 -7,750 LF 473 X21535734
TOCOPHEROLS 160-1,600 (-7,780) FR X21514607 (X21535734)
ALPHA-TOCOTRIENOL 0.3-1.5 FR X17263473
BETA-TOCOTRIENOL 2.7-13.5 FR X17263473
DELTA-TOCOTRIENOL 0.2-1 FR X17263473
GAMMA-TOCOTRIENOL <0.01-<0.05 FR X17263473
TOLUENE FR AAS170:142
TRIGONELLINE 0.6 SD PAN
4-ALPHA-14-ALPHA-24-TRIMETHYL-CHOLESTA-8(24)-DIEN-3-BETA-OL SD PAN
2,3,5-TRIMETHYLPYRAZINE FR AAS170:142
TRISHOMOCAPSAICIN FR WO2
TRYPTOPHAN 110-1,500(-2120) FR USA
TRYPTOPHAN-PYRROLO-OXYGENASE LF PAN
TYROSINE 180-2,455 (-3,425) FR USA
2-UNDECANONE FR AAS170:141
VALERIC-ACID RE PAN
VALINE 360-4,910 (-6,855) FR USA
VANILLIC-ACID-4-BETA-D-GLUCOSIDE FR WO3
VANILLYL-AMIDE FR HHB
VANILLOYL-GLUCOSE FR WO3
VANILLYL-CAPROYLAMIDE FR PAN
VANILLYL-DECANAMIDE FR PAN
VANILLYL-OCTANAMIDE FR PAN
VIOLAXANTHIN 2-800 FR JBH HHB PH2 TEU JAF44:711 X15186108 X21535519
VIT-B-6 2-23 FR USA
VIT-E 19-100 FR X17263473
VIT-P FR WO2
WATER 70,000-937,000 FR PED WOI USG (CF = 10X)
XANTHOPHYLL PL JSG
XANTHOPHYLL-EPOXIDE FR HHB
P-XYLENE FR AAS170:142
XYLOSE FR HHB
ZEAXANTHIN 0.18-1,525 FR JAF44:711 JAF48:1713 X15186108
cis-ZEAXANTHIN 0-35 FR X15186108
9-CIS-ZEAXANTHIN 2-32 FR JAF44:711
13-CIS-ZEAXANTHIN 2-43 FR JAF44:711
15-CIS-ZEAXANTHIN 0-9 FR JAF44:711
ZINC 1-77 FR PED USA USG
ZIRCONIUM 1.4-2 FR USG
(AAS=ACTA AGRIC SCAND SUPPL 22:1980.)
(H20=91%; ZMB=11.1 X APB)

James A. (Jim) Duke is a PhD economic botanist and ethnobotanist.. He holds an AB (1952), MA (1955) and PhD (1961), all from the University of North Carolina, Chapel Hill. Jim worked with the Missouri Botanical Garden until 1963, joining the USDA until 1965, then joining Battelle Columbus Laboratories for ecological and ethnobotanical studies in the Sea Level Canal Survey in Panama and Colombia. In 1971 he returned to USDA, Beltsville working on an alternative crops program. Between 1977–1982, he directed the USDA program, collecting plants from China, Ecuador, Panama and Syria, in collaboration with the NCI Cancer-Screening Program. That is when he started compiling his phytochemical database, still online and growing at the USDA. Retiring in 1995, he wrote *The Green Pharmacy*. This is just one of over 30 books he has published. In retirement, Duke has worked as a consultant with AllHerb, Nature's Herbs, and developed his famous Green Farmacy Garden, where he has hosted Tai Sophia Institute teaching tours as Distinguished Lecturer. He is still hosting garden tours at the Green Farmacy Garden, and working on a new book, *Herbistatins, Green Farmacy Herbal Alternatives to Synthetic Statin Drugs*.

Fire Cider. Karen O'Brien

Herb of the Year™ Selection

How the Herb of the Year™ is Selected

Every year since 1995, the International Herb Association has chosen an Herb of the Year™ to highlight. The Horticultural Committee evaluates possible choices based on their being outstanding in at least two of the three major categories: medicinal, culinary, or decorative. Many other herb organizations support the herb of the year selection and we work together to educate the public about these herbs during the year.

Herbs of the Year™: Past, Present and Future:

1995	Fennel	2008	Calendula
1996	Monarda	2009	Bay Laurel
1997	Thyme	2010	Dill
1998	Mint	2011	Horseradish
1999	Lavender	2012	Rose
2000	Rosemary	2013	Elderberry
2001	Sage	2014	Artemisia
2002	Echinacea	2015	Savory
2003	Basil	2016	Capsicum
2004	Garlic	2017	Corinadrum
2005	Oregano & Marjoram	2018	Humulus
2006	Scented Geraniums	2019	Agastache
2007	Lemon Balm	2020	Rubus

Join the IHA

ASSOCIATE WITH OTHER herb businesses and like-minded folks, network and have fun while you are doing it!

Membership Levels:

$500	Sponsor
$100	Business/Professional
$25	Additional member from your business
$100	Individual/Hobbyist
$25	Full-time Student
$50	Educator
$50	Small Business Start-up (first year of membership)

Log onto www.iherb.org to see what we are all about!

Membership includes:

Your business information listed on www.iherb.org
Membership directory
Herb of the Year™ publication
Quarterly newsletters
Online herbal support
Discounts on conference fees
Promotional support for IHA's Herb of the Year™ program and National Herb Week
Support for National Herb Day
Association with a network of diverse herbal businesses

Recipes

Stuffed Peppers á la Tony and Michael 6
John's Spicy Eggplant 7
Liptauer Cheese 8
Honey-Glazed, Super Chile Chicken 9
Hot Pepper Mustard 16
Ethiopian Berbere Paste 17
Mole Poblano de Guajolote 18
To finish the sauce: 19
Mexican Chocolate Cookies 20
Cream of Poblano Soup with Jack Cheese Crust 24
Breakfast Migas with Anaheims 25
Southwest Broken Spaghetti 26
Blackberry Chipotle Fool 27
The Pepper Oil 32
The Ginger Tincture 33
The Ointment 34
Chile-Infused Olive Oil with Herbal Healers 38
Hot Pepper Infused Vinegar 39
How to Roast or Grill Chile Peppers 41
Homemade Sriracha-Style Hot Sauce 42
Charlene's Jalapeño Poppers with Bacon 43
Firecracker Shrimp 44
Marion's Habanero Shrub 48
Blueberry Jalapeño Jelly 53
Cacahuatl Chili 74
Mole Rojo 76
Mole Verde 79
Holy Mole Ice Cream 81
Harissa 90
Pulled Chicken and Beans 91
Turkish-Stuffed Baked Eggplant 92
Hot Veggie-Oatmeal Crumble 93

Savory Oatmeal Topping 94
Fish Tacos with Two Kinds of Slaw 114
Batter Fried Fish 115
Fish Taco Slaw 116
Spicy Sweet Jicama Salad 117
Pickled Hot Peppers 120
Calypso Peach Salsa 121
Piccalilli 122
Tomato Catsup 124
Smoked Jalapeños in Adobo Sauce 129
Red Pepper Paste 175
Mary Vetrice Lee's San Antonio Chili-Stew 177
Fish Pepper Dip 183
Fiery Vinaigrette 184
Hot Pepper Vinegar 185
Herbed and Hot Chili Sauce 186
Lucille's Tomato Soup 188
Chile Pistachio Butter 189
Lemon-Paprika-Garlic Chicken 206
Paprika Butter 207
Paprika Pork Rub 208
Spice Rub 208
Paprika Cabbage Wedges 209
Paprika Cheese Crackers with Rosemary and Savory 210
"Instant" Hot Sauce from Dried Peppers 216
Garlic and Mixed Chile Hot Sauce 217
Quick and Easy Hot Sauce 218
Homemade Sriracha-Style Sauce 220
Honey with a Kick 237
Cayenne Hot Salve 238
Cayenne Tincture 240

Color Insert credits

Page 1
Top left: Fish pepper foliage, Karen O'Brien; Top right: Hinklehatz pepper flower and fruit, Karen O'Brien; Bottom left: Piquin pepper, Diann Nance; Bottom right: Fresh pepper ristra, Pat Crocker.

Page 2
Top left: Hinklehatz peppers in vinegar, Karen O'Brien; Top right: Roasting peppers, Susan Belsinger; Bottom: Sizzling salsa, Karen O'Brien.

Page 3
Top: Pepper Harvest, Marge Powell; Middle: Many colorful peppers, Susan Belsinger; Bottom: Selection of just harvested chiles, Susan Belsinger.

Page 4
Dried chile wreath, Susan Belsinger; Spice market, Pat Crocker.

Cover Credits

Front background
Basket of just harvested red hot chiles, Susan Belsinger.

Left overprint
Peppers, garlic, and herbs, Susan Belsinger

Middle overprint
Basket of hot peppers, Susan Belsinger

Right overprint
Ornamental pepper, Susan Belsinger

Back cover, left to right
Lemon drop peppers, Susan Belsinger; Red hot pepper jelly, Susan Belsinger; Long hot peppers, Susan Belsinger

Notes:

Notes:

Notes:

Notes:

Notes: